# Soviet-American
# Horizons
# on the Pacific

# Soviet-American Horizons on the Pacific

*Edited by*

JOHN J. STEPHAN

*and*

V. P. CHICHKANOV

UNIVERSITY OF HAWAII PRESS

HONOLULU

**Library of Congress Cataloging-in-Publication Data**
Main entry under title:

Soviet-American horizons on the Pacific.

Includes bibliographies and index.
1.   United States—Foreign economic relations—Soviet
Union—History—Addresses, essays, lectures.   2.   Soviet
Union—Foreign economic relations—United States—History
—Addresses, essays, lectures.   3.   Pacific Area—Commerce
—History—Addresses, essays, lectures.   4.   Pacific
States—Economic conditions—Addresses, essays, lectures.
5.   Soviet Far East (R.S.F.S.R.)—Economic conditions—Ad-
dresses, essays, lectures.   I.   Stephan, John J.
II.   Chichkanov, Valeriĭ Petrovich.
HF1456.5.S624S68   1986        337.73047'099        85-16535
ISBN 0-8248-1020-1

You Russians and we Americans—our countries so distant, so unlike at first glance . . . and yet in certain features, and vastest ones, so resembling each other. The variety of stock—elements and tongues to be resolutely fused in a common Identity and Union at all hazards—the idea, perennial through the ages, that they both have their historic and divine mission—the fervent element of manly friendship throughout the whole people . . . the grand expanse of territorial limits and boundaries—the unformed and nebulous state of many things, not yet permanently settled, but agreed on all hands to be the preparations of an infinitely greater future . . . the deathless aspirations at the inmost centre of each great community, so vehement, so mysterious, so abysmic—are certainly features you Russians and we Americans possess in common.

Walt Whitman, 1881

Both countries [the United States and Russia] overflow with strength and resiliency, with a spirit of organization and tenacity which knows no obstacles. . . . Both began with a complete break with tradition. Both spread over endless valleys, searching for their frontiers. Both—from different directions—reached across awesome expanses, building towns, settlements, and colonies, to the shores of the Pacific Ocean, the "Mediterranean of the future."

Alexander Herzen, 1858

# A NOTE ON TRANSLITERATION

In the notes, transliteration of Russian words follows the system employed by the Library of Congress. In the text, certain modifications have been made: (1) the apostrophe denoting the Russian soft sign has been omitted; (2) *g* has been represented by *v* in the endings *ovo* and *evo;* and (3) *ia, io, iu,* and *e* are written *ya, yo, yu,* and *ye* when they form the first letter of a word (e.g., Iakutsk—Yakutsk).

# Contents

U.S.-USSR and the Pacific

# Foreword

WHEN, in 1984, I introduced two resolutions in the United States Congress calling for Soviet-American scientific and cultural cooperation,* my colleagues expressed surprise that such initiatives should come from a representative of an island state in the middle of the Pacific Ocean. U.S.-USSR relations are commonly viewed as a component of U.S.-European relations. The Pacific dimension has not gained the recognition that it deserves.

*Soviet-American Horizons on the Pacific* is a major milestone in correcting this parochialism. The histories of both the United States and the Soviet Union contain a common theme: transcontinental movement toward the Pacific. The American Far West and the Soviet Far East, moreover, share a dynamism expressed in their rapidly developing regional economies and in the energetic spirit of their inhabitants.

I was born on the island of Kauai and lived in a little town bordering the Hanapepe River. About 170 years ago a representative of the Russian-American Company came from Alaska to Kauai, established friendly relations with the island's chief, and gave Russian names to a number of local sites. The Hanapepe River was renamed the Don.

*Soviet-American Horizons on the Pacific* revives our awareness of this historical heritage and offers a provocative, realistic agenda for future economic cooperation, taking into account constraints as well as opportunities. The book is a pioneering and inspiring example of how our people can work together in one of the world's most rapidly developing regions, the Pacific Basin.

The Honorable SPARK M. MATSUNAGA
U.S. Senator from Hawaii

---

*A resolution calling for renewed U.S.-USSR cooperation in space, and a resolution aimed at strengthening government support for U.S.-USSR scientific and cultural exchanges in areas such as oceanography, medicine, and energy resources.

# Foreword

IT IS A PLEASURE to undertake the request of this volume's editors, both of whom I know and respect, to prepare a short foreword for Soviet and American readers. The underlying idea of this joint endeavor—to illuminate relatively unstudied aspects of Soviet-American relations in the Pacific region—struck me as intrinsically interesting and important.

We in the Soviet Union do not wish and indeed cannot renounce our deep and manifold ties with Europe. Our state was born on the European continent. Much, very much in our history is associated with Europe. Such is also the case with the United States, for which Europe has been a source of cultural traditions and immigrants. It is not surprising that Soviets and Americans have perceived each other through a European prism, giving little thought to our Pacific commonalities. Yet it is in the Pacific area where we are neighbors, very close neighbors. Only three miles separate Big Diomede Island (USSR) from Little Diomede Island (U.S.) in the Bering Strait.

Today a special responsibility rests upon our two countries for the future, indeed for the survival, of human civilization. At the same time the role of the Pacific region in global security is growing in pace with the Pacific's increasing political and economic importance.

In order to cope with the complex issues of our times, it behooves us to seek greater mutual understanding. This volume represents one of the first joint Soviet-American scholarly efforts to address the above task. The authors examine geographic, historical, economic, and scientific ties that have for over two centuries linked our countries across the Pacific. Special attention is devoted to economics and to science, both of which have the potential of exerting a salutary influence on Soviet-American relations in general.

As a contribution to improved understanding between our two countries, so important for the normalization of relations between East and West, the publication of this volume is to be welcomed.

Academician G. A. ARBATOV
Director, Institute of the USA and Canada
USSR Academy of Sciences

# Introduction
# from the American Editor

WELL OVER A CENTURY AGO young Russian officers are said to have gathered in the study of Governor-General N. N. Muraviev* in the Siberian town of Irkutsk to discuss the prospects for a United States of Siberia, federated across the Pacific Ocean with the United States of America.[1] This volume makes no such proposal. But it does suggest that at a time of deepening economic and cultural relations among Pacific Basin countries, the United States and the Soviet Union have an opportunity to build mutually beneficial ties across the Pacific, ties based on geographical propinquity, a legacy of trade and cooperation, and contemporary economic complementarities.

The idea of a joint Soviet-American study of the above topic grew out of discussions in Khabarovsk with V. P. Chichkanov, a distinguished economist. Khabarovsk is an economic, cultural, and scientific center of the Soviet Far East. Since 1966 I have had the privilege of visiting Khabarovsk regularly, including 1979 when this picturesque city on the Amur River hosted the Fourteenth Pacific Science Congress. Valerii Petrovich and I became acquainted in 1981. He had recently come to Khabarovsk to assume the directorship of the Institute of Economic Research, a component of the Far East Science Center in Vladivostok. Our conversations during 1981 and into 1982 revealed a number of common interests and shared convictions.

We sensed, for one, that Americans and Russians (meaning here all Soviet citizens, not just those of Russian nationality) alike know less about each other's Pacific region territories than about each other's core areas, the U.S. East Coast and Eastern Europe respec-

---

*Nikolai Nikolaevich Muraviev (1809–1881), energetic and farseeing governor-general of Eastern Siberia from 1847 to 1861. He was honored with the title Count Muraviev-Amurskii after having reunited the Amur region with Russia in 1858.

tively. To most Soviet observers the American Far West seems remote and exotic. For their part, Americans as a whole have only the vaguest intimations of nonmilitary aspects of the Soviet presence in the Pacific. President Gerald Ford's deliberate omission of any mention of the USSR in his 1975 "Pacific Doctrine" speech together with the absence of the USSR from most discussions of the Pacific Community concept since 1980 reinforce popular perceptions of the Soviet Union as a European country with a landlocked Siberian backyard. Yet the Soviet Far East's maritime frontiers (16,700 miles) exceed those of the continental United States (14,225).[2]

We agreed, further, that both the United States and the Soviet Union are increasing their involvement in the Pacific region. The American Far West and Soviet Far East are assuming more significance in their respective national economies. In 1977, American trade in the Pacific surpassed American commerce for that year in the Atlantic. The Far East* plays an increasingly important role in the Soviet economy as a source of raw materials and marine products. Completion of the Baikal-Amur Railroad, or BAM, the "gateway to Siberian resources" in the apt words of Theodore Shabad and Victor L. Mote,[3] should strengthen Soviet participation in an international division of labor in the Pacific Basin.

Russians and Americans are moving toward the Pacific as travelers, temporary workers, and permanent residents. This trend is perhaps stronger in the United States, where it forms a historical tradition. Since 1819 the population center of the United States has moved steadily westward with each census. In 1982 the center crossed the Mississippi River.[4] In 1983 the Census Bureau predicted that by A.D. 2000 a majority of Americans will be living on the Pacific and in the American South.[5]

Siberia and the Far East have long been important themes in Russian and Soviet literature. Today more than ever before, Siberia and the Far East figure in the lives and works of the USSR's most popular writers: Georgii Markov, Viktor Astafiev, Valentin Rasputin, Pyotr Proskurin, and Vasilii Shukshin to name just a few. Why are Soviet readers drawn to areas east of the Urals? Open spaces, natural grandeur, mineral wealth, and romance account for part of the pull. So does nostalgia for a simple, if hard, life. Personal qualities commonly attributed to Siberians—directness, self-reliance, bigness

---

*Here and hereafter in this volume, the expression "Far East" denotes the Soviet Far East.

of spirit, a concern for the natural environment—are also admired.[6] Interestingly, such qualities are also associated with Americans who live in the western part of the United States.

We also agreed that the histories of the American Far West and the Russian Far East are interconnected. Cultural differences and political vicissitudes have not prevented Russians and Americans from trading and working with each other in the Pacific for two hundred years. These historical associations have traces in regional toponymy. Witness Russian place names in Alaska (Shelikhov Strait, Baranov Island, Pavlov Bay, etc.) and California (Russian River). Conversely there is no question about the inspiration for Amerika Bay (near Vladivostok) and Lake Jack London (in the Magadan District).

After several conversations we decided in February of 1982 to prepare a book on Soviet-American economic relations in the Pacific with special attention to the Soviet Far East and American Far West. We decided that the book would be addressed to nonspecialists.

In identifying specific objects of analysis, we came up with the following questions: What are the salient geographical characteristics of the American Far West and the Soviet Far East? How did American and Russian economic interests develop in the Pacific region? What trends are currently shaping the magnitude and structure of the economies of the American Far West and the Soviet Far East? How do these trends impinge on the potential for each region's future involvement in the Pacific Basin? What is the record of Russian-American and Soviet-American trade in the Pacific? Do economic complementarities between the American Far West and the Soviet Far East exist? If so, can these complementarities be translated into trade and investment? What incentives and constraints govern prospects for economic and scientific cooperation?

The task of putting together such a study and of bringing it out as a book in both the United States and in the Soviet Union, given the international climate of 1982–1985, was fraught with pitfalls. Although a Soviet-American study of early Russian-American relations had been published in Moscow and Washington in 1980,[7] we felt that our joint project with its contemporary and regional foci had only one precedent.[8] Common sense therefore dictated that we proceed cautiously, move step by step, and maintain close contact through regular meetings. Fortunately we were able to meet frequently, either in Khabarovsk or in Honolulu.

At the outset of this cooperative effort, guidelines were established

and observed by contributors from both countries. Each editor
began by selecting scholars from among his own countrymen and
invited each to prepare a chapter about one aspect (e.g., geography,
history, current trends) of the subject. All then agreed that the focus
would be on economic and scientific topics. Polemics were excluded.
It was further decided that each editor, in consultation with the
coeditor and contributor, would enjoy the prerogative of editing
each chapter. On one matter the American and Soviet coeditors
were unable to reach an agreement by the time the American edition
of this volume went to press. During the review process of the Rus-
sian-language edition, a Soviet referee suggested adding a critical
commentary to chapters written by American authors. In the interest of maintaining reciprocity, the American authors expressed hope
that this proposal would not be implemented when the Soviet edition
of this joint monograph is published in 1986 by Progress Publishers,
Moscow. The translation of American chapters into Russian and
Soviet chapters into English was to be done in Khabarovsk. I welcomed the last arrangement, for as translator of the Russian-lan-
guage contributions, I was afforded the opportunity to work with
each of the Soviet authors as well as with the translator of the American chapters. A spacious and well-equipped office was placed at our
disposal.

As the work got underway in the spring of 1982, several ad hoc
adjustments brought all participants closer together. Each American
and Soviet coauthor became aware of his or her counterpart (author
of a chapter on an analogous topic). Initial drafts were translated
and read by counterpart authors as well as the coeditors. Revised
drafts were then prepared on the basis of sometimes extensive commentary. Each author received and approved the translation of his
or her chapter. Those authors who could not read the language of
translation consulted specialists. Investment of extra time and effort
by all participants justified itself not only editorially. It also deepened
mutual understanding and respect among Soviet and American
coauthors, who did not let methodological and ideological differences preclude a fruitful intellectual dialogue.

Without the help of institutions and individuals, both American and
Soviet, this work would not have been completed. Sustained support
was given by the USSR Academy of Sciences. Noteworthy in this
respect are Academician N. A. Shilo, member of the Academy's
Presidium and until 1985 chairman of the Far East Science Center
in Vladivostok, his successor A. D. Shcheglov, and I. V. Milovidov

of the Academy's Foreign Relations Department in Moscow. Academician Yu. A. Kosygin, director of the Institute of Tectonics and Geophysics in Khabarovsk, lent wise counsel, as did A. I. Krushanov, deputy chairman of the Far East Science Center and director of the Institute of History, Archaeology, and Ethnography of Peoples of the Far East in Vladivostok. Stephen Uhalley, Jr., director of the Center for Asian and Pacific Studies at the University of Hawaii graciously sponsored Dr. Chichkanov's visit to Honolulu and gave personal encouragement to a number of this volume's contributors. Each author is to be thanked for punctually completing drafts and for submitting to multiple editorial reviews with patience, understanding, and good humor.

The editors are grateful to the U.S. Department of State and to the USSR Ministry of Foreign Affairs for expediting unprecedented mobility between Honolulu and Khabarovsk.

A number of Soviet and American individuals have generously given of their time and expertise: George Akita, N. N. Bolkhovitinov, Georgiana Chave, Basil Dmytryshyn, Roland J. Fuchs, James R. Gibson, V. I. Ivanov, Mead Kirkpatrick, K. V. Malakhovskii, Victor L. Mote, D. V. Petrov, Richard A. Pierce, Pat Polansky, Don Raleigh, Theodore Shabad, V. Vrevskii, John A. White, Allen S. Whiting, Everett A. Wingert, and Ella Wiswell.

N. G. Nekhaenko and V. A. Slyusarev, Vladivostok and Khabarovsk scientific secretaries representing the Far East Science Center, ably assisted by S. V. Kharlamova, provided space for the translation work.

Attentive readers may notice an imbalance in the composition of this volume's authorial *kollektiv*. Chapters by eight Americans appear but only seven are by Soviets. The discrepancy is more apparent than real. L. K. Zhukova, translator of the American chapters, merits inclusion as the eighth Soviet author. All participants in the project have reason to be grateful to her.

This volume has had the good fortune of meticulous and expert editorial advice from Patricia Crosby of the University of Hawaii Press.

This work does not pretend to offer an authoritative treatment of Soviet-American economic relations in the Pacific. Rather it is designed to raise the level of awareness and to stimulate discussion of a neglected topic in both countries. Its contributors hope that it will lead to further analogous cooperative efforts in the interests of strengthening mutual tolerance and understanding between the Soviet and American peoples.

## NOTES

1. P. Kropotkin, *Memoirs of a Revolutionist* (New York: Horizon Press, 1968), p. 169.

2. E. I. Dolgopolova, *U karty mirovogo okeana* (Moscow: Voenizdat, 1980), pp. 167, 382.

3. Theodore Shabad and Victor L. Mote, *Gateway to Siberian Resources (the BAM)* (New York: John Wiley & Sons, 1977).

4. *New York Times,* 6 June 1982.

5. *Time,* 19 September 1983.

6. Klaus Mehnert, *The Russians and Their Favorite Books* (Stanford: Hoover Institution Press, 1983), p. 76.

7. *The United States and Russia: The Beginning of Relations, 1765–1815,* ed. N. N. Bashkina, et al. (Washington: GPO, 1980). *Rossiia i SSHA: stanovlenie otnoshenii 1765–1815* (Moscow: Nauka, 1980).

8. *Soviet Far East and Pacific Northwest,* ed. by Robert Mosse (Seattle: University of Washington Press, 1944).

# Introduction
# from the Soviet Editor

IN THE MIDDLE of the nineteenth century, Friedrich Engels wrote that the Pacific Ocean would someday inherit the unifying role that the Mediterranean had played from antiquity through the Middle Ages and that the Atlantic had assumed with the Age of Exploration. Few today would gainsay this prediction. Scientific progress has in our time transformed the Pacific Ocean from a barrier into an avenue between nations and peoples. Across its waters intermingle the interests of socialist, capitalist, and developing countries, among whom stand out the Soviet Union, America, China, and Japan.

Of the multitude of important and difficult tasks facing the peoples and governments of Pacific Basin countries, none is more pressing than that of strengthening peace. It is clear to economists that international trade and long-term economic ties not only reinforce stability and stimulate healthy growth but promote a general atmosphere of trust, mutual respect, and a readiness to seek mutually acceptable solutions to thorny issues. Economic and scientific cooperation, cultural interchange, and international movements of people and information all help dispel prejudices and deepen mutual understanding, whether in the Pacific Basin or in the world as a whole.

In the present unsettled international environment, a widening of regional cooperation in the Pacific Basin is a practicable and effective means to strengthen peace, trust, and security. In the Soviet Union any step toward regional ties is regarded as a positive phenomenon. Nor do we doubt that a majority of Americans share this view.

Two regions with a tremendous economic potential face each other across the North Pacific: the Soviet Far East and the American Far West. It has been a timely and commendable task for fifteen

Soviet and American scholars to acquaint readers in both countries with these regions. They have united their efforts and come to grips with what in many ways is a unique, pioneering work.

The work seeks to achieve the following four goals. First, it sets out to describe the physical geography of the Soviet Far East and the American Pacific states, juxtaposing their differences and illuminating shared traits of their natural environments. Second, it traces the historical development of each country's economic interests in the Pacific region, with due attention to Russian-American commerce. Third, it measures the scale and analyzes the structure of the Soviet Far Eastern and American Far Western regional economies, relating contemporary trends to roles which these two areas might play in the Pacific Basin. Fourth, it hypothesizes a framework of economic complementarity between our Far East and the American Far West, identifying incentives and constraints bearing upon perspectives for regional economic and scientific cooperation. These issues are, furthermore, addressed here from both Soviet and American points of view.

Although this is not the place to recapitulate arguments and conclusions, I should like nonetheless to make a few observations. In the pages of this collective work, references are made to the lure of the Pacific for Russians and Americans alike. Various motives led them to the shores of this great ocean, not the least of which was the lure of romance. For example, at the beginning of the last century a group of young aristocrats, fated later to participate in the December 1825 uprising in St. Petersburg and to be remembered as Decembrists, decided to establish on Sakhalin a republic modeled after the United States of North America.

More than anything, however, it was economic considerations that attracted Russians to the Far East. Bit by bit inhabitants of Russia's central provinces moved closer to the Pacific in search of land and a better life. Eastward migration assumed a mass character in the middle of the nineteenth century, about the same time that Americans started to settle the Pacific shores of North America in significant numbers. Is there not something symbolic in this coincidence?

The history of Russian-American relations is rich in symbols, and a number of these are treated in this volume. Let us look at an example that does not appear in the text but which in my opinion deserves mention. Mikhail Aleksandrovich Bestuzhev (1800–1871), a Decembrist condemned to permanent exile in the eastern borders of the

Russian Empire, wound up thirty years later being dispatched by an Amur River trading company to America to purchase paddle wheel steamers. Bad weather prevented Bestuzhev from reaching the United States, but during the course of his attempt he encountered a Cossack battalion descending the Amur, looking for a suitable spot to establish a post on this great river. Bestuzhev advised the battalion commander to locate the post on high ground overlooking the Amur near its junction with the Ussuri River. The commander took this advice. On the site of this post (called Khabarovka), there eventually grew up a city named Khabarovsk, where a good portion of this book was written and translated.

Such examples are good symbols, for they reflect the strivings of peoples of both great countries to build positive relations across the Pacific. This volume contains any number of such historical episodes. Yet with all due respect to our ancestors' deeds, our main focus here is contemporary: to show how the USSR and U.S. might use their geographical propinquity and economic complementarities to activate their relations in the Pacific Basin. An important objective of the Soviet authors has been to highlight the USSR's economic potential in this region, a potential which we feel is not always fully appreciated outside of our country.

Since Soviet rule was established in 1922, the Far East has been transformed into an industrialized region under the leadership of the Communist Party. We feel that the area's potential remains great. Enormous reserves of natural resources await the time when they will be placed at the service of the country and, under favorable international conditions, at the service of other states, notably those of the Pacific Basin.

In realizing this potential a valuable contribution, in our opinion, can be made by regional cooperation with the U.S. Pacific states. Astute observers have identified a dozen fields of knowledge and enterprise where bilateral ties might bring significant results. At the same time, no one can deny that the potential for mutually beneficial interaction between the two regions is hardly being utilized. Completion of the Baikal-Amur Railroad may stimulate new thinking about international economic cooperation in the North Pacific.

Among the contributors to this work are scholars from the USSR Academy of Sciences' Institute of the USA and Canada, the University of California, the University of Washington, and the East-West Center for Scientific and Cultural Interchange in Honolulu. The host institutions are the Institute of Economic Research of the Far

East Science Center of the USSR Academy of Sciences and the University of Hawaii.

There is no sense in concealing that at times our joint efforts were saddled with complexities. After all, Soviet and American contributors have different ideologies and different methodological approaches to their topics. At the same time, work on this volume brought us closer together. We were animated by a vision of trans-Pacific cooperation and by a determination to convey this vision convincingly to our readers. We were united by respect for the knowledge and professionalism of our colleagues, with whom we shared scientific interests and, in a majority of cases, residence in the Pacific region. Of inestimable utility were the frequent visits to Khabarovsk by the American coeditor, John J. Stephan, and a visit by myself to Honolulu.

The contributors have been united in their opinion that this volume must have a scholarly basis. At the same time, we have tried to make the text accessible to nonspecialist readers in both the Soviet Union and in the United States. To achieve this we stressed conciseness and minimized technical jargon. Conciseness required restricting details and perhaps in some areas depth as well. We ask our readers to forgive this. A hefty book could, of course, be written about the subject covered in each of our chapters.

Parallel editions of this study are appearing in the Soviet Union and in the United States in Russian and English respectively. In general the two editions are identical. However, taking into account differences in the background of Soviet and American readers, some adjustments have been made by mutual agreement of the coeditors. These concern largely the removal or addition of explanatory material. The America edition includes an appendix on cities in the Soviet Far East by V. G. Smoliak. The Soviet edition has an appendix on cities of the American Far West prepared by John B. Richards.

All American chapters were translated into Russian by L. K. Zhukova under the supervision of E. B. Kovrigin. John Stephan has translated all the Soviet contributions.

# Soviet-American
# Horizons
# on the Pacific

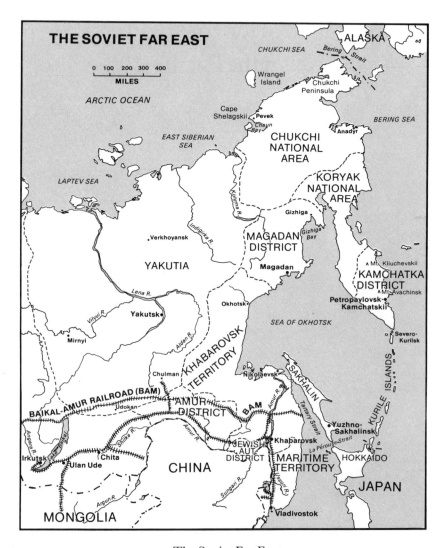

The Soviet Far East

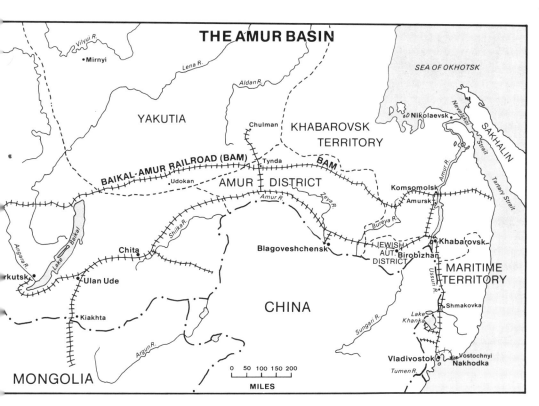

The Amur Basin

# The Soviet Far East

## E. B. KOVRIGIN

THE FAR EAST. These words evoke in Soviet citizens twin associations—distance and romance. The distance is both real and illusory. Although Trans-Siberian express trains take a week to reach Vladivostok from Moscow, Ilyushin-62s whisk passengers over the same territory in less than eight hours. The romance, on the other hand, remains steadfastly real. Anyone who visits the Soviet Far East cannot forget its exotic natural majesty. Nowhere does the land seem so alive, so pristine. Nowhere do so many contrasts and paradoxes leap to the eye. Where else do grapevines wrap themselves around fir trees? Where else do tigers hunt arctic reindeer? Ginseng, geysers, volcanoes, king crabs, and salmon—in our country these are found only in the Far East.

The Far East has generous physical proportions. It stretches from the polar ice cap 3,000 miles southward to rice plantations on the Korean frontier. Its 2,500-mile breadth straddles five of the USSR's eleven time zones. When the Moscow Kremlin bells strike midnight, people in Khabarovsk are getting up. In Kamchatka they are already at work.

The Far East is a treasure trove of mineral and biological resources. It contains more than a third of the USSR's forests, a quarter of the USSR's energy resources, a fifth of the USSR's biological marine resources, and a sizeable portion of the country's precious metals. This natural wealth has international significance. Yet the task of development is fraught with obstacles. More than 80 percent of the territory falls within the permafrost zone, where the ground is permanently frozen at depths reaching up to a mile.

Although both Soviet and foreign literature occasionally subsume all territory east of the Urals in the Russian Republic (RSFSR) under the rubric "Siberia," Siberia and the Far East are distinct areas both geographically and economically. In terms of physical geography, the Far East's western boundary runs from the juncture of the Shilka and Argun rivers (tributaries of the Amur) along the Stanovoi and Dzhugdzhur ranges and Kolyma uplands to Chaun Bay on the coast of the East Siberian Sea.[1] The Far East's northernmost point, Wrangel Island, lies on the same latitude as does Alaska's northern tip, Point Barrow. Its southern extremity, where the Tumen River flows into the Sea of Japan, shares a latitude with Detroit, Michigan.

The Far East is an entity unto itself, for it lies at the juncture of the world's greatest continent and greatest ocean. "This meeting point," in the words of V. V. Nikolskaia, "is exactly where our planet's dissymmetry reveals itself."[2] Kamchatka's Mount Kliuchevskii (15,912 feet above sea level) is quite close to the Kurile-Kamchatka Trench (reaching depths of 30,000 feet below sea level), the two points spanning nearly nine vertical miles.

For purposes of economic geography, the Yakut Autonomous Soviet Socialist Republic (hereafter Yakutia) is included in the Far East, although its natural environment comes closer to that of Eastern Siberia. Yakutia's economic ties with the rest of the Far East have been strengthened by completion of the Baikal-Amur Railroad, which provides direct access to the Pacific littoral.

The Far East's 2,400,000 square miles (including Yakutia) accounts for more than a quarter of the USSR. Ten Frances could fit into the Far East with room left over for Italy and West Germany. Yakutia's area is equivalent to a third of the United States. The Khabarovsk region is double the area of Japan.

If the Far East is spatially impressive, it remains nonetheless thinly inhabited. The region's 1983 population (7,297,000) only slightly exceeded that of Hokkaido, Japan's northernmost island. Table 1 gives an outline of the Far East's spatial and demographic magnitudes.

The Far East is located at the interstices of several nations. Its southern edge forms the USSR's frontier with China and the People's Democratic Republic of Korea. Sakhalin comes to within twenty-six miles of Hokkaido, just across the La Pérouse Strait. Less than two miles separate Hokkaido from the southernmost islands of the Kurile archipelago. The Bering Strait (fifty-five miles) divides Eurasia from North America. The Soviet-American frontier and international dateline run through a group of small islands in the strait. Just 4.5 miles of water separate Big Diomede (Ratmanov) Island, USSR, from Little Diomede Island, U.S.

TABLE I
**Area and Population of the Soviet Far East**

| Administrative Unit (Administrative Center) | Area (in Thousands of Sq. Mi.) | Population, 1983 (in Thousands) |
|---|---|---|
| Kamchatka District, including Koryak National Area (Petropavlovsk-Kamchatskii) | 182.4 | 415 |
| Magadan District, including Chukchi National Area (Magadan) | 463 | 510 |
| Amur District (Blagoveshchensk) | 140.4 | 1,007 |
| Sakhalin District (Yuzhno-Sakhalinsk) | 33.6 | 679 |
| Maritime Territory (Vladivostok) | 64 | 2,079 |
| Khabarovsk Territory, including Jewish Autonomous District (Khabarovsk) | 318.4 | 1,663 |
| Yakutia (Yakutsk) | 1,198.2 | 944 |
| TOTAL | 2,400 | 7,297 |

## Geology

The Far East has a complex and rich geological past. Minister of Geology E. A. Kozlovskii has written, "This is a unique region, allowing us to study the formation of the earth's crust from the earliest periods until the present."[3]

Mountains dominate most of the Far East. Lowlands are wedged between ranges or cling to rivers and seacoasts. Although Far Eastern peaks, most of which are three thousand to six thousand feet in height, cannot rival those of the Himalayas or Andes, a few are quite impressive. In particular, peaks well over six thousand feet are not uncommon in the Dzhugdzhur Range along the Okhotsk seaboard. Mount Kliuchevskii, rising nearly three miles above sea level, is the largest active volcano in Eurasia. Picturesque hills undulate across the southern part of the Maritime Territory.

While on a visit to the Far East in 1890, Anton Chekhov recorded his impressions of the Amur estuary. "Asia ends here, and it might be said that the Amur would flow into the Great Ocean if Sakhalin Island did not stand astride its path."[4] Sakhalin, a long, slender island lying roughly parallel to the continent, is separated from the mainland by the Tartary Strait, which narrows toward the north to form the four-mile Nevelskoi Strait, named in honor of a Russian captain (later admiral) who in 1849 conclusively established that Sakhalin was an island and that it was possible to navigate ships from the Amur into the ocean.*

The Far East's northern reaches—the Yakutia Plateau, Kolyma Basin, and Chukotskii (Chukchi) Peninsula—are almost entirely composed of mountain systems interspersed with tundralike river plains.

Approximately midway along the Far East's Pacific littoral extends the 750-mile Kamchatka Peninsula. In the distant geological past, Kamchatka was an island. Seismic and glacial activity eventually fused it with the Eurasian landmass. Through the length of the peninsula run two parallel ranges with asymmetric slopes. These ranges plunge steeply toward the Pacific in the east and gently incline toward the Sea of Okhotsk in the west. Glaciers cover much of central Kamchatka. Seen from the air, the peninsula presents a magnificent spectacle of untamed, rocky majesty.

Kamchatka and the Kurile Islands are the only region of the USSR with active volcanoes. Eruptions occur almost annually, at times leaving new cones. Writing about Kamchatka in the eighteenth century, the noted Russian traveler Stepan P. Krasheninnikov recorded how Kamchadal natives characterized Mount Avachinsk. They spoke of it, Krasheninnikov wrote, as a "burning mountain" which since ancient times had "constantly smoked" and on occasion belched out molten lava and ash-laden clouds.[5] Along Kamchatka's Pacific coast stretches a chain of hot geysers redolent of Old Faithful in Wyoming's Yellowstone National Park. The Valley of Geysers in the Kronotskii Natural Reserve is one of the most dramatically beautiful natural scenes in the USSR.

Between Kamchatka and Hokkaido stretches a 650-mile insular arc—the Kuriles—dividing the Pacific Ocean from the Sea of Okhotsk. Consisting of some thirty major islands and many islets and rocky outcroppings, the Kuriles are mostly of volcanic origin.

---

*The Japanese explorer Mamiya Rinzō ascertained Sakhalin's insularity in 1809, but his discovery was not widely known in Europe until many years later. —AMERICAN EDITOR

Like Kamchatka, the archipelago forms a segment of the Pacific's seismically active "rim of fire," where earthquakes and seaquakes frequently occur. Some of these disturbances unleash sea swells that, upon approaching land, rear up into giant waves (tsunami) of awesome destructive force. In 1952 a tsunami over forty feet in height struck the town of Severo-Kurilsk on the island of Paramushir in the northern Kuriles, causing severe damage.

The Soviet government has since created a network of tsunami warning stations which monitor seismic shocks and, if the occasion requires, sound the alert. Soviet-American cooperation in tsunami research, inaugurated in the early 1970s, has proven mutually beneficial, for the Pacific littorals of the Far East and American Far West alike are subject to tidal waves.

## Mineral and Fuel Resources

A long geologic history and active tectonic processes have richly endowed the Far East with mineral resources. More than seventy-nine varieties of valuable deposits are found here, including gold, diamonds, tin, zinc, iron ore, coal, oil, and natural gas. In some cases proven reserves are huge.

Nonferrous and precious metals are found in a wide belt along the Pacific coastline. Gold prospectors tried their luck along the Aldan, Zeya, Bureya, and Amgun rivers and on the Chukchi Peninsula well before the Revolution. In Soviet times gold mining became a large-scale industry in the Kolyma River Basin of the Magadan District. Today the Far East continues to supply the USSR with most of its gold.

Extraction of nonferrous metals in the Far East is a major branch of the USSR's mining industry. Geologists have demonstrated that the Far East has the richest deposits of zinc in the country, deposits located in the Sikhote-Alin Mountains of the Maritime Territory, southern reaches of the Khabarovsk Territory, in Yakutia, and on the Chukchi Peninsula. Cassiterite, a tin-rich mineral with significant traces of wolfram, copper, lead, zinc, and bismuth, is attracting special interest, as have aluminum deposits in the Khabarovsk Territory and copper ore at Udokan in southern Yakutia.

Important iron ore deposits have been uncovered in the Jewish Autonomous District, the Amur District, and in southern Yakutia. Manganese has been found in the Khabarovsk Territory, and titanium deposits have turned up along the Maritime Territory coast. Recently discovered coking coal at Chulman and Lena in southern Yakutia are going to supply a significant portion of the country's metallurgical industry. The Lena field alone is the second largest in the USSR, putting it far ahead of traditional coal-mining areas in the Amur and Sakhalin districts and in the Maritime Territory.

The Far East is generously endowed with natural gas and oil. Gas deposits in Yakutia are becoming accessible through railroad and pipeline construction and are assuming international economic significance. Two pipelines are carrying north Sakhalin oil under the Tartary Strait to refineries at the industrial city of Komsomolsk-na-Amure.[6] Parallel pipelines are being laid in anticipation of transporting gas from offshore areas along Sakhalin's Okhotsk seaboard. Geologists believe that oil and gas will also be found in the shelf zones of Magadan and Kamchatka districts.

Other minerals are also found in abundance. Apatite and phosphate are ample for meeting regional demand for fertilizers. The regional building-materials industry can rely on local sources for cement, clay, stone, tuff (porous volcanic rock), pumice, vermiculite, and gravel. From the 1950s the region around Mirnyi in Yakutia began yielding fabulous diamonds. Subsequently, diamonds have also been found further north on the Vilyui Plateau.

Nature's bounty includes two hundred fifty mineral springs distributed throughout the Far East. Regional sanatoriums enjoy national as well as local popularity, notably those at Kuldur in the Khabarovsk Territory and at Shmakovka in the Maritime Territory. Paratunka Hot Springs near Petropavlovsk-Kamchatskii features outdoor bathing in midwinter. Geothermal energy on Kamchatka generates electric power and heats greenhouses for year-round fresh vegetables. The Pauzhetskaia Geothermal Electric Power Plant is the only one of its kind in the USSR.

At present minerals and fuels represent the Far East's best hope for economic growth. A lack of transport has until now constrained development of mineral wealth, but the newly completed Baikal-Amur Railroad should reduce bottlenecks and help the region achieve its productive potential.

Geologists have conducted extensive but not exhaustive surveys in the Far East. The region remains relatively unexplored compared to the rest of the country and probably still holds some surprises.

## Climate and Agriculture

It is not easy to generalize about the climate of a region that extends from the arctic to the temperate zone with subtropical flora. The weather in most of the Far East has a monsoon character, with seasonal changes in wind direction. Winter winds are from the northwest, the west, and the southwest, blowing dry, clear, cold air across the Far East except for Kamchatka and the Chukchi Peninsula. In summer the Hawaiian anticyclone brings warm, humid air and heavy rains. Typhoons strike the Maritime Territory, Kamchatka, and the Kuriles in late summer. At times these typhoons penetrate inland to Khabarovsk and further west, causing extensive flooding such as that which inundated the Amur Basin in August of 1981. Precipitation in the southern part of the Far East has been known to reach eleven inches in twenty-four hours, equivalent to more than six months average rainfall in Moscow.[7]

Precipitation varies considerably within the Far East. Kamchatka and the Kuriles have on the average forty inches of rain and snow annually, but the Kolyma Basin gets less than a fifth of that. As a rule more than half of the precipitation occurs during the summer months. Summer humidity can reach 90 percent and more. In the Kuriles this humidity can assume the form of thick fogs that blanket the islands for weeks, making navigation treacherous. Winter precipitation in inland areas is sparse. Snow falls only several times a season. Indeed, winter months are the sunniest time of year. Khabarovsk, for example, enjoys twenty-seven sunny days in an average winter month.

Far Eastern temperatures vary in accordance with latitude, altitude, and the influence of ocean currents. In general, year-round temperatures are lower than in other parts of the USSR at equivalent latitudes. Siberian frosts grip most of the territory in winter. The coldest recorded temperature in the northern hemisphere (−95.8 degrees Fahrenheit) was registered at Oymyakon in Yakutia. Winter frosts are one of the main factors limiting economic activity. The need for special construction techniques and high fuel consumption greatly increase development costs. In some years the cold is so severe that rivers freeze to the bottom, killing millions of fish. But it is easy to overdramatize Far Eastern winters. This time of year has its compensations. An invigorating nip in the air, bright sunshine, a cloudless sky, and a thick carpet of snow covering a silent windless landscape all combine to win the hearts of residents and visitors alike.

V. P. Sysoev, a sensitive observer of nature in the Far East, has written that the region's summer climate resembles that of northern India.[8] Ninety-degree heat and 98 percent humidity can wilt the toughest denizen of this area. But specialists hold out the hope that construction of flood control installations in the Amur Basin could improve the area's climate, cooling summers and warming winters.[9]

The most congenial climate in the Far East is probably found along the southern coast of the Maritime Territory, an area which offers superb sites for relaxation, as more and more Soviet tourists are discovering. By general consensus autumn is the best time of year. In the Maritime Territory, the southern reaches of the Khabarovsk Territory, and on Sakhalin, warm, dry, Indian summers continue right into October. We call it the "velvet season."

In his 1981 study of Siberia and East Asia, the American scholar Allen S. Whiting noted that "a basic problem far more challenging than climate confronts the developers of East Asian Siberia, the phenomenon of permafrost."[10] Indeed, permafrost is a problem for us. Only southern Kamchatka, the Kuriles, the Maritime Territory, and most of Sakhalin and the Amur Valley are free of it. Not by chance are those regions the most developed and populated.

Permafrost does have certain advantages. For example, in the mining industry, shafts can be dug in frozen ground without supports. Permafrost prevents drainage of surface moisture and thus helps support vegetation in areas of low rainfall. On the other hand, the melting and refreezing of surface soils, with attendant swellings and deformations, pose special problems for the construction of buildings, railbeds, and roads.

Climatic characteristics of the Far East together with the region's mountainous terrain do not create favorable conditions for developing agriculture. In the south, excessively damp soils are hard to cultivate. The further north one goes, the shorter the growing season. Consequently, per capita acreage under cultivation in the Far East is one of the lowest in the USSR.

What good land there is can be found in the three southern plains: Zeya-Bureya, mid-Amur, and Lake Khanka. The Amur and Maritime regions have virtually a monopoly on soybean production in the USSR. Here also are grown wheat, barley, oats, and buckwheat. Harvests, however, are below national norms. These plains also yield good crops of potatoes, cabbage, cucumbers, and tomatoes, all of which are consumed locally.

Fertile soils and a long (200-day) growing season in the Maritime Territory allow for a number of crops, such as rice and grain, that are atypical for the Russian Republic, but unfortunately, heavy summer monsoon rains saturate cultivated areas and inhibit harvesting. When completed, Amur flood control projects are expected to boost agricultural productivity.

Although permafrost soils limit agriculture in northern parts of the Far East, abundant natural ground vegetation creates favorable conditions for livestock raising. Reindeer continue to provide a living for sections of the aboriginal population. Recently in Yakutia considerable attention has been accorded to horses as the basis for a meat industry.

Limited arable land and an inclement climate make it unlikely that the Far East will supply itself with agricultural products such as grains and fruits in the foreseeable future. Except for potatoes, soybeans, eggs, poultry, and fish, food products will probably continue to be imported from the rest of the country. Nonetheless, economists assure us that improved utilization of local resources will ameliorate supplies of meat, dairy products, and vegetables.

## Hydrology

More than any other region of the USSR, the Far East has a maritime environment. Its shores are washed by the East Siberian, Chukchi, Bering, Okhotsk, and Japan seas. Kamchatka and the Kuriles face directly on the Pacific. The Far Eastern littoral (16,700 miles) accounts for more than half of the USSR's maritime frontiers (27,000 miles).

Proximity of the ocean influences Far Eastern life-styles and economic activities. Of the Maritime Territory's 2 million inhabitants, about 100,000 go to sea every year. The Pacific and adjacent seas supply some 40 percent of the country's fish. There are abundant hauls of herring, cod, flounder, halibut, mackerel, and mollusks. Waters around Kamchatka and the Kuriles provide almost 100 percent of the Soviet crab and salmon catch.

All sorts of sea mammals can be found in Far Eastern waters. Sperm whales, finbacks, humpback whales, and blue whales appear in the summer months along the Okhotsk, Bering, and Chukchi coasts. Walruses live in the arctic seas.

Marine flora are also a valuable resource of the Pacific littoral. Around the Kurile Islands are clustered kelp plantations. In accordance with a bilateral agreement, Japanese fishermen from Hokkaido harvest kelp in Soviet waters around the southern Kuriles under the surveillance of Soviet inspectors.

Tides reach record heights along our Pacific coasts and may someday become an important supplementary source of electric energy. The Okhotsk seacoast, where forty-foot tides have been recorded, offers attractive possibilities for the construction of tidal power stations.

The Pacific and Arctic oceans have for us an important logistic significance. Through them passes the Northern Sea Route linking Vladivostok with Murmansk and Arkhangelsk in European Russia. Ice poses formidable obstacles at such high latitudes, and only three Far Eastern ports (Vladivostok, Nakhodka, Vostochnyi) are ice free. Others must be kept open by icebreakers. Ships can travel along the arctic coast only in summer. Even then they travel in convoys behind icebreakers, an operation fraught with difficulties and uncertainties.

The risks run by arctic convoys were graphically demonstrated in September and October of 1983 when unexpectedly early freezing of the Chukchi Sea trapped dozens of eastbound ships. A rescue operation was mounted from Pevek, northernmost port in the USSR, and for several weeks the nation held its breath while the icebreakers *Leonid Brezhnev, Yermak,* and others tried to free the ships from the grip of massive ice floes. One freighter sank and over thirty other vessels required extensive repairs.[11] Maintaining year-round movement along the Northern Sea Route remains a high-priority task which technology and human ingenuity will someday solve.

Because mountains approach close to the coastline, Far Eastern rivers are relatively short. Only four of them flow for over six hundred miles: the Amur, Kolyma, Anadyr, and Zeya. Most rivers here have swift currents and sharply elevated water levels during the monsoon season, especially in the wake of typhoons when wide expanses of the taiga are flooded. In open, flat areas, riverbeds become sinuous and break up into innumerable tributary channels and rivulets. All rivers freeze over in winter. The Kolyma Basin, emptying into the Arctic Ocean, can be icebound for more than half of the year. In areas without roads, rivers serve as transport arteries.

Steamers and barges ply their sinuous courses in summer. In winter their frozen surfaces serve as roads for lorries.

The Amur, the Far East's greatest river, extends with its tributary the Argun for 2,800 miles. Its basin sprawls over most of the southern part of the Far East. Unlike Siberian rivers, which flow from south to north into the Arctic Ocean, the Amur moves from west to east, from the Siberian interior toward the Pacific. Virtually its entire length is navigable during the summer and early autumn, though a longish icebound interval lasting from November to April somewhat diminishes the river's logistic significance. Nonetheless, "Father Amur," as it is popularly called, remains the most important inland waterway in the Far East. Along its shores are cities such as Blagoveshchensk, Khabarovsk, Komsomolsk, and Nikolaevsk.

The Amur's is significant for more than transportation. Zoologists have identified 105 types of fish in the Amur Basin, a record for the northern hemisphere. Among these, salmon are particularly valuable as a commercial product.

Far Eastern rivers have an enormous hydroelectric potential, but steps to utilize this potential have begun only comparatively recently. A hydroelectric station has been built on the Zeya, and similar facilities are being constructed on the Bureya and Kolyma. Smaller rivers also have hydroelectric potential which will be tapped to serve the region's highly dispersed population.

Nature has endowed the Far East with thousands of lakes. They are distributed in low-lying areas and in volcanically active Kamchatka and the Kurile Islands, where they have formed in craters. For the most part the lakes are small, with Lake Khanka the largest, measuring fifty-three by sixty miles. Located in the southern corner of the Maritime Territory, Khanka is divided by the frontier with China, to which the northern quarter belongs. American readers may be interested to learn that in the Magadan District there is a lake named after Jack London, a writer whose unforgettable evocations of the American Far West, Hawaii, and the North and South Pacific have long commanded the admiration of Soviet readers.[12]

## Flora and Fauna

One can fly for hours over the Far East, and the taiga below seems to have no limits. This expanse of moist subarctic coniferous forest covers everything except the treeless northern tundra and some agricultural oases in the south. The taiga's most majestic tree is the Korean cedar, which has been known to reach a height of 120 feet and has a lifespan of over half a millennium. These venerable giants long served as the main source of timber before their depletion prompted conservation measures. Today the forest industry relies heavily upon the Daurian larch, which in addition to making modest demands on soil nutrients offers wood suitable both for cellulose and for construction. Among conifers of the Far Eastern taiga, the Ayan spruce, various types of fir, and the yew stand out.

The taiga supports about two hundred fifty types of trees and over two thousand different plants. Some six hundred of these plants, including the much sought-after ginseng (locally called the "root of life") are used for medicinal purposes. Over a hundred varieties of edible mushrooms, nuts, and berries enrich local diets. Many Far Eastern plants are found nowhere else in the country. One example is bamboo, which grows on Sakhalin and in the southern Kuriles. Sakhalin and the Kuriles are, moreover, the scene of plant gigantism, where leaves loom like verdant panoplies. Scientists have yet to explain the causes of such botanical anomalies.

Any number of landscapes occur in the Far East. Alpine meadows grace mountain slopes, while swamps dominate low-lying areas. Observers are struck by the proximity of northern and subtropical flora. For example, in the Ussuri taiga stretching across much of the southern Khabarovsk and Maritime territories, ferns, nuts, grapes, orchids, and cork trees thrive among northern conifers. Lotus plants with rose-colored blossoms are held in delicate suspension on the waters of Lake Khanka.

The Ussuri taiga's unique botanical life is explained by the absence of glaciation, which at one time covered most of Siberia. Spared an icy mantle, the Amur-Ussuri valleys and southern Sakhalin continue to host pre-glacial vegetation. The Ussuri taiga thus holds clues to ancient flora such as the Korean cedar and the yew tree, which date from the Neocene.

In the northern tundra along the arctic coast, faunas in many respects resemble those of North America, here one finds the Canadian crane and white duck, and on Wrangel Island, polar bears live undisturbed. Some animals are unique to the Far East, among them a rare species of polar fox on the Komandorskii Islands and the Okhotsk reindeer.

Coastal waters teem with furbearing amphibians. Treasured at one time for its pelts was the sea otter. This predator was itself hunted almost to extermination a half-century ago. Law now restricts the hunting of seals, furseals, and sea otters.

The Kurile Islands are nesting areas for hundreds of types of birds, some quite rare. Here, for example, one meets the storm petrel, a sea bird which has already vanished from neighboring Japan. In the Maritime Territory can be found about half of the avian species in the USSR. Most of them are migratory. Protection of migratory birds such as the Siberian crane has been coordinated between the Soviet Union and Japan by a special governmental convention concluded in 1973.[13]

The Far Eastern taiga shelters many denizens of the forest: bears, wolves, elk, and boar. It is also full of furbearing animals: sable, ermine, fox, squirrel, and marten, some of which have commercial significance. The quest for pelts brought Russians to the Pacific in the seventeenth century. The Far East currently supplies the country with a third of its furs.

The richest variety of fauna (some seven hundred species) can be found in the Ussuri taiga. Here the predatory marten hunts roe, and the brown bear coexists with the tree-dwelling white-chested Himalayan bear. The Ussuri taiga is also home to the spotted reindeer, from whose antlers is prepared *pantakrin,* a highly valued medicine. Here alone is found the black sable, whose pelts command the highest prices in the world. Also unique to the area are the Manchurian antelope and the East Siberian leopard.

The very symbol of Far Eastern fauna is the Ussuri tiger. Despite an awesome appearance, this lord of the taiga rarely attacks humans unless provoked. The Ussuri tiger even helps to preserve nature's equilibrium by chasing away predators and hunting only when it is hungry. Thanks to strict preservation laws and vigilant game wardens, the Ussuri tiger population has stabilized, reassuring concerned environmentalists and wildlife lovers.

The rich variety of Far Eastern fauna belies its vulnerability. Some species exist only in small numbers, a dozen-or-so living relics on the verge of extinction. Gone irrevocably are others. The sea cow, whose entire population lived in the Komandorskii Islands, was killed off by hunters in the eighteenth century. Today many regional animals are listed in the USSR's "Red Book" of endangered species and are protected by law. Far Easterners treasure their wildlife and have helped create a network of preserves where fauna and flora are shielded from human predators.

# People

Ultimately the Far East's greatest resource is its people. The region's population is small, but ethnic varieties are considerable. From ancient times the expanses between the Bering Strait and the Amur Basin were inhabited by tribes speaking Paleoasiatic and Tungusic languages: Chukchi and Koryaks (both related to North American Aleuts and Eskimos), Evenki, Nanai (formerly called Goldy), Orochi, Nivkhi (Gilyaks), Ulchi, Udegei, and others. An influx of Slavs from west of the Urals began in the seventeenth century and swelled in the latter half of the nineteenth century.

Eastward migration across Siberia gradually brought the Far East's natural wealth into the Russian Empire's economy. Economic integration both stimulated and was a result of trade. To the seventeenth-century forts (Yakutsk, Okhotsk) were added eighteenth-century ports (Bolsheretsk, Petropavlovsk) and in the nineteenth-century trading and adminstrative centers such as Nikolaevsk (1850), Blagoveshchensk (1856), Khabarovsk (1858), and Vladivostok (1860).

With some exceptions, most of them in the seventeenth and eighteenth centuries, contacts between Russians and the native population during the above process of migration and settlement were peaceful and mutually beneficial. Russians brought economic, technical, and cultural accoutrements which (vodka excepted) had a positive influence on local life-styles. For their part, natives used their knowledge of the taiga to help the Russians as hunters and guides. Cartographers and geologists were particularly indebted to natives for this assistance. A well-known example of such cooperation was the friendship between the naturalist and explorer V. K. Arseniev and the Goldy Dersu Uzala. Arseniev recalled his companion in a 1923 book, which was subsequently translated into many languages.[14] In 1975 Arseniev's story was made into a Soviet-Japanese film directed by Akira Kurosawa.

The establishment of Soviet power in the Far East in 1922, followed by ambitious industrialization projects, quickened the pace of settlement and changed the region's demographic structure. Hundreds of thousands of young people flocked eastward to help turn the taiga into a productive base for the benefit of the whole country. In the 1930s the "Khetagurov movement"* inspired many girls and unmarried women to come east. A new generation appeared, a generation for whom the Far East was home.

Insofar as the whole country took part in the Far East's settlement and industrialization, a genuinely international community grew up there. Russians predominate, but there are many Ukrainians, Belorussians, Jews, and representatives of other peoples of the USSR. Thousands of Koreans emigrated to the Russian Far East in the nineteenth and early twentieth centuries. In addition, some forty thousand Koreans became residents of the Soviet Far East when southern Sakhalin, under Japanese occupation since 1905, was liberated by the Red Army in 1945 and shortly thereafter incorporated into the USSR.

There are more than a dozen aboriginal minorities in the Far East, many of whom were saved under Soviet rule from degeneration and perhaps even extinction. The largest single group, Yakuts, number some 330,000. There are in addition more than 50,000 members of other ethnic minorities native to the Far East. These people preserve their customs and languages yet at the same time use Russian as a means of universal communication, giving them access to the multinational culture of the whole country. Aboriginal peoples are making a substantive contribution to the Far East's development as teachers, doctors, scientists, and administrators, as well as in traditional occupations such as hunting, herding, and fishing.

Although the Far East occupies a quarter of the USSR's territory, it accounts for only 2.7 percent of the country's population. Most people live on the southern edge of the region along the Trans-Siberian Railroad and in the Amur and Ussuri valleys. In the north, where nature seems to have pooled its forces for the struggle with humanity, the population has developed around historical settlements or near concentrations of natural resources.

The Far East has a bright future. Socio-economic planning is stressing the interdependence of healthy development and the maintenance of a delicate ecological equilibrium. Symbolic of our hopes is the Baikal-Amur Railroad, along which new towns are appearing

---

*So named after eighteen-year-old Valentina Semenovna Khetagurova, who came to the Far East in 1932 as the wife of a military officer. In 1937 she issued an exhortation to young female compatriots to participate in the region's development.—AMERICAN EDITOR

in the virgin taiga. These towns are inhabited by people who have come from all over the USSR to build the railroad and who have decided to make the Far East their new home. Their multinational backgrounds and love of nature strengthen the best traditions of the Far East.

## NOTES

1. *Fizicheskaia geografiia SSSR: Aziatskaia chast'* (Moscow: Vysshaia shkola, 1978), p. 407.

2. V. V. Nikol'skaia, *Fizicheskaia geografiia Dal'nego Vostoka* (Moscow: Vysshaia shkola, 1981), p. 4.

3. E. A. Kozlovskii, *Geologi otkryvaiut bogatstva nedr* (Moscow: Nedra, 1980), p. 20.

4. A. P. Chekhov, *Polnoe sobranie sochinenii,* vol. 10 (Moscow: Goslitizdat, 1948), p. 148.

5. N. G. Fradkin, *S. P. Krasheninnikov* (Moscow: Mysl', 1974), p. 25.

6. Kozlovskii, *Geologi,* p. 79.

7. *Sovetskii Soiuz. Rossiiskaia federatsiia. Dal'nii Vostok* (Moscow: Mysl', 1971), p. 27.

8. V. P. Sysoev, *Zolotaia Rigma* (Moscow: Sovetskaia Rossiia, 1983), p. 6.

9. Nikol'skaia, *Fizicheskaia geografiia,* p. 99.

10. Allen S. Whiting, *Siberian Development and East Asia: Threat or Promise?* (Stanford: Stanford University Press, 1981), p. 26.

11. *Pravda,* 20 October 1983; *Sovetskaia Rossiia,* 22 October 1983.

12. K. G. Pysin, *O pamiatnikakh prirody Rossii* (Moscow: Sovetskaia Rossiia, 1982), p. 54.

13. *Iaponiia 1974: Ezhegodnik* (Moscow: Nauka, 1975), p. 299.

14. Vladimir Klavdievich Arseniev, *Dersu the Trapper,* trans. Malcolm Burr. (New York: E. P. Dutton, 1941).

# The American Far West

KATHLEEN BRADEN

JOHN B. RICHARDS

FOR THE PURPOSES of this volume, we define the American Far West as the five Pacific states: California, Oregon, Washington, Hawaii, and Alaska. Are these states bound together by common characteristics other than being washed by the waters of the Pacific Ocean? Discerning regional character is no simple task. Yet there does seem to be a basis for these five states sharing something both important and tangible. Together they account for more than a quarter of the territory of the United States. Their magnitude is matched by rich endowments in natural resources. Moreover, youth, diversity, and dynamism characterize both the economies and peoples of these states. Finally, the Far West is becoming ever more closely involved with countries and cultures of the Asia-Pacific region.

All five states have an extended shoreline on the Pacific. Each has established substantial trade links with other nations around the Pacific rim. Air travel, telecommunications, and modern ocean shipping have contributed to a growing perception of the Pacific as a link rather than a barrier between regions and peoples around it.

The confluence of Asian, European, and African migrations to the Pacific states has led to a high degree of regional ethnic diversity. The Native American and Asian component of the population base in all five states is greater than in most other parts of the country. While some social tensions and economic inequalities are apparent, a large variety of ethnic groups have coexisted peacefully in the Pacific states, a phenomenon epitomized by Hawaii, where no single race forms a majority of the population. Ethnic diversity enrichens and invigorates the region's cultural life.

A large portion of the Far Western territory is publicly owned. In Alaska more than 90 percent of the land is controlled by the federal government. Recent legislation, however, has returned some 40 million acres to Alaskan hands. The movement to transfer control of the land from federal to state jurisdiction has been popularly dubbed the "sagebrush rebellion" after a shrub indigenous to the American West.

The Far West's population has been growing at a rate above the national average. Much of this is a result of the "sunbelt" phenomenon—a demographic shift away from the Northeast and Midwest toward the South and Southwest. About 90 percent of net population growth of the United States occurred in its southern and western regions during the 1970s, and the trend is not expected to change.

The Far West has a youthful population. Whereas the median age for the country as a whole is about thirty, figures for the Pacific states tend to be in the upper twenties. Despite some fluctuations in local economies, employment opportunities in the region have been expanding at a rate adequate to accommodate the bulk of migration from the other parts of the nation and from Mexico.

Certain cultural traits serve to unify the region despite its ethnic diversity. Far Westerners tend to share a number of perceptions: a sense of distinctness from states east of the Rocky Mountains, a buoyant optimism and vitality, and a deep concern for the natural environment, for preserving natural beauty in the face of economic development.

The Far West contains several subregions. Alaskan planners commonly identify six within that state alone. Even the casual observer can see that the humid, maritime sections of Washington and Oregon have more in common with each other than they have with the dry, continental expanses east of the Cascades. California folklore even contains the notion that northern California would be better off if it seceded from the rest of the state. Climatic differences underscore the existence of subregions: Alaska's arctic, Washington and Oregon's temperate climes, southern California's Mediterranean ambience, and Hawaii's tropics. Such differences suggest that grouping the Pacific states by virtue of their common Pacific littoral involves an element of arbitrariness. On the other hand, it can also be argued that intraregional diversity promotes unity by laying the foundation for economic interaction. Also, by sharing a Pacific littoral, these states have unique opportunities for establishing economic and cultural ties with Oceania, Asia, and the Soviet Far East.

# Geomorphology

The state of Alaska is divided into nine geomorphological subregions: (1) the coast range of southeastern Alaska; (2) the St. Elias Mountains, which join the Alaskan panhandle to the rest of the state; (3) the Chugach-Kenai Mountains and Kodiak; (4) the Wrangell Mountains; (5) the Alaska Range, including Mount McKinley (20,300 feet), the highest point in North America; (6) the Aleutian Range from Mount Spurr to Attu Island; (7) the interior lowlands and plains; (8) the Brooks Range; and (9) the arctic slope. Volcanoes and glaciation are found throughout Alaska, making the state literally a land of "fire and ice."

California is a land of natural beauty and tectonic instability. Mountains jut out into the ocean to create a dramatic coastline. Yet behind the picturesque Pacific littoral run two major fault patterns. An earthquake along the San Andreas Fault in 1906 left San Francisco in ruins. Most Californians are aware that such a natural disaster could recur at any time.

Moving inland, the 400-mile-long, 50-mile-wide valley stretching through most of the state's length forms one of the world's major structural depressions. Bordering the valley to the east is the Sierra Nevada Range, a massive fault block of Paleozoic-Mesozoic Age. The west slope descending to the central California valley is gentle, but the eastern face is rather steep. Lake Tahoe, 6,200 feet high with a depth of more than 1,600 feet, is a depressed block between the Sierra Nevada Range and the Carson Range to the east.

Much of southern California is extremely arid. Death Valley and the Mohave Desert are among the driest spots on earth. In recent years, attempts have been made to bring water to the area by diverting the course of rivers.

The Hawaiian archipelago extends 1,600 miles across the mid-Pacific, approximately equidistant at its eastern and western extremities from California and Japan respectively. There are eight main islands as well as dozens of unpopulated islets and atolls. All the Hawaiian Islands form a ridge of cones which rise from the Pacific Ocean floor. Volcanic eruptions occur regularly on the island of Hawaii at the Kilauea Crater.

A line of coastal mountains extending from Canada to California form the westernmost geomorphologic region of Oregon and Washington. Washington's Olympics are the highest peaks of the coastal range, led by Mount Olympus (7,954 feet). Further south the coastal range gives way to hills. The Oregon coast shows evidence of moderate folding, and its elevations are plateaulike in contrast with Washington's more rugged and dramatic littoral.

The Cascade Range, running from north to south through Washington and Oregon, contains active volcanoes such as Mount St. Helens, which erupted in 1980 with destructive effects. North of Seattle the Cascades exhibit rock types and faulting similar to California's Sierra Nevadas. Glaciers are found throughout the Cascades among the higher peaks such as Mount Rainier. Mount Mazama in the Oregon Cascades exploded in prehistoric times to form a crater in which has formed a lake with depths of two thousand feet, second only to those of Lake Baikal in Eastern Siberia.

Washington and Oregon's eastern sections form part of the Columbia intermontane region, bounded by the Cascades and the Rocky Mountains. The area is characterized by vast lava flows, loess deposits, and basalt. Loess deposits in southeastern Washington have created a rich farming oasis.

The American continental shelf on the Pacific reaches its greatest extent off southern California, where submarine banks are crisscrossed by troughs and ridges. North of San Francisco the shelf narrows to less than twenty miles. Glacial troughs intersect the shelf off the Washington and Alaska coasts.

## Minerals and Fossil Fuels

More than $4 billion worth of minerals were extracted from California in 1977, of which $2.6 billion were from petroleum. California is also a major producer of asbestos, boron minerals, calcium chloride, natural carbon dioxide, cement, diatomite, feldspar, gypsum, iron ore, lithium minerals, magnesium compounds, mercury, perlite, potassium salts, pumice, rare earth metal concentrates, sand, gravel, sodium carbonate, natural sodium sulfate, and tungsten concentrate. Rich though California's resources are, increased extraction cannot indefinitely keep pace with the population growth rate. Major deposits have already been worked out, and urban growth encroaches upon others. Moreover, environmental-protection measures have introduced significant increases in the cost of extraction and refining, which in turn raise prices and affect sales. California's experience here may serve as an example to Pacific Basin countries considering the consequences of a developmental strategy of maximum extraction at maximum speed.

With the completion of the trans-Alaskan oil pipeline, Alaska joined California as a major petroleum producer. Although profitability declined somewhat as a result of the 1983 oil glut, petroleum gives 450,000 Alaskans the highest per capita personal income ($17,194 in 1983) in the United States. With an estimated 10 billion barrels of proven oil reserves and over 30 trillion cubic feet of natural gas reserves, Alaskan deposits represent 29 percent and 13 percent respectively of U.S. totals. Unproven reserves may be four times this amount. Besides being a major oil producer, Alaska is the nation's second largest producer of sand and gravel. The state is also an important source of copper, gold, and silver.

Washington's 1977 mineral output of $216 million was roughly double that of Oregon. Oregon ranks fourth after California, Nevada, and Washington in the production of diatomite, is the nation's most important producer of nickel, and leads in the production of pumice. Washington is the nation's second largest producer of olivine and is a minor producer of cement, clays, copper, gold, gypsum, lead, lime, peat, pumice, silver, building stone, talc, tungsten, uranium, and zinc. Neither Washington nor Oregon produces significant amounts of fossil fuels, probably because of a tradition of relying on low-cost hydroelectric power. Both states face rising power costs, however, and are looking to additional energy sources. Oil appears to be an alternative to expanded use of nuclear power. In 1982, permits were granted for exploratory drilling for petroleum in the Seattle watershed, but public protests led to their revocation.

Hawaii produces rock and clay products, including concrete for local construction and lime for use in refining sugar. Coral is harvested for the making of jewelry. The discovery of manganese nodules on the ocean floor southeast of Hawaii has attracted the interest of German, French, Japanese, and American firms. These nodules are about 25 percent manganese by weight and 3 percent cobalt, copper, and nickel. This rich mineral mix may make nodule harvesting economically feasible within the foreseeable future. Construction of a nodule refinement plant at Puna on the island of Hawaii has been considered. Volcanic activity creates a potential for developing geothermal energy in Hawaii, as well as in California and Washington.

In the short run, mineral exports from Pacific states depend upon the exploitation of reserves in California and Alaska. In the long run, improved extraction technologies and seabed deposits may afford other Pacific states export opportunities. Current indications are that the mineral trade will increase in the Pacific Basin and that the U.S. Pacific states will take part in this growth.

## Hydrology

Alaska's water resources are similar to those of the Soviet Far East, except that precipitation does not have such marked seasonal fluctuations. Precipitation varies sharply within the other four Pacific states. In Washington, Oregon, and Hawaii these contrasts derive from the influence of mountains. In Hawaii precipitation is determined by the interaction of mountains and prevailing winds. Rainfall levels in the mountains of Kauai are the highest on earth, yet the lee sides of some of the islands can be arid. While mountains also play a role in California's rainfall variations, the latitudinal difference of ten degrees between the temperate north and Mediterranean-like south is probably more important.

Warm onshore westerlies bring humid air and relatively abundant rainfall to the coastal (western) slopes of the Cascades in Washington and Oregon. However, the hills and plateaus of eastern Washington and Oregon are semiarid. Agriculture is supported by irrigation water from the Columbia and Snake rivers. Rivers flowing down the western slopes of the Cascades could provide hydroelectric power. However, the desire to preserve these streams and their watersheds for fish spawning, recreation, and forestry has put a brake on dam construction.

Agriculture in California's San Joaquin, Central, and Imperial valleys is made possible by bringing water from the north by aqueduct and by canal from the Colorado River. Competition for water is intense and has promoted more efficient utilization, including computerized control of irrigation at both farm and regional levels. A growing awareness of the costs engendered by evaporation and salting further encourages the adoption of advanced irrigation technology.

## Soils, Agriculture, and Forestry

California's soils vary widely and generally are inferior to the prairie soils of the Great Plains. Yet coupled with a Mediterranean climate and imported water, they make California the seventh largest producer of agricultural products in the world and the leading agricultural state in the United States.

Large, efficient, mechanized farms are typical of California's agricultural structure. Most of the farming occurs in the Central Valley, which makes up a sixth of the state's area. A dry climate, long growing season, and irrigation water from the Sierra Nevada Range combine to make the Central Valley one of the most productive agricultural regions in the world. Other agricultural regions include the wine-producing Napa and Sonoma valleys north of San Francisco and the Salinas Valley near Monterey on the Pacific coast.

A list of agricultural products from California would take up several pages. Most types of fruits and vegetables are grown in the state, including citrus fruits, lettuce, tomatoes, grapes (California produces 80 percent of U.S. wines), wheat, hops, barley, corn, and sugar beets. California is second only to Texas in cotton and to Iowa in livestock production.

Oregon and Washington's soil resources are divided between the humid soils west of the Cascade crest and subhumid soils to the east. Bog soils are found near the Pacific coast. East of the mountains are basaltic and loessal soils which are highly productive when irrigated.

The heart of Oregon's agricultural sector is the Willamette Valley, a 180-mile by 60-mile region running from north to south in the western part of the state. A mild climate and plentiful moisture creates favorable conditions for vegetable, dairy, and livestock production. East of the Cascades, Oregon is a land of wheat farming and grazing.

The climate and agricultural patterns of Washington are similar to those of Oregon. The Puget Sound lowland supports vegetable and dairy farms, while the eastern slopes of the Cascades provide rich harvests of apples which have made the state nationally famous. Further east, the Yakima Valley is a major fruit and vegetable-growing area. Eastern Washington, parts of which are irrigated with water from the Columbia River, is one of the largest wheat-producing regions in the nation. Washington state wines are beginning to make an impression on the national marketplace.

Alaska's arable soils are largely alluvial and located in the southern valleys or near the state capital at Fairbanks. In the north the soils are quite humid as a result of poor drainage, due to permafrost, and low evaporation rates.

Alaska produces barely 10 percent of its food needs. Given the dominance of the fishing industry, land-based food production plays a negligible role in supplying the state. The Matanuska Valley, located some fifty miles northeast of Anchorage, accounts for three-quarters of Alaska's agriculture. Long summer days permit the cultivation of some vegetables in this valley, but marketing difficulties as well as climate restrict its agricultural output. Experimental crops in barley and rapeseed suggest that a potential may exist for exporting these crops to Pacific markets. Nonetheless, the state has a thousand times more arable land than is currently under cultivation.

In contrast, of the Pacific states Hawaii has the largest proportion of its land (48 percent) in agriculture. Hawaii's soils vary from place to place, but all are volcanic in origin and have a relatively high degree of acidity. Hawaii's tropical climate has allowed the state to specialize in sugar and pineapples, but their importance in the state's economy is declining. Cattle are raised on the island of Hawaii and supply a portion of local demand for meat.

Climate has a pervasive influence on the mainland Pacific states' forest industry. A mild climate and abundant rainfall on the western slopes of the Cascades have created conditions for the commercial cultivation of Douglas fir, cedar, hemlock, and spruce and the processing of these woods into pulp, paper, lumber, and composition board. In northern California, cedar and redwood have developed as products enjoying national and international markets.

Recently several factors have troubled the regional forest industry. First, the California redwood industry has suffered from decreasing stocks of this tree and from the campaigns of conservationists. Second, the pulp industry has been identified as a major polluter, and environmental-protection laws, particularly in Washington and Oregon, have added to production costs by imposing strict controls that diminish both pollution and competitiveness. Third, exports of roundwood to Japan have aroused protests against the exporting of forestry products that could be processed locally. Fourth, the recent downturn in demand for forest products both in Japan and in the United States has created concern of unemployment.

## Biological Marine Resources

In 1977 some 28 percent of the world catch of fish came from the North Pacific. Yet barely a tenth of that share came from the Northeast Pacific. More than half of the world's fishing boats of over one hundred gross tons operate in the North Pacific. Only a small percentage of these are American however. One reason for this imbalance is that, unlike the Russians and Japanese, who maintain large fishing fleets in the North Pacific, Americans are not as dependent upon fish as a source of protein. Moreover, the American market values only a limited number of fish species such as salmon, halibut, shrimp, and crab.

When the United States began enforcing a 200-nautical-mile offshore commercial protection zone in 1977, international maritime relations along the American Pacific littoral entered a new phase. One positive repercussion of this measure has been cooperation between American trawlers and Soviet and Japanese processing ships within the 200-mile limit.

Marine resources along the U.S. Pacific littoral are increasingly subject to the negative consequences of shipping and waste disposal. The great circle route to Asia passes along the Pacific coast and Aleutian Islands, creating a concentration of marine traffic in waters where mineral exploration and fishing are actively pursued. The discharge of shipborne wastes in these lanes can endanger sea life and constitutes a source of mounting concern.

## Trade, Transportation, and Tourism

The Pacific states provide the United States with broad access to the Pacific Basin. Alaska, Hawaii, California, Oregon, and Washington not only generate exports but serve as trans-shipment points for commodity flows between the rest of the nation and Asian-Pacific countries.

Alaska's location has both constrained and encouraged the state's economic development. Its distance from the other U.S. states raises transportation costs. Yet by lying on the polar routes connecting North America, Asia, and Europe, Alaska has become a key link in intercontinental air transportation.

North Slope oil and the trans-Alaskan pipeline have dramatically enhanced Alaska's trade. During the 1970s the state carried a trade deficit because of heavy imports of machinery, equipment, and materials for pipeline construction. In the 1980s, oil exports have shifted the trade balance in the state's favor. Foreign customers, notably Japan, may play an increasing role in maintaining the momentum of Alaska's extractive industries, cushioning periods of low demand for petroleum products on the American West Coast.

Alaska looks increasingly to East Asia for trade opportunities. In 1978 more than 65 percent of the state's trade was with East Asia, of which Japan accounted for 90 percent. Other Pacific Basin trade partners include: Singapore, Canada, Indonesia, and Panama for Alaskan imports; Canada, India, Taiwan, and the Republic of Korea for the state's exports of petroleum, forest products, fish, and ammonia.

California's long coastline forms the geographic basis for a strong transportation infrastructure. Moreover, the state has a well-developed highway network. Highways along with air and rail links serve as the main ligaments supporting a complex regional economy. Major port facilities at San Diego, Los Angeles-Long Beach, and Oakland-San Francisco make California the principle gateway for American commerce in Asia and the Pacific.

Both agricultural and manufactured products figure prominently in California's external trade. Many Pacific Basin nations locate their American headquarters in San Francisco or Los Angeles. A large population (23.7 million in 1984) and a high degree of urbanization make California an important market for exports from Japan, the Republic of Korea, Taiwan, Hong Kong, the Philippines, Singapore, Indonesia, Canada, Australia, and New Zealand.

Washington's main ports, Seattle and Tacoma, derive a large share of their income from Pacific Basin trade. One may drive along the Seattle waterfront and see Japanese motor vehicles being rolled off ships for distribution throughout the U.S. Wheat loaded at Seattle "tops off" vessels which take on cargoes at ports along the Columbia River. Informed opinion believes that Washington's trade will increasingly emphasize distant destinations. Diversification of the state's economic base suggests that traditional export items such as aircraft, wheat, apples, and forest products will soon be supplemented by exports of high-technology electronic equipment. Export services such as banking and insurance are gaining significance. Possible construction of oil, gas, and other bulk commodity shipment facilities in Washington may further enlarge the range of the state's trade activities.

The Columbia River system serves as Oregon's main gateway to the Pacific. It provides a corridor from the rich agricultural hinterland to ocean ports from which forest and food products can be shipped to Asian and Pacific countries.

Hawaii occupies a geographically strategic position as an American outpost in the Pacific. The islands play an important role as a trans-shipment point in the U.S.-Pacific trade. At the same time, high transport costs dictated by Hawaii's distance from the American mainland make almost all products more expensive in the local Hawaiian market.

From the 1950s until 1968, Hawaii enjoyed a favorable balance of payments with the rest of the United States and with foreign countries. Since 1968, however, the state has experienced growing deficits. Some of the deficits are offset by mounting foreign investment in the local economy, notably by Japanese nationals. Foreign investment tends to be concentrated in the tourist industry, a fact demonstrated by the high proportion of Japanese-owned hotels. The presence of foreign capital is also evident in retail businesses and in real estate. There is no doubt that foreign investment has stimulated the Hawaiian economy and has created employment opportunities for the local population. At the same time, it has contributed to high land prices, provoking some local criticism. Hawaii's leading trade partners in the Pacific are Japan, Hong Kong, the Republic of Korea, Indonesia, China, and Australia. Indonesia supplies Hawaii with the bulk of its petroleum. The Hawaii state government has been making efforts to interest multinational corporations in the idea of establishing their Asia-Pacific regional headquarters in the islands.

Containerization and airline industry deregulation have had a noticeable influence on the transportation infrastructure of the Pacific states. Containerization tends to increase the level of interaction between distant points at the expense of shorter linkages. Moreover, it channels cargo movements through a few large ports. Deregulation has witnessed the merger of small air carriers and, as in the case of containerization, has led to the concentration of service on a few large cities at the expense of smaller, less heavily traveled destinations.

Alaska is linked to the rest of the continental United States by air, shipping, and the Alcan Highway, much of which is still unpaved. Construction of a gas pipeline to parallel the Alcan is under consideration. Much of the oil from the trans-Alaskan pipeline is shipped to California refineries, but a significant amount is traded to foreign countries in return for shipments of oil to U.S. East Coast ports.

Californians are dependent on motor vehicles to an extent surprising even to Americans. Cars rivals people in numbers, with one automobile for every 1.4 persons. This statistic does not take into account trucks, buses, and motorcycles. Los Angeles and Oakland-

San Francisco are major hubs for national and international air routes. Inland linkages are provided by rail, superhighway, and pipeline networks. International marine traffic is concentrated in Los Angeles and Long Beach, which together occupy first place among West Coast ports in terms of cargo turnover. Washington tends to follow California's pattern of transportation, depending heavily upon the automobile. Trains are largely confined to hauling freight.

Hawaii has air and sea links with the American mainland. The Matson Navigation Lines, a traditional leader in cargo transport, faces increasing competition from ocean-going barges. During the 1960s and 1970s air transport made deep inroads into freight haulage between the U.S. mainland and Hawaii. The trend continues despite rising costs of aviation fuel. Interisland passenger service is by air. Hydrofoils also carried passengers for a while during the 1970s but were eventually taken out of service as unprofitable. Interisland freight is handled by cargo planes and barges.

During the 1970s and early 1980s tourism made large strides in the Pacific states. In California it is a major industry. Millions of foreign and American visitors flock to the state every year. Tourists spent over $12 billion there in 1979 alone. Attractions include the climate, natural scenery, and California's irrepressible cultural vitality, popularly symbolized by the glamour of Hollywood, pervasive "alternate" life-styles, and the fantasy kingdom of Disneyland.

California's booming tourist industry, however, is a mixed blessing. It is putting visible strains on the natural environment. Visitor levels at national parks such as Yosemite skyrocket during the summer months. Waves of vacationers converge in automobiles and campers, bringing congestion and leaving litter. Dune buggies and trail bikes threaten to damage the delicate equilibrium of southern California's sand dunes.

Distance no longer serves as a deterrent to mass tourism in Hawaii. Jumbo jets bring millions to the islands from the mainland United States and Asia each year. In 1984, 4.8 million tourists (including a million from Japan) visited the islands. Tourism has surpassed agriculture as the state's major industry. Among the five Pacific states, Hawaii ranks second to California in income from tourism.

Tourists have been actively courted by the state of Washington since 1981 when a national advertising campaign was launched to lure American visitors to "the other Washington." The visitor industry has concentrated around Puget Sound and in national and state parks. In 1979, tourists spent $1.9 billion in Washington. Development of Mount St. Helens' volcano area as a scenic attraction underlies the state's commitment to maximizing access to natural beauty while protecting the natural environment.

Fueled by an influx of visitors from California, tourism became one of Oregon's fastest growing industries during the 1970s. Tourism is perceived by some Oregonians as having deleterious effects on the human as well as the natural environment. Oregon's ambivalence is not a unique reaction. Its dilemma is shared to various degrees by the other Pacific states. Tourism has come to be seen by more and more as needing guided, not rampant, development. Yet placing any restrictions on the volume of outside visitors raises not only political but constitutional problems. A half-measure taken by Oregon is to charge, for the time being at least, higher entrance fees for nonresidents at certain parks.

## Demographic and Social Profiles

California and Hawaii are the most highly urbanized states in the Far West. Alaska, Oregon, and Washington, on the other hand, fall below the national average of urbanization levels. In 1980 the region's major metropolitan areas were Los Angeles-Long Beach (7,477,503), San Francisco-Oakland (3,250,630), Seattle-Everett (1,607,469), and Portland (1,242,594). The city and county of Honolulu (762,534) accounted for nearly 80 percent of Hawaii's population in 1980. In the same year, more than 40 percent of Alaskans (174,431 out of 401,851) lived in the city of Anchorage.

The Far West is ethnically diverse. There are concentrations of Native Americans in every state of the region except Hawaii. Each of the mainland Pacific states has federal Indian reservations. There are seventy-eight in California alone. Eskimos and Aleuts constitute a significant portion of Alaska's population. Other regional minority groups include blacks, Hispanics, Filipinos, and Asians.

Blacks, Native Americans, and Hispanics tend to have comparatively lower living standards and higher rates of unemployment. Asian-Americans have been more successful in entering the country's economic mainstream. Japanese-Americans and Korean-Americans enjoy one of the highest levels of per capita income in the United States.

California and Hawaii stand out as having unusual population structures. Hispanics have played a significant role in the cultural and economic life of the state and today form a major source of agricultural labor. In 1980 they numbered 4.5 million, or 20 percent of the state's population. Hispanic farm workers emerged as a strong labor force in the 1960s with the organization of the United Farm Workers, chartered under the American Federation of Labor and the Council of Industrial Organizations (AFL-CIO). The organizational success of the United Farm Workers crowned years of struggle, marked by popular support in the form of consumer boycotts of farm produce.

Hawaii's complex ethnic history began when the earliest settlers, Polynesian maritime migrants from Tahiti and the Marquesas, arrived during the first millennium A.D. Capt. James Cook's discovery of the island in 1778 inaugurated two centuries of settlement by Asians and Europeans. Meanwhile, the aboriginal Hawaiians, numbering an estimated 400,000 in 1778, were decimated by disease and their population fell to 56,897 in 1872. Today there are less than 10,000 "pure" Hawaiians, but the number of part-Hawaiians (of mixed ancestry) has been steadily growing. In 1980 Hawaiians and part-Hawaiians numbered 115,500, or 12 percent, of the state's total population of 964,691. Japanese-Americans (239,748) and Filipino-Americans (133,940) account for approximately 25 percent and 14 percent respectively of the state's inhabitants. Hawaii also has significant numbers of Chinese-Americans (56,285) and Korean-Americans (17,962) as well as more recent immigrants from Samoa (14,073) and Vietnam (3,463). Disparities exist in income levels among the various ethnic groups. Moreover, certain groups are found in greater concentrations in specific parts of Hawaii's economy and government. Nonetheless, relatively good relations among the state's diverse peoples make Hawaii an encouraging example of a multiethnic society.

## Conclusion

In this chapter we have sought to identify salient characteristics of the physical and economic geography of the American Far West. We believe that California, Oregon, Washington, Alaska, and Hawaii have much more in common than a shoreline on the Pacific Ocean. They are linked by both the possibilities and problems of developing natural resources. They are inhabited by a young population, a significant portion of which consists of immigrants or the children and grandchildren of immigrants from Pacific region nations as well as other parts of the United States. Finally, the Far West is becoming an ever more important factor in the complex, multiple ties linking the United States to an emerging community of Pacific rim nations.

# Russia and the Pacific to 1917

## B. N. Slavinskii

THIS EXAMINATION of the origins and pre-revolutionary development of Russian economic interests in the Pacific region begins with the seventeenth century. The term "Pacific region" as used here encompasses Northeast Asia and North America as well as Oceania. Within this temporal and spatial framework, relations with China, Japan, and the United States deserve special scrutiny, insofar as they illuminate both the incentives and constraints for imperial Russia's economic activities in the region.

Over the course of three hundred years, the tsarist regime, chronically absorbed by European issues, accorded the Pacific region only erratic attention. Moreover, the Pacific's remoteness from European Russia, unfavorable climatic conditions, and cumbersome communications also handicapped our country's position on the Pacific and help explain the sale of Russian America (Alaska) in 1867, alienation of the Kurile Islands to Japan in 1875, and reverses sustained in the Russo-Japanese War of 1904–1905.

## Early Contacts with the Pacific

Assimilation of the enormous territories which today make up the Soviet Far East constitutes a logical culmination of an eastward movement begun four hundred years ago by Russian pioneers. Less than six decades elapsed from Yermak's expedition across the Ural Mountains into Western Siberia (1584) and the appearance of Ivan Moskvitin on the shores of the Sea of Okhotsk (1639). During the last half of the seventeenth century, Russians explored and settled both the northeastern extremity of Eurasia and the Amur River.

The exploration of northeastern Eurasia was carried out by small numbers of Cossacks traveling immense distances under appallingly difficult conditions. Expeditions along the Lena and Kolyma rivers passed through the coldest part of the continent. In 1648 Semyon Dezhnev made an epic odyssey around Siberia's northeastern tip, passing from the Arctic into the Pacific Ocean through straits separating Eurasia and North America.

Meanwhile, other groups explored the Okhotsk littoral. In 1647 the fort of Okhotsk was established, becoming Russia's first Pacific port. Okhotsk subsequently served as a regional provisioning center and, until 1851, the main base for the Siberian Flotilla, forerunner of the Pacific Fleet.

The earliest attempts to explore Kamchatka date from 1686. However, Vladimir Atlasov made the first significant contributions to opening this huge peninsula in 1697–1699 by constructing a network of forts and preparing geographical and ethnographical reports.

Russian contacts with the Kurile Islands date from 1654 when a Cossack detachment sailed along the arc. In 1700 Semyon Remezov gave the Kuriles their cartographical debut in Russia by including them in his map of Kamchatka. Further knowledge of the Kuriles was gained by a series of Russian expeditions during the eighteenth century.

Exploration and settlement of the Amur region occurred simultaneously with that of maritime Northeast Asia. Cossack expeditions in 1643–1646 and 1649–1653 surveyed the Amur River and called attention to the area's ample natural endowments. The leader of one of these expeditions, Yerofei Khabarov, established a number of fortified outposts. Russian settlers that followed in the wake of these expeditions undertook herculean efforts under inhospitable natural circumstances to raise livestock and till the soil.

The eastward movement of Russians was not seriously hampered by Siberia's aboriginal tribes. Most of these were nomadic or seminomadic peoples living at a low level of economic development. Absorption of Siberian and Far Eastern tribes by Russia should be considered a progressive phenomenon. As Friedrich Engels remarked, "Russia actually plays a progressive role in relation to the East."[1]

At this time the tsarist regime supported the exploitation of Far Eastern territories mainly for pecuniary reasons. During the seventeenth century about one-third of state treasury receipts came from furs, and most of these came from Siberia and the Far East. Political considerations of course also played a role, namely, the search for an outlet to the Pacific Ocean.

Tsar Peter the Great (reigned 1689–1725) showed a particular interest in strengthening Russia's position in the Far East. Aware of the critical importance of reliable access to the oceans, he did much to consolidate the country's position on the Pacific. On his orders, shipbuilding facilities were constructed, regular maritime communications between Okhotsk and Kamchatka were established, and research on the whole North Pacific littoral from Japan to America was activated.

Peter understood that the power of the Russian state could be enhanced by trade ties with Asia as well as Europe. He conjectured that economic ties with Japan, China, and even India could be opened and maintained via Russia's arctic coastline, providing, that is, that a strait affording access to the Pacific existed between the Asian and American continents. These considerations gave birth to a series of initiatives, the most important of which were the First (1725–1730) and Second (1733–1743) Kamchatka expeditions, led by a Dane in Russian service, Vitus Bering.

The Kamchatkan expeditions made a significant contribution to our knowledge of the North Pacific. They revealed, first, that Asia and America were not connected as a single landmass but divided by a strait, a strait which today bears Bering's name.* Second, they discovered Alaska and the Aleutian Islands. Furthermore, thanks to the scholarship of Stephan P. Krasheninnikov, G. F. Müller, and others, they yielded a large amount of geographical and ethnographical information about Eastern Siberia and the North Pacific. Finally, these expeditions opened a sea route to Japan.

## Origin and Development of Russian-Chinese Trade

Russia's position in the Far East during the last half of the seventeenth century was quite weak. Distance and poor communications complicated the task of provisioning outposts around the Sea of Okhotsk and along the Amur River. Seeking to establish trade relations with China, the Russian government dispatched a number of embassies to Peking.

During this period, the Manchu rulers of the newly established

---

*Semyon Dezhnev's 1648 report, which would have alerted Russia's leaders to the existence of a water route from the Arctic to the Pacific, did not become generally known until 1736 when it was discovered in a Yakutsk archive. AMERICAN EDITOR

Ch'ing dynasty conducted foreign relations within the traditional Chinese framework of the tribute system. The hierarchical assumptions underlying the tribute system complicated the task of Russian envoys seeking to establish diplomatic and trade relations on the basis of equality. Moreover, the Manchus, capitalizing upon the strategic advantages accruing from the proximity and magnitude of their military forces, attempted by armed incursions to squeeze the Russians out of the Amur region.

Absorbed by efforts to strengthen its western and southern frontiers, the Russian state was in no position to send heavy reinforcements to the Far East. Consequently, the tsarist government was obliged to sign the Treaty of Nerchinsk (1689), which demarcated the Russian-Chinese border in a manner that deprived Russia of most of its recent acquisitions along the Amur. Although the loss of the Amur was temporary, it nevertheless marked a serious setback for Russian interests in the Pacific area.

Following the Treaty of Nerchinsk, Russian-Chinese trade consisted of caravans dispatched by the Russian government to Peking. From 1693 to 1754 seventeen caravans brought some two billion rubles worth of furs to China. In exchange for Russian sable, black fox, ermine, beaver, and squirrel the Chinese traded gold, silver, pearls, precious stones, porcelain, silk, and other luxuries. The Russian government treated this trade as a state monopoly. Indeed, it turned out to be a lucrative source of income for the state treasury.

Russian-Chinese trade was put on a different basis in 1727 with the conclusion of the Treaty of Kiakhta. The treaty provided that commercial relations be conducted at two frontier stations, Nerchinsk and Kiakhta. Kiakhta subsequently became the sole venue for these exchanges. During the "Kiakhta system's" first century, the bulk of Russian exports continued to be furs, followed by other animal products, mirrors, and clocks. China exported mainly silk. Silk exports grew from Rub 61,700 in 1728 to Rub 173,000 in 1751. The Russian market for Chinese silks, however, declined thereafter in the face of European competition. Chinese cotton fabric enjoyed popularity in Russia and by 1760 constituted 60 percent (Rub 257,000) of total Russian imports from China. Other Chinese products passing through Kiakhta included rhubarb and tobacco.[2]

In 1760 the Kiakhta trade amounted to Rub 1,358,000, or 7.3 percent of Russia's total foreign commerce and over 60 percent of Russia's commerce with Asia. Thereafter the volume of trade increased, partially as a result of growing demand for Chinese tea, which by the early nineteenth century had become a fixture in Russian households.

The Kiakhta trade had a salutary influence on the economies of both countries. For one, it stimulated the fur and animal-skin industries in Siberia. Toward the end of the eighteenth century, thriving tanneries could be found in Irkutsk, Tobolsk, and Tiumen, processing animal products for the Chinese market.

The Kiakhta trade also promoted improved communications in Siberia. After completion of the Moscow-Ekaterinburg Track in 1763, preparations for the Great Siberian Track were launched, following a route that led from Ekaterinburg through Tiumen, Tomsk, Mariinsk, Krasnoiarsk, and Irkutsk, with a branch to Kiakhta. The Great Siberian Track served as an artery along which peasant settlers moved into Siberia.

The first decade of the nineteenth century witnessed an upsurge of the Kiakhta trade, partially because the Napoleonic Wars constrained Russian commerce with Europe. Between 1800 and 1824 turnover nearly doubled, from Rub 8.4 million to Rub 16 million. Meanwhile, Russian exports to China changed in composition. The proportion of furs declined from 90 percent to less than 50 percent. Chinese imports of Russian cloth grew steadily, until by 1820 they outdistanced by more than two times the volume of cloth imports reaching Canton from England and the United States.

Tea retained its preeminence among Russian imports from the Heavenly Kingdom, accounting for nearly 90 percent of goods (by value) coming through Kiakhta. A significant portion of this Chinese tea was re-exported by Russia to Europe, thereby illustrating how Siberia had come to serve as a link between East Asia and the West.

Improvements in maritime communications between Europe and the Far East eventually made the sea route to China quicker and cheaper than the land route across Siberia. After reaching its peak in 1824, the Kiakhta trade leveled off and then entered a period of gradual decline.

## Russian Expeditions in the Pacific

The Russian-American Company, chartered in 1799 by Tsar Paul and led by among others the colorful Aleksandr Baranov, was given a state monopoly over all resources along the North Pacific littoral.

Over the next six decades the company not only engaged in the fur trade but carried out exploration and established the first Russian settlements in North America, from Alaska to California.

One of the company's most pressing problems was how to provision far-flung Russian settlements on the Pacific. The trans-Siberian land route was costly and cumbersome. Consequently, efforts were made starting in the early nineteenth century to supply Russia's North Pacific outposts by sea. This involved carrying provisions halfway around the world from Kronshtadt, an island and port in the Gulf of Finland near St. Petersburg. The task fell to the Imperial Russian Navy, which undertook to carry it out by a series of circumglobal expeditions.

The first Russian circumglobal expedition was launched in 1803 under the command of Capts. Ivan Kruzenshtern and Yurii Lisianskii. During the next half century, over forty similar naval voyages were made from Kronshtadt to the Pacific. The best-known are those of Vasilii Golovnin (1807–1813, 1817–1819), Otto von Kotzebue (1816–1818, 1823–1826), Ferdinand Wrangel (1825–1827), and Fyodr Litke (1826–1829). These voyages not only brought supplies to Russian settlements on the Pacific, they also shed light on alternate sources of provisions, notably from Japan, Hawaii, the Philippines, and the United States. These expeditions also conducted scientific research in a broad variety of fields, from cartography and botany to ethnography and climatology.

Russian expeditions did not limit themselves to areas north of the equator. Capts. Fadei Bellingshausen and Mikhail Lazarev led their ships in 1819–1821 through archipelagoes in the South Pacific to discover the shores of Antarctica.* Some one hundred fifty Pacific islands, capes, bays, and other landmarks today bear Russian names, eloquently testifying to the discoveries of these navigators.

Russians also made a decisive contribution to clarifying the elusive geography of Sakhalin, a long, slender island about the size of Ireland lying astride the mouth of the Amur River and extending southward toward Hokkaido, separating the Sea of Okhotsk from the Sea of Japan. In 1644, Cossacks descending the Amur heard of and caught sight of what local natives called "Sagalin Anga Hata" ("island at the end of the river"). However, European and Russian

---

*The discovery of Antarctica is a matter of different interpretations. Some sources credit an American, Capt. Nathaniel Palmer, who sighted a coast in 1820 which Captain Bellingshausen subsequently called "Palmer's Land" when referring to Antarctica—AMERICAN EDITOR

surveying expeditions in the late eighteenth and early nineteenth centuries came to the conclusion that Sakhalin was a peninsula attached to the Asian continent by a narrow isthmus. In 1849 Capt. Gennadii Nevelskoi conclusively demonstrated Sakhalin's insularity and showed, moreover, that the Amur River had a navigable outlet to the sea. This discovery had important strategic as well as economic significance and served to reinforce Russia's growing interest in the Far East.

Another notable Russian navigator was Stepan Makarov, widely known as a brilliant naval commander who met a heroic death during the Russo-Japanese War. As a young captain in 1886–1889, Makarov conducted oceanographic research around the Pacific on the corvette *Vityaz*. Makarov won international distinction through his scientific publications about this expedition, notably by a book entitled *Vityaz and the Pacific Ocean*.

Discussion of Russian scientific activities in the Pacific Basin during the nineteenth century would not be complete without mention of Nikolai Miklukho-Maklai. During the course of six visits to Papua New Guinea starting in 1871, Miklukho-Maklai conducted ethnographical research yielding unusual insights into this Melanesian culture.

## The Sale of Alaska

Russia's position in the Pacific for most of the nineteenth century remained relatively weak. Although the empire had extensive possessions around the basin's northern rim, these territories were sparsely populated. It is estimated that in 1860 about twenty-six thousand people lived in the Okhotsk-Kamchatka region. Russian America's population at this time was only about ten thousand.* Such people as there were lived in small, scattered communities.

The tsarist government, preoccupied by problems in Europe, devoted only intermittent attention to developing the productive and strategic potentials of Russia's Pacific territories. Such neglect resulted in weak resistance to American inroads in the Pacific North-

---

*According to an 1862 census of Russian America, less than 600 of the inhabitants were Russian. The remainder were Tlingits, Aleuts, Eskimos, and Creoles. The total population was 10,156 (James R. Gibson, *Imperial Russia in Frontier America* [New York: Oxford University Press, 1976], p. 26).—American editor

west, which began in the late eighteenth century and gathered momentum after the incorporation of California and the Oregon Territory into the Union, the gold rush of 1849, and a general upsurge of American commercial activity in the Pacific starting in the 1840s.

American entrepreneurial activity made itself felt on Russia's Pacific territories. New England whalers operated virtually unimpeded along the coasts of Siberia and Russian America. American businessmen openly discussed the commercial penetration of Sakhalin and the Amur.

These developments did not prevent Russia and the United States from enjoying civil and even cordial relations during most of the nineteenth century. For one thing, the logic of Russian-American cooperation found adherents such as Thomas Jefferson, who in 1807 declared that Russia was among all countries the United States' firmest friend.[3] Moreover, the tsarist government perceived that the United States might serve as a counterweight to England and France, whose international policies not infrequently ran contrary to those of St. Petersburg. Thus, Russia morally supported the Union during the American Civil War, going so far as to send a naval squadron to New York and San Francisco in 1863 as an expression of goodwill. The gesture captured the North's popular imagination and evoked praise from, among others, the American naval minister.[4]

Aware of the weakness of its position on the Pacific, St. Petersburg understood that it could not defend Alaska from American and British encroachment. This awareness became acute during the Crimean War (1854–1856), which graphically revealed Russian America's strategic vulnerability. Moreover, by this time the Russian-American Company, burdened by debt and unprofitable enterprises, was not justifying the expectations of its shareholders.

The tsar's brother Grand Duke Konstantin analyzed this situation in 1857 and affirmed in a letter to Foreign Minister A. M. Gorchakov: "The North American states, following the natural course of affairs, will seek control over all North America. Therefore, sooner or later they will come into direct contact with us and doubtlessly will take over our colonies, and we shall never be in a position to regain them." The grand duke went on to suggest that Russian America be sold to the United States and thereby "resolve in a friendly and convenient way an issue which otherwise would be resolved to our disadvantage, moreover by conquest."[5]

Giving preference to the United States over England in disposing of Alaska, the tsarist government hoped that Washington would help Russia to revise certain concessions made to England and France in the Treaty of Paris (1856). In addition, any weakening of England in North America and in the Pacific was regarded as redounding to Russia's advantage in the Far East.

The 1867 sale of Alaska and the Aleutian Islands to the United States for a mere $7,200,000 revealed the tsarist government's inability to defend Russian America. It also brought an end to age of Russian pioneers on the American continent.

## The Search for Trade Ties with Japan

Russia made efforts to establish contact with Japan at the outset of the eighteenth century. The underlying motivation was an awareness that the Okhotsk-Kamchatka region and Russian America could be provisioned more cheaply and effectively from Japan than from Europe. As Commerce Minister N. P. Rumiantsev wrote Tsar Alexander I in 1803, "Nature itself, placing Russia next to Japan and affording them access to each other by sea, has given us trade advantages over all other trading states."[6]

Such considerations underlay a series of official and unofficial attempts to open commercial relations with Japan during the eighteenth and early nineteenth centuries. Notable among these was the first official embassy, led by Capt. Adam Laxman, which reached Ezo (renamed Hokkaido in 1869) in 1792, bringing with it some Japanese castaways whose storm-tossed ship had drifted to Russian America a decade earlier. Notwithstanding Japan's self-imposed seclusion policy, Laxman received from shogunal authorities a license to visit Nagasaki, a port under direct shogunal administration where strictly regulated trade was conducted with the Chinese and the Dutch. Using this license, Nikolai Rezanov, an official of the Russian-American Company, sailed into Nagasaki in 1804 and broached the prospect of opening trade relations in the Kurile Islands. After a delay of several months, Rezanov's proposal was declined by the shogunate, which regarded any alteration of the seclusion laws as a dangerous precedent that might jeopardize the foundations of Japan's feudal system.

The official basis for Russian-Japanese trade was laid much later, in 1855, when the two countries concluded the Treaty of Shimoda.

This treaty provided for the establishment of diplomatic relations and the opening of three Japanese ports to Russian vessels. A commercial treaty was signed in 1858, providing for trade, extraterritorial rights for Russian citizens, and tariff schedules. Russian ships were given access to Hakodate, Shimoda, Niigata, Hyogo (Kobe), and Nagasaki, and limitations were placed on Japan's rights to levy import tariffs.

Siberian merchants had high hopes of trade with Japan, expecting that Japanese ships would call at Nikolaevsk (a port on the lower Amur), bringing vegetables and grain for local consumption and for redistribution to the interior and to settlements around the Okhotsk littoral. These hopes were not immediately realized. Trade in the late 1850s and early 1860s got off to a slow start. Ignorance about each other's markets and logistic obstacles constrained the level of exchanges. Merchants exporting goods to Japan faced formidable transport problems. They had to move these goods by land to Sretensk for trans-shipment by river to Nikolaevsk. Once in Nikolaevsk these goods faced yet another trans-shipment, as well as delays of up to a year. Maritime traffic around Nikolaevsk was restricted to a short ice-free season. Once the Amur estuary and Nevelskoi Strait froze over in the fall, all shipments were held up until the following spring. Delays raised costs and diminished the competitiveness of Russian goods. Moreover, Siberia's staple trade item, furs, enjoyed only limited demand in Japan. Russian candles met with more success. Conversely, although rice found a ready market in Russia, Japanese authorities forbade its export.[7]

Russia's weak position on the Pacific, the sale of Alaska, and the growing British and American challenge to Russian interests in Northeast Asia obliged the tsarist government to strengthen the defenses of its Far Eastern territories. A weak link in the security of this region was Sakhalin, whose position was left ambiguous by the Treaty of Shimoda. The treaty defined Sakhalin as a joint Russian-Japanese possession. Its location at the mouth of the Amur River, however, made it the shield of Eastern Siberia and invested the island with considerable strategic significance for Russia. In order to gain Japan's recognition of Russia's unquestioned sovereignty over all of Sakhalin, the tsarist government conceded to Japan the central and northern Kurile Islands in the Treaty of St. Petersburg (1875).

Settlement of the Russian-Japanese frontier issue in the mid-1870s coincided with a steady growth of trade between the two countries. Although their numbers did not match that of British and

American vessels, Russian ships visited Japanese shores with increasing frequency, especially Hakodate (where Russian culture exercised considerable influence), Kobe, and Nagasaki (where the Russian Pacific Squadron wintered during the 1880s). By 1903, bilateral trade had reached approximately $6 million, with Russia enjoying a favorable balance of about $2 million. Some 98 percent of Russian exports to Japan emanated from Asiatic parts of the empire. They included kerosene, soybean cakes, and fish. Exports to Japan from European Russia consisted largely of lump sugar and textiles.

After the Russo-Japanese War Japanese exports to Russia far outstripped imports. The reopening of Vladivostok as a free-trade port in 1905 eliminated tariff obstacles. At the same time, the growing sophistication of its economy enabled Japan to supply a wider range of products. By 1912, Japan was shipping to Russia coal, camphor, ginger, bamboo, mats, glue, ceramics, lacquer, wax, fruits, vegetables, salt, soya, soda, ironware, medicines, beer, tea, soap, glassware, clothing, and cotton goods. Japanese imports included flax, bran, calico, dried fish, paper products, timber, soybeans, furs, leather, iron ore, lead, and zinc. This commerce led to the establishment of Japanese communities in Vladivostok, Khabarovsk, Nikolaevsk, Blagoveshchensk, and Chita. These communities consisted largely of merchants, bank representatives, retail-store owners, barbers, and prostitutes.

In the years before World War I, Russian-Japanese trade for all its growth still amounted to only a small proportion of Japan's external commerce. In 1910, for example, Japan's leading trading partners were the United States (accounting for 23 percent of Japan's foreign trade), China (21 percent), and England (13 percent). Russia's share fell short of 1 percent.[8]

The outbreak of World War I, however, precipitated a surge of Russian imports from Japan. Japan shipped goods to Vladivostok that could not otherwise reach Russia through Baltic and Black Sea ports because of hostilities in Europe. These goods included foodstuffs, clothing, and military ordnance. By 1916, the year in which St. Petersburg and Tokyo concluded an alliance which coordinated their interests in Manchuria and their strategy against the Central Powers, bilateral trade had reached unprecedented levels: Rub 119 million of trade, of which over 98 percent consisted of Japanese exports.[9] This acute trade imbalance was not corrected before the October Revolution. And it was accompanied by extensive Japanese economic penetration into the Russian Far East as well as domination of the fisheries along Russia's Pacific littoral.

## Deepening Economic Ties with China

As a result of the Opium War (1839–1842), China's economy became subject to penetration by British, French, and American capital. With the opening of treaty ports along China's coast and with the outbreak of the T'aiping Rebellion (1850), China's Manchu rulers experienced growing difficulties in preserving the Heavenly Kingdom's territorial integrity. This process obliged Russia to devote greater attention to its own Far Eastern territories, which since the Crimean War had been increasingly falling within the scope of Western economic and strategic calculations. Repossession of the Amur region, ceded to China in the Treaty of Nerchinsk, assumed particular urgency. As the energetic and farseeing governor-general of Eastern Siberia, Nikolai N. Muraviev, wrote, "Who controls the Amur estuary controls Siberia."[10]

Negotiations between Russia and China culminating in the treaties of Aigun (1858) and Peking (1860) brought the Amur question to a peaceful settlement. Russia regained sovereignty over the Amur River's left bank and extended its rule to what is today the Maritime Territory, thereby guaranteeing access to the Pacific through an ice-free port (Vladivostok) and opening the way for more intensive commercial activity in the Asia-Pacific region.

The last four decades of the nineteenth century witnessed a remarkable development of new towns in the Russian Far East, a number of which became the scene of active Russian-Chinese commerce and the objects of Chinese migration. Khabarovka, a military post established in 1858 on the Amur near its confluence with the Ussuri River, grew into an administrative and transportation center which in 1893 officially assumed the name Khabarovsk. Vladivostok, founded in 1860 at the southern extremity of the Maritime Territory, became in the 1870s Russia's main gateway to the Pacific, surpassing in economic significance older ports such as Nikolaevsk and Okhotsk.

Settlement and development of the Amur region gave Russian-Chinese trade a new regional complexion in the last four decades of the nineteenth century. In accordance with an 1862 agreement, a

38-mile strip on each side of the Far Eastern sector of the Russian-
Chinese frontier was designated a free-trade zone. Manchurian
flour, grain, vegetable oils, and textiles found ready markets
throughout Russia's eastern territories. Conversely, gold, furs, antelope horns, and ginseng flowed from the Russian Far East into
China. Because of the prevalence of contraband, it is difficult to
establish with precision the magnitude of these regional exchanges.
In 1894 the official border trade amounted to over Rub 2 million.[11]
This figure, however, represents only a fraction of the total.

Insofar as the Tientsin Treaty (1858) granted Russia most-
favored-nation status, Russian citizens enjoyed the same privileges
as English, Americans, French, and other imperial powers active in
China, that is, freedom of trade and extraterritorial enclaves within
the treaty ports. After over a century of operating within the restric-
tive guidelines established by the Kiakhta Treaty, Russian merchants gained direct maritime access to China, and that on an equal
footing with the Western powers.

The weakness of its naval forces in the East Asia and Pacific
regions prevented Russia from taking full advantage of commercial
opportunities in China. Until 1880 Russian ships occasionally called
at the treaty ports, but most of these vessels were on scientific expeditions or were carrying cargoes from Europe to ports in the Russian
Far East.

Russian-Chinese maritime commerce entered a new phase in
1880 when the Volunteer Fleet (formed in 1878 on the basis of private contributions) inaugurated regular service between Odessa and
Vladivostok. Originally engaged in domestic transport, these ships
came to be used also for foreign trade. On their return passages to
Europe from Vladivostok, they called at Canton and Shanghai,
picking up cargoes of tea, raw silk, and brocade. Thanks to the Volunteer Fleet, Russian-Chinese trade made a comeback in the late
nineteenth century. Maritime commerce grew steadily during the
1880s until by the early 1890s it matched the volume of trade at
Kiakhta—some Rub 14 million annually. Russian exports, however,
stagnated both at Kiakhta and in the treaty ports. Consisting largely
of paper products, cotton fabric, and metal ware, they amounted to
less than Rub 35,000 annually.

In addition to supporting commerce with China, the Volunteer
Fleet also brought settlers from European Russia to the Far East.
From 1883 until 1905, over three hundred thousand people took this
route. This migration consisted of soldiers assigned to Far Eastern

garrisons, peasants attracted by land grants in the Amur and Maritime territories, and convicts and exiles destined for a penal colony on Sakhalin.

Maritime transport alone could not cope with mounting logistical demands arising from Russia's growing interests in the Far East and Pacific. The need for effective communications between Europe and East Asia eventually led to one of the world's great construction projects—the Trans-Siberian Railroad, a 5,000-mile steel filament linking European Russia with the Far East. The Trans-Siberian inaugurated a new age for Russia's economic interests in the Pacific.

The idea of building a railroad across Siberia was widely discussed in Russian commercial and industrial circles during the 1870s and 1880s. Capital requirements for such an undertaking precluded private initiatives. Government participation, on the other hand, was hampered by preoccupation with the Balkans and the strained state of the imperial treasury. Official circles in St. Petersburg were not prepared at this time to divert large amounts of capital to a project that did not seem to deserve such high priority.

This lukewarm attitude changed during the late 1880s and early 1890s in the face of growing English economic penetration of China and tangible American interest in financing railroad construction in Manchuria. The tsarist government's decision, in 1890, to build a railroad across Siberia was largely due to the urging of Sergei Witte. Witte, an energetic advisor to Tsar Alexander III and a subsequent minister of finance, entertained a bold vision of extending Russian economic enterprise into China as a means to accelerate the development of the Russian Far East as well as to strengthen the foundations of Imperial Russia at a time of momentous socioeconomic changes.

Sending his son Crown Prince Nicholas on a tour of Asia in 1891, Tsar Alexander entrusted him with the task of overseeing the inauguration of work on the Ussuri Railroad, a 540-mile segment of the Trans-Siberian connecting Vladivostok and Khabarovsk.[12] The Ussuri line was completed in 1899, five years after Nicholas had ascended the throne. As the nineteenth century drew to an end, Russia saw its first railroad on the Pacific.

Construction of the Trans-Siberian meanwhile proceeded during the 1890s. Work started on the Cheliabinsk-Ob River section in 1892, on the Ob-Krasnoiarsk segment in 1893, and on the Krasnoiarsk-Irkutsk section in 1894. Construction of the line around Lake Baikal, a difficult stretch requiring many tunnels, began in

1895. Most of the Trans-Siberian west of Lake Baikal was completed
by 1904, but the trans-Baikal and Amur lines were not linked with
the Ussuri line until the eve of the October Revolution. The final
link, a mile-long bridge across the Amur River at Khabarovsk, was
finished in 1916.

Insofar as the Far Eastern section of the Trans-Siberian involved a
detour to the north following the course of the Amur River, the idea
of a shorter route cutting across Manchuria to Vladivostok occurred
to a number of officials in St. Petersburg in the early 1890s. In addition to reducing the distance to Vladivostok, a railroad across Manchuria promised to serve as an instrument for the Russian economic
penetration of China. Aware of the political and strategic implications of such a project, Finance Minister Witte nonetheless stressed
its economic benefits in a memorandum submitted to the tsar in
1892. "The construction of such a branch line could hardly meet
serious obstacles in the near future. On the contrary it would promote our trade with China, increase revenues from the Trans-Siberian line, and strengthen our position in international commerce."[13]

Witte's prognosis was partially borne out by events during the
1890s. After its defeat in the Sino-Japanese War (1894–1895), Peking found it politically expedient to respond favorably to St. Petersburg's initiatives. Consequently, in 1895 China accepted a low-
interest Russian loan (floated with French capital) to help pay the
war indemnity owed to Japan. In 1896, China and Russia concluded a treaty aimed at restraining Japanese encroachment on their
respective territories. In 1898, China agreed to a 25-year lease to
Russia of two ports, Port Arthur and Dalny,* on the tip of the
Liaotung Peninsula which juts from southern Manchuria into the
Yellow Sea. As part of the 1896 and 1898 agreements, St. Petersburg
secured the right to construct across Chinese territory two intercon-
necting rail systems. The Chinese-Eastern Railroad, as the inter-
locking system came to be known, consisted of a line cutting diago-
nally across central Manchuria linking the trans-Baikal sector of the
Trans-Siberian line with the port of Vladivostok, and a branch of
this line running southward from central Manchuria to Port Arthur.
The Chinese-Eastern Railroad (CER) was constructed during
1896–1903 and led not only to a dramatic growth of Russian economic activity in northeastern China but to the appearance of a sizeable Russian community in the rail center of Harbin.

---

*Named Dalny, or Dairen, from 1905 to 1945, this port is now called Dalian.

Russia's economic penetration of Manchuria in 1895–1904 stimulated the economies of the Amur and Maritime territories. Provisioning CER construction sites and Liaotung Peninsula ports precipitated a boom in Amur and Sungari River steamship traffic. A number of Nikolaevsk and Vladivostok commercial enterprises expanded their operations into Manchuria, opening branches in Harbin and Dalny.

This blossoming of Russian enterprise was interrupted by war with Japan in 1904. The war's unsuccessful outcome, codified by the Treaty of Portsmouth (1905), deprived Russia of a number of gains made in the decade preceding 1904 (the Port Arthur and Dalny leaseholds, most of the southern spur of the CER, economic preeminence in southern Manchuria) and marginally reduced the empire's position on the Pacific by the cession of southern Sakhalin. Nonetheless, these losses did not blunt the growth of Russian economic interests in northern Manchuria. Nor did they reduce the momentum of economic development in the Russian Far East. Indeed, the stabilization of Russian-Japanese political relations through a series of agreements in which the two powers adjusted their respective interests in Manchuria and Mongolia created an atmosphere conducive to international economic cooperation. After 1905 the Chinese-Eastern Railroad, in conjunction with the Trans-Siberian Railroad, became an important international communication system, a direct rail link between Europe and the Far East. It is true that the cooperative character of this undertaking was not absolutely complete since the CER's southern spur, renamed the South Manchurian Railroad when Japan assumed control of it in 1905, posed a competitive alternative to the Pacific.

Construction of the CER and ancillary enterprises also had repercussions on the Chinese economy. Of the $475 million of Russian capital investments in China (second only to England's $607 million) on the eve of World War I,[14] almost all was concentrated in the northeastern province of Manchuria, which helps explain this region's extraordinary development in the first decades of the twentieth century.

Russian-Chinese trade between 1895 and 1914 more than doubled (from Rub 47 million to Rub 118 million). China enjoyed a favorable balance thanks in part to heavy Russian imports of tea. In 1915, Russia accounted for 65.2 percent of total Chinese tea exports.[15] Moreover, Chinese meat, grain, and soybeans figured prominently among foodstuffs consumed in the Amur and Maritime territories. Russian exports to China continued to consist largely of cotton cloth, leather, furs, and metal ware. While the contents of trade remained relatively stable, the trade routes shifted. The traditional caravan route through Kiakhta receded in favor of the rail line from trans-Baikalia into Manchuria, the Amur River and its tributaries (Sungari and Ussuri), and steamship service from Odessa to Tientsin and Shanghai.

Military and political forces again intruded upon Russian-Chinese economic relations on the eve of World War I. The fall of the Ch'ing dynasty in 1911 inaugurated two decades of internal disunity and instability, conditions under which earlier trade practices proved difficult to maintain. For its part, Russia soon thereafter was caught up in upheavals which in the short run interrupted trade with China but in the longer run laid the foundations for a new economic relationship between two socialist states.

## Conclusion

In contemplating the history of Russian economic activities in the Far East and Pacific before 1917, certain thematic inferences come to mind. The first is that Russia's international commerce in the Pacific arose from and remained inextricably tied to the provisioning needs of Eastern Siberia and (until 1867) Russian America. This interconnection assumed particularly clear form in the case of the Russian-American Company.

Second, China offered Russia the first and most diversified market in the Far East. Over two hundred years of bilateral commerce took various forms: missions to Peking, the Kiakhta system, border trade, and treaty-port trade. These modes of economic interchange waxed and waned, but taken collectively they offered both countries benefits. Pre-1917 border trade with China along the Amur prefigured Soviet-Chinese border trade of the 1950s and, after an interim of suspension, in the 1980s.

Third, the history of Russian-Japanese economic relations demonstrates that both countries were able to surmount difficulties and to engage in mutually beneficial commerce by taking advantage of geographic proximity.

Fourth, Russian-American economic relations before 1917, despite friction arising from disparate approaches to questions of access and use of natural wealth along the North Pacific littoral, contain valuable lessons for the present. There is today no objective barrier to Soviet-American economic cooperation in the Pacific. No frontier dispute mars Soviet-American geographical propinquity. Scientists of both nations have demonstrated the feasibility of working together to solve problems and explore natural phenomena in the Pacific region: biological resources of the Bering Strait, vulcanism, tidal waves, to name a few. As other authors in this book point out, there is reason to believe that cooperation can be extended to the economic sphere.

## NOTES

1. Karl Marx and Friedrich Engels, *Sochineniia,* 2d ed., vol. 27 (Moscow: Gos. izdat. polit. literatury, 1962), p. 241.

2. M. I. Sladkovskii, *Istoriia torgovo-ekonomicheskikh otnoshenii narodov SSSR s Kitaem (do 1917 g.)* (Moscow: Nauka, 1974), pp. 143–144.

3. *Rossiia i SSHA: stanovlenie otnoshenii, 1765–1815,* ed. N. N. Bolkhovitinov et al. (Moscow: Nauka, 1980), p. 307.

4. Alexander DeConde, *A History of American Foreign Policy* (New York: Charles Scribner's Sons, 1963), pp. 252, 261.

5. S. B. Okun, *Rossiisko-Amerikanskaia kompaniia* (Moscow-Leningrad: Gos. izdat. sotsekonomicheskoi literatury, 1939), p. 228.

6. Ministry of Foreign Affairs, *Vneshniaia politika Rossii XIX i nachala XX veka,* Seriia 1, tom 1 (Moscow: Gos. izdat. polit. literatury, 1960), p. 387.

7. S. I. Novakovskii, *K voprosu o russko-iaponskikh torgovykh otnosheniiakh* (Kiev: Tipografiia Chokolova, 1915), p. 8.

8. Ibid., p. 9.

9. Tsentral'nyi gosudarstvennyi arkhiv Primorskogo kraia, f373, op. 1, d. 9, L.144.

10. Ivan Barsukov, *Graf Nikolai Nikolaevich Murav'ev-Amurskii,* vol. 1 (Moscow: Sinodal'naia tipografiia, 1891), p. 669.

11. Dmitrii Pozdneev, ed., *Opisanie Man'chzhurii,* vol. 2 (St. Petersburg: Ministerstvo finansov, 1897), tables 6 and 10.

12. *Aziatskaia Rossiia,* vol. 2 (St. Petersburg: Izdanie tovarichestvo M. O. Vol'f, 1914), p. 516.

13. E. Kh. Nilus, comp., *Istoricheskii obzor Kitaiskoi vostochnoi zheleznoi dorogi, 1896–1923* (Harbin: Obshchestvo KVZHD, 1924), p. 14.

14. Sladkovskii, *Istoriia,* p. 335.

15. Ho Ping-yin, *The Foreign Trade of China* (Shanghai, 1935), p. 368.

# American Economic Interests in the Pacific to 1945

FRANKLIN C. L. NG

As A NATION facing two oceans the United States has long engaged in commerce throughout the Atlantic and the Pacific. While considerable attention has been devoted to American economic relationships with Europe, ties with Asia and the Pacific have yet to receive the systematic scrutiny they deserve. These ties can be traced back to the eighteenth century when Boston merchants entered the Canton trade. In the nineteenth century, against a background of American expansion across the continent to the Pacific, they multiplied to include the Philippines, Siberia, Hawaii, Japan, British and Dutch possessions in Southeast Asia, Thailand (then Siam), Australia, New Zealand, and various Pacific island groups. The acquisition and development of the American Far West has had a direct and sustained impact upon American economic involvement throughout the Pacific Basin.

Settlement of the American West constitutes a colorful chapter in the country's history. Accounts of explorers and pioneers crossing the continent and laying the foundations of a young nation have animated the imaginations of several generations. The opening of virgin lands, encounters with Indians, and the rugged individualism fostered by frontier life are themes that have cast a spell on Americans. These themes are the very substance of national mythology and folklore. They also serve to highlight the growing importance of the Pacific in American economic life.

The appearance of American traders on the Pacific occurred shortly after the Revolution as an indirect consequence of having been excluded from the British mercantile system in general and the British West Indies in particular. The China trade presented itself as an alternative to grim economic prospects in the Atlantic. The China trade began in 1784 when the *Empress of China* sailed from New York to Canton. The vessel carried a cargo of ginseng and returned laden with tea, silks, and porcelain. The handsome profits that this venture reaped for investors prompted emulation. Sino-American trade grew steadily in the late eighteenth and early nineteenth centuries. The New Englanders imported tea, silks, porcelain, and cotton cloth. From 1790 to 1833 Chinese tea exports to the United States quadrupled.[1] Americans, like Russians, were acquiring a strong taste for this beverage.

The Canton trade, while financially attractive, confronted American merchants with unforeseen complications. All commercial transactions with the Chinese had to be conducted through an intricate "Canton system" which required all foreign merchants* to work through special guilds. Although Westerners found the system cumbersome and frustrating, they had little choice but to operate within it.

Another source of frustration for American merchants was the difficulty they encountered in finding commodities that would command a market in China. The United States was still predominantly an agricultural country whose main exports (cotton, grain, tobacco) enjoyed only a modest demand in the Heavenly Kingdom. Quicksilver, woolens, and cotton cloths also found only limited acceptance in China. Exports of ginseng seldom exceeded $200,000 annually. Americans were consequently obliged to redress the trade imbalance by paying for their purchases in China in specie or offering bills of exchange derived from sales of Southern cotton to England. Unsatisfied with the export of gold, American merchants experimented with various alternatives.

One of these was furs, which thanks to Manchu sartorial fashion did enjoy a certain vogue in China. Americans started bringing furs to Canton before the end of the eighteenth century from various sources: the Mississippi Valley, the Falkland Islands, and the Northwest coast of North America (Pacific Northwest). A triangular trade developed along the Pacific Northwest coast with New England merchants supplying settlements in Russian America with provisions in exchange for furs resold in Canton. From 1805 to 1834 nearly 1,800,000 fur seal pelts valued at $3,500,000 reached Canton. American exports of sea otter pelts from the Pacific Northwest during this period totaled $4 million.[2] By the 1820s, however, the fur trade declined as a result of the depletion of animal resources.

---

*Russian merchants were not permitted to trade at Canton until 1858. Their commercial access to China was restricted to the village of Kiakhta near the Russian frontier with Mongolia.

Americans also exported sandalwood, bêche-de-mer, and opium to China. The Chinese valued sandalwood for its fragrance and used it for incense, perfumes, and medicines. Merchants brought sandalwood from Fiji, the Marquesas, and Hawaii, but supplies were soon exhausted by overexploitation. After reaching a peak of $268,220 in 1822, sandalwood sales in Canton declined.[3] The Chinese prized bêche-de-mer (also known as sea cucumber or trepang) as a culinary delicacy used primarily in soups. In their search for bêche-de-mer, Americans scoured the East Indies, Australia, and islands throughout the South Pacific.

American merchants also exported Turkish opium to China. Opium enjoyed a ready market, and its sales soon reversed the outward flow of specie. However profitable, the sale of opium was illegal, and attempts by Manchu authorities to curb illicit traffic in the drug led to war with England. The Opium War (1839–1842) resulted in China's being forced to abandon the Canton system and to open several new trade ports in which Westerners enjoyed extraterritorial rights. The United States, which operated in the shadow of the British in China, acquired all the rights and privileges accorded to England in the newly opened "treaty ports."

Throughout the first half of the nineteenth century, American commerce in the Pacific centered around China, where it was second only to that of Great Britain. This trade had several consequences for the economic development of the United States. Among them was that commercial activity in China promoted American shipping in the Pacific. The re-export of Chinese commodities to third countries stimulated the American carrying trade and clipper trade. Increased American shipping in turn led seaports such as Boston, New York, Philadelphia, Providence, and Baltimore to develop enterprises servicing this trade, notably banking, insurance, shipbuilding, and warehousing.

Another consequence was that American businessmen learned entrepreneurial skills and new management techniques in order to deal with multiple markets in the Asia and Pacific regions. These techniques were subsequently applied to the management of large, complex industrial and financial enterprises.

Finally, the China trade yielded capital for reinvestment into the American economy. A prominent China trader, John Murray Forbes, and his Boston associates invested profits in the Chicago, Burlington, and Quincy railroad systems in the Midwest.[4] The Philadelphia businessman Stephen Girard ploughed China trade earnings into real estate, coal, railroads, and shipping. Further examples of this pattern are quite numerous.

The steady westward expansion of the United States across the North American continent during the first seven decades of the nineteenth century prepared the foundations for a dramatically enhanced level of commercial activity in the Pacific area. America's westward movement was sustained by a deep-seated conviction of the country's "manifest destiny" to span the continent. Idealism, rugged individualism, a sense of boundless possibilities, a willingness to take risks, the lure of wealth, and the search for new frontiers were all ingredients in the complex psychology underlying such rhetoric as "Go West, young man!" This sense of possibility and national purpose was implemented by a series of treaties, land purchases, and outright annexations. The Louisiana Purchase (1803), the purchase of Florida (1819), the annexation of Texas (1845) and the Oregon Territory (1846), the acquisition of California and the Southwest (1848), the Gadsen Purchase (1853), and the purchase of Alaska (1867) served as milestones for an expansionist movement.

Territorial expansion went hand in hand with the quickening pace of industrialization after the Civil War. Favored with abundant and rich land, a large and increasing (thanks to immigration) pool of labor, the increasing availability of domestic and foreign capital, and resourceful entrepreneurs, the American economy gathered momentum.

These trends stimulated and in some ways constrained American trade in the Pacific. On the one hand, Americans became increasingly preoccupied with opportunities for internal economic growth, with attendant domestic investment patterns. Moreover, as domestic markets developed, the American economy became less dependent upon foreign trade. At the same time, acquisition of the Far West, particularly California, afforded entrepreneurs direct access to Asia and Pacific markets. Starting in the 1850s Californians became active participants in trans-Pacific commerce with China, Hawaii, and, after 1858, Japan.

By the 1890s the incentives had definitely outweighed the constraints guiding American commercial involvement in the Pacific Basin. Improved agricultural technologies and mechanized production left American farmers with large surpluses which the vicissitudinous domestic market could not always absorb. Industrialists and manufacturers fell into an analogous predicament. Meanwhile, completion of a transcontinental railway network opened concrete prospects for exporting American goods to Asia and the Pacific. Indeed, railroad construction and Pacific trade were closely linked. Great Northern Railway Company organizer James J. Hill made this connection explicit, writing in 1897, "When we built the Great Northern Railway to the Pacific coast, we knew that it was necessary to look to Asia for a part of out traffic."[5]

Hill was not alone. Other Americans toward the turn of the century displayed renewed interest in developing markets in Asia and the Pacific for exports from the United States. Their arguments invoked strategic and philosophical as well as economic reasons for an enhanced American presence in the Pacific. Capt. Alfred Thayer Mahan, Rear Adm. Stephen B. Luce, Rep. Henry Cabot Lodge, and Sen. Albert J. Beveridge stressed the importance of a strong navy, coaling stations, and naval bases to protect American commerce in the Pacific. Evangelical pronouncements and social Darwinist injunctions about the "survival of the fittest" provided a religious and philosophical justification for growing American interests throughout the Pacific Basin.

As the United States expanded its markets and strengthened its strategic position in the Pacific during the 1890s, it became embroiled in disputes with both European and Asian powers. Washington contested claims to Samoa with Great Britain and Germany before acquiring the eastern half of the island chain in 1899. The annexation of Hawaii in 1898 sowed the seeds for rivalry with imperial Japan. Acquisition of the Philippines and Guam as a result of the Spanish-American War (1898) brought American territory to the western Pacific at the doorstep of East Asia.

Despite the acquisition of extensive possessions in the Pacific, the United States continued to direct the bulk of its trade toward Europe and the Americas. In 1890, 58 percent of U.S. exports went to Great Britain and France, while 6.2 percent went to Canada and Mexico. Less than 1 percent went to Japan and China. These proportions shifted only marginally during the next two decades, although trade with China and Japan grew in absolute terms.[6]

By 1890 Japan had surpassed China as the United States' leading trade partner in the Pacific, a position Japan would retain until 1940, despite a deterioration of political relations during the 1930s. The largest American imports from Japan before World War I were silk and silk manufactures, followed by tea. Other imports included crude camphor, copper manufactures, chinaware, fibers, and matting. American exports were led by unmanufactured cotton, followed by wheat flour, electrical machinery, steam engines and loco-motive parts, and mineral and refined oils.

The British East Indies ranked second in American Asia-Pacific commerce during the first decade of this century. In 1907 the United States imported merchandise worth $84 million and exported $9 million. Imports were chiefly chemicals, drugs, dyes, wood, tin, India rubber, and unground spices. Exports were principally ma-chinery, pipes and fittings, other iron and steel manufactures, meat and dairy products, and tobacco.[7]

China ranked third in trade with the United States in the Pacific region at this time. Its exports consisted (in order of value) of raw silk, tea, hides and skins, and wool. China imported from the United States foodstuffs, cotton cloths, mineral and refined oils, and tobacco.

Fourth place in American Asia-Pacific trade at this time was Brit-ish Oceania, including Australia and New Zealand. In 1907 this region shipped about $17 million worth of exports (chemical gums, fibers and vegetables, hides and skins, unmanufactured wool) to the United States and imported over $32 million worth of iron and steel manufactures, wire, mineral oils, tobacco, wood and wood manu-factures, cotton manufactures, and cars and carriages.

The Netherlands East Indies occupied fifth place in American Pacific trade in the first decade of this century. Exports to the United States included sugar, coffee, wood, unground spices, and chemical drugs and dyes. The United States exported mineral and refined oils (interesting in view of Indonesia's massive petroleum exports to the United States in recent years), various types of machinery, and bicy-cles. As in the case of the British East Indies, the United States car-ried a trade deficit of several million dollars annually.

In sixth place in American trade in the Pacific region was the Brit-ish colony of Hong Kong. In 1907 its total exports to the United States were somewhat less than $3 million while imports exceeded $8 million. The United States imported from Hong Kong chemicals, drugs, dyes, vegetable oils, matting, rice and rice flour, unground spices, and tea. It exported wheat flour, ginseng, mineral oils, and refined oils.

American-Korean diplomatic relations dated from 1882, but trade between the two countries remained modest thereafter. After the Russo-Japanese War (1904–1905) Korea fell within Japan's sphere of influence, not a propitious development for American commerce there in view of growing Japanese-American rivalry in the Asia-Pacific area. Nonetheless, the United States shipped over a million dollars of rails, machinery, iron and steel manufactures, and oil to Korea in 1907, possibly for use in Japanese enterprises. Korea's annexation by Japan in 1910 cut off this market for American goods.

American economic relations with Hawaii can be traced to the early nineteenth century when sandalwood merchants and later whalers called at the islands. Subsequently an influential American community formed around missionaries and sugar planters. In 1893 a group of Americans overthrew the last Hawaiian monarch, Queen Liliuokalani and established a republic in the hope of annexation by the United States. In 1898 the United States did annex the islands through the instrument of a joint resolution of Congress. Thereafter trade between the United States and the Territory of Hawaii grew steadily, rising from somewhat over $18 million in 1897 to nearly $44 million in 1907, with Hawaii enjoying a favorable balance. Hawaiian exports were led by sugar (over 98 percent), followed by small amounts of fruits, coffee, hides, and rice. Hawaii imported a wide variety of foodstuffs that could not be grown or raised on the islands, together with clothing and manufactured items.

Acquisition of the Philippines in 1898 both promoted trade and created a relationship of Philippine dependency on the American market for raw materials such as sugar, hemp, and copra. Philippine imports included a wide range of manufactured items, mineral oils, meat, and dairy products. American-Philippine trade grew from $4.5 million in 1897 to over $20 million in 1907, the bulk of growth consisting of American exports.

Mention should be made of American trade with Siam (Thailand) which, though modest, continued through much of the nineteenth and early twentieth centuries after the two countries established diplomatic relations in 1833. In 1907 the United States imported $65,581 worth of commodities, mostly spices, and exported mineral oils, iron and steel manufactures, and other items valued collectively at $376,738.

American economic involvement in the Pacific on the eve of World War I was not limited to trade. In 1914, American direct foreign investment totaled $2.65 billion, or about 7 percent of the national GNP. An overwhelming amount of this investment was in four areas: Canada ($618 million), Mexico ($587 million), Europe ($573 million), and South America ($371 million).[8] Asia accounted for only $120 million, or less than 5 percent of the total. Oceania's portion was a infinitesimal $17 million (.07 percent).

While Pacific region countries received a modest share of American overseas investment at this time, the impact on certain nations cannot be called insignificant. American firms such as Western Electric and American Tobacco maintained important economic interests in Japan, as did the Standard Vacuum Company in China.

Education and technology transfer also played an important role in the American economic presence in Asia and the Pacific during the late nineteenth and early twentieth centuries. In their efforts to modernize, China, Japan, and other Asia-Pacific countries sent thousands of their young people to study at American schools and universities. At the same time, these countries imported large amounts of American technology, everything from automobiles to Singer sewing machines. American agricultural machinery made important contributions to the development of Siberia and the Russian Far East, as is noted elsewhere in this volume. American farm machinery, barns, and agricultural techniques were also found in Australia and in Japan's northern island of Hokkaido.

The American economic relationship with Asia and the Pacific was also shaped by the eastward movement of Asians to Hawaii and California during the last half of the nineteenth and the early twentieth centuries. Coming from China, Japan (including Okinawa), Korea, and the Philippines, Asian immigrants more often than not expected to remain in the United States only long enough to accumulate a certain amount of capital through their labor. Many did return to their homelands, but a larger number became reconciled to spending the rest of their lives in America and raising families there.

The labor of Asian immigrants helped to tranform the urban and rural landscape of the American West. Chinese from Kwangtung Province worked on the great transcontinental railways. Chinese, Japanese, and Filipinos provided labor for land reclamation, irrigation, and farms in Hawaii and California. Asians helped to promote crafts and foreign trade with Pacific rim countries. Japanese immigrants helped to establish a silk industry in New York State.[9]

For all their contributions to the American economy, Asians met with prejudice and discrimination as well as with opportunity in the United States. Particularly on the West Coast, specters of economic competition and of a "yellow peril" led to social ostracism and occasionally to violence. Antimiscegenation laws, alien land acts, and immigrant restriction and exclusion so injured the interests and sensibilities of Asians that they at times provoked international repercussions. In 1905 a boycott against American goods was carried out in China in retaliation against the treatment of Chinese immigrants in the United States. In 1906 and 1907, Japan remonstrated against the discriminatory treatment accorded its citizens in San Francisco's public schools, obliging President Theodore Roosevelt to take both diplomatic and domestic steps to rectify the situation. The Exclusion Act of 1924 deeply injured Japanese sensibilities and provoked indignation that probably contributed indirectly to a deterioration of Japanese-American relations in the 1930s.

The treatment of Asian immigrants in the United States and reactions among Asian nations testified to serious gaps in perceptions across the Pacific. Americans believed that their aims in Asia differed from those of their European competitors, but such self-flattering assessments were rarely shared either in Asia or in Europe, including Russia. The Open Door Notes of 1899 and 1900 notwithstanding, the United States was prepared to seek a coaling station or a sphere of influence off the China coast. After 1905, railway schemes, consortia plans, and neutralization proposals emanating from the United States contributed to nationalistic forces in China and provoked negative reactions from Japan and Russia. During the 1920s and even the 1930s, Washington's proclamations of upholding China's territorial integrity and criticism of Japan's continental expansion were hard to reconcile with the sustained preference among American investors and traders for Japan as a market.

The broad patterns of American economic relations in Asia and the Pacific during the two decades preceding the Second World War leave little doubt about the paramount importance of Japan. Japan continued to be the United States' leading trade partner, followed by the British East Indies, China, the Dutch East Indies, the Philippines, Australia, and New Zealand. Japan's principal export to the United States was silk until 1930 when the stock market crash and the Great Depression precipitated a plunge in American demand for that commodity. The United States exported to Japan cotton and petroleum products. Japan's prominence in American Pacific trade slipped only after 1939 when the United States announced the abrogation of the 1911 commercial treaty and started to take steps to limit the export of scrap metals and petroleum products to Japan.

World War II proved to be but a temporary interruption in a

remarkable Japanese-American economic relationship, the durability and magnitude of which attracts considerable commentary today. While it is debatable to what extent the $2.2 billion in American foreign aid to Japan in 1945–1952 contributed to that country's remarkable postwar economic recovery, there can be no doubt that Japan since 1952 has been America's most important economic partner in Asia and has directly contributed to the phenomenal growth of American economic interests in the Pacific region in recent years.

Today East Asia and the Pacific are of unprecedented economic importance for the United States. When it is recalled that in 1890 less than 1 percent of American exports went to China and Japan, the transformation of the Asia-Pacific market is nothing short of remarkable. In 1977, American trade in the Pacific surpassed that in the Atlantic. Aside from Canada, Japan is the United States' most important trade partner. Economic ties with China, Taiwan, Hong Kong, the Republic of Korea, ASEAN nations (Singapore, Thailand, Indonesia, Malaysia, Brunei, and the Philippines) have become stronger and more significant for the American economy. In 1984, exports accounted for 20 percent of the United States' industrial output, twice the proportion of 1972. East Asian and Pacific countries purchased $52 billion in American goods and services in 1983 and provided 1.3 million Americans with jobs. Never before has the economy of the United States been so closely interconnected with economies of the Pacific region.[10]

The expansion and growing complexity of American economic interests in the Pacific region has brought its share of problems. The economic development of Japan, Taiwan, Hong Kong, South Korea, and Singapore has made these countries formidable competitors with American enterprises. The international movement of capital has complicated trade balances and introduced multilateral trade and investment networks throughout the Pacific, affording the United States and Japan opportunities for both cooperation and sometimes severe competition.

Some Americans whose economic well-being has been adversely affected by economic competition of Japan and other East Asian countries have succumbed to protectionist impulses. A protectionist response to economic challenges emanating from East Asia and the Pacific would surely undermine long-term American interests. Perhaps one of the greatest tasks facing Pacific nations today is to recognize their interdependence and to find practical approaches to harmonizing multilateral interests without sacrificing the dynamism and vitality that has characterized the region's economies since the 1960s.

NOTES

1. Timothy Pitkin, *A Statistical View of the Commerce of the United States of America* (New Haven: Durrie & Peck, 1835), pp. 246–247, 301.

2. Shu-lun Pan, *The Trade of the United States with China* (New York: China Trade Bureau, 1924), p. 11.

3. Pitkin, *Statistical View*, p. 304.

4. Arthur M. Johnson and Barry E. Supple, *Boston Capitalists and Western Railroads: A Study in the Nineteenth-Century Railroad Investment Process* (Cambridge: Harvard University Press, 1967), pp. 24, 157–160.

5. Howard B. Schonberger, *Transportation to the Seaboard: The "Communication Revolution" and American Foreign Policy, 1860–1900* (Westport, Conn.: Greenwood, 1971), p. 218.

6. Bureau of the Census, *Historical Statistics of the United States, Colonial Times to the Present* (Stamford, Conn.: Fairfield, 1965), p. 550.

7. Trade statistics for the United States with Asia-Pacific countries from 1907 to 1920 are drawn from Bureau of Statistics, Department of Commerce and Labor, *The Foreign Commerce and Navigation of the United States* (Washington: GPO, 1958), pp. 28–29, 36–37, 50–51, 1137–1149.

8. Mira Wilkins, *The Emergence of Multinational Enterprise: American Business Abroad from the Colonial Era* (Cambridge: Harvard University Press, 1970), pp. 201–203.

9. T. Scott Miyakawa, "Early New York Issei: Founders of Japanese-American Trade," in Hilary Conroy and T. Scott Miyakawa, eds., *East Across the Pacific* (Santa Barbara, Calif.: Clio Press, 1972), pp. 158, 172–175.

10. W. Allen Wallis, "The Near West: America and the Pacific," Current Policy No. 578 (9 May 1984) of the Bureau of Public Affairs, United States Department of State.

# Russian-American Economic Relations in the Pacific: A Historical Perspective

JOHN J. STEPHAN

RUSSIAN-AMERICAN economic ties in the Pacific area antedate the establishment of diplomatic relations between Washington and St. Petersburg in 1809. In the late eighteenth century the North Pacific became a meeting ground for converging Russian eastward and American westward movements. Economic links developed as a result of shared interests arising from commercial opportunities in China, Japan, Siberia, and the Northwest Coast.* Although not immune from disruptive influences, these ties persisted for a hundred and fifty years, surviving a variety of political vicissitudes.

A number of constraints have interrupted Russian-American commerce in the Pacific. Differences in social and economic systems, red tape, mutual distrust, difficulties in reaching agreement on interest rates and credit terms, and congressional linkage of most-favored-nation (MFN) terms with Soviet emigration policies have directly or indirectly inhibited trade. Additional constraints are peculiar to the Pacific region: the growing but still limited capacities of Soviet ports, a limited consumer market in the Soviet Far East, transportation bottlenecks, nonparticipation of the United States in the Soviet Far East's coastal trade system, and an inadequate awareness in both countries about each other's Pacific markets.

These obstacles, together with a common preoccupation with immediate issues, have tended to obscure an earlier tradition of Russian-American commerce in the Pacific. This chapter proposes to illuminate that tradition by reconstructing its historical development.

---

*"Siberia" in this chapter refers to all Russian territories from the Ural Mountains to the Pacific littoral. "The Northwest Coast" refers to the Pacific coast of North America from northern California to the Bering Strait.

## Origins, 1784–1832

Trade between the United States and Russia, following the example of Boston ships which called at Russian Baltic ports in the 1760s,[1] dates from 1784 when a merchantman from Salem, Massachusetts, sailed into Kronshtadt with a cargo of West Indian sugar. The sugar was exchanged for hemp, canvas, iron, and ducks.[2] Although the first trickle of Russian-American commerce flowed across the Atlantic, the Pacific soon assumed a significant role in trade between the two countries.

The Pacific as an arena of Russian-American commerce was foreseen by an American named John Ledyard (1751–1789). Ledyard, visited Kamchatka as a member of Capt. James Cook's last voyage (1776–1779). He thereafter began to entertain thoughts of Russian-American trade across the North Pacific. Ledyard succeeded in interesting Thomas Jefferson in 1785 but evoked only a lukewarm response in Russia, where his inquisitiveness aroused official suspicions. After a journey across Siberia, he was politely but firmly asked to leave. Though unrealized in his lifetime, Ledyard's visions were prescient, for economic forces in the late eighteenth century were creating conditions favorable to the opening of Russian-American trade in the Pacific.[3]

Furs had attracted Russians across Siberia to the Okhotsk Sea and Kamchatka in the seventeenth century and to the Aleutian Islands and Alaska in the eighteenth century. From the beginning, supply problems plagued the Russian fur trade. Outposts along the North Pacific rim were chronically short of food, clothing, and other necessities. Poor soil and harsh climatic conditions precluded agriculture. Until the middle of the nineteenth century, food had to be brought around the world by sea from European Russia or by land across Siberia. Grain grown near Lake Baikal and livestock raised in Yakutia supplied the Okhotsk region until 1800. The costs of this overland route can be gauged from the fact that in 1800 provisions in Kamchatka cost up to thirty-two times more than in Irkutsk.[4]

A number of attempts were made to improve the provisioning of Russia's North Pacific settlements. Japan was approached by a succession of private and official missions starting in 1739, but the self-imposed isolation maintained by the Tokugawa shogunate discouraged trade until 1858. It was not until the 1890s that Japan began to play a significant role in supplying commodities to the Russian Far East.

Efforts were also made to open trade with Spanish colonies in the Philippines, California, and Peru, but with generally disappointing results. A number of Russian naval officers, among them Ivan Kruzenshtern and Vasilii Golovnin, showed an interest in California as a provisioning base. A director of the Russian-American Company, Nikolai Rezanov, established ties with Spanish officials in San Francisco in 1806, but Rezanov's untimely death prevented these ties from maturing into a solution to Russian America's food problems. In 1812 the Russian-American Company founded an agricultural colony just north of San Francisco at Ross; however, Ross yielded only modest amounts of grain.[5]

There was no shortage of ideas about provisioning. Plans for a Russian Pacific trade complex encompassing Siberia, Alaska, California, Japan, Canton, and the Philippines were brought to the attention of the government in 1813 by an American entrepreneur named Peter Dobell. Letters of recommendation from the governor of Kamchatka and the governor-general of Siberia helped Dobell secure the title of Russian consul general in Manila in 1817, but the American's proposals fell victim to opposition in St. Petersburg.[6]

During the second decade of the nineteenth century, the Hawaiian Islands briefly figured as a potential provisioning base for Russian America. Dobell favored the arc's annexation. Georg Anton Schäffer, an employee of the Russian-American Company, made an abortive attempt in 1815–1817 to bring the island of Kauai into the empire.[7] However, St. Petersburg ignored Dobell's proposal and disassociated itself from Schäffer's unauthorized gambits.

Russian-American trade in the Pacific owed its genesis to the convergence of two forces: the Russian-American Company's need for supplies and the calculations of New England merchants looking for furs. During the first decades of Russian-American economic interaction, neither St. Petersburg nor Washington formulated a clear, consistent policy toward the North Pacific. Russian naval and mercantile views of the Pacific often conflicted. Even within the Russian-American Company, opinions diverged over whether or not to trade with the "Bostonians."[8]

Starting in the late 1780s, Boston merchants were drawn by the fur trade to the Northwest Coast. They began collecting sea otter skins in Nootka Sound as early as 1789. By the 1790s a triangular

trade pattern involving Boston, the Northwest Coast, and Canton
had taken shape. Sooner or later the Russian fur trade and the Bos-
tonian Canton trade were bound to intersect, giving birth to a Russian-American economic relationship in the Pacific.

Trade began in 1799 when an American ship visited Sitka Island
(now Baranov Island) off the coast of Alaska. During the next thirteen years Russians and Americans concluded a series of local
arrangements. Starting in 1803 the Bostonians leased, with Russian-
American Company permission, Aleut natives to hunt sea otters
along the California coast. In 1804 American merchants began selling Russian furs in Canton. Thanks to competition among the New
Englanders, the Russian-American Company was buying provisions in 1811 at half the prices paid in 1803. This Northwest Coast
trade totaled $590,000 between 1803 and 1812.[9] According to the
Soviet historian N. N. Bolkhovitinov, these exchanges "proved
profitable to both sides."[10]

During 1810–1812 there were signs that Russians and Americans
were considering measures to systematize their trade on the Northwest Coast. In 1810 an official in St. Petersburg is said to have suggested to the American minister, John Quincy Adams, that the
United States handle trade between Russian America and Canton.[11]
John Jacob Astor was at this time showing an interest in buying
Russian furs for resale on the China market. Astor's negotiations
with the Russian-American Company in 1812 led to a contract giving him exclusive rights to provision Russian settlements on the
Northwest Coast and to transport Russian furs to Canton. In return
for these privileges Astor promised not to trade illegally with the
Alaskan natives (American arms sales to the latter caused company
officials considerable concern).

The War of 1812 prevented Astor from fulfilling this contract. But
in 1819 American merchants were again frequenting the Northwest
Coast. Some extended their operations to Kamchatka. When the
Englishman John Dundas Cochrane completed his pedestrian odyssey across Siberia to Kamchatka in 1821, he noted an American vessel in Petropavlovsk's harbor.[12]

The degree to which St. Petersburg tolerated American economic
penetration of the North Pacific littoral after 1800 may have been
related to a larger geopolitical consideration. Individuals within the
government recognized that Britain and the United States were
rivals on the Northwest Coast. British maritime power and imperial

ambitions created a political atmosphere conducive to a rapproche-
ment of Russian and American commercial interests. St. Petersburg
and Washington had a common stake in free trade and the rights of
neutrals, each of which was vulnerable to British interference. A
confluence of Russian-American interests can be traced to the
"armed neutrality" proclaimed by Empress Catherine in 1780,
which, by upholding the rights of neutrals on the high seas,
indirectly benefitted American traders. The idea of the United
States as a "natural ally"[13] to counterbalance Great Britain ran
through Russian foreign policy strategy for much of the nineteenth
century. A number of accommodations to the United States, not to
mention the sale of Alaska in 1867, are in part attributable to the
"British factor."

The British factor, however, did not always suffice to overshadow
differences of Russian and American economic interests in the
Pacific.[14] After 1810 St. Petersburg grew increasingly sensitive to
what it regarded as American encroachments on a preserve of the
Russian-American Company. The company sustained financial
losses from the diversion of furs from Kiakhta (Russia's single trading post with China) to Canton. Faced with falling profits and
galvanized by warnings from naval officers, the Russian-American
Company directors prohibited further commerce with foreigners in
1820. In 1821, upon renewing the company's charter, Tsar Alexander I issued a ukase which claimed the Pacific coast north of the fifty-
first parallel (the northern tip of Vancouver Island) and barred foreign vessels from approaching to within a hundred miles of the
North Pacific littoral. The 1821 ukase had the effect of placing Russian settlements along the Northwest Coast in jeopardy, for they
were deprived of the opportunity to obtain supplies from American
merchants.

Problems of access to the North Pacific's resources were resolved
to the satisfaction of both sides in 1824 by the first formal agreement
between the United States and Russia defining guidelines for navigation, trade, and fishing in the Pacific. The 1824 Convention
assured both parties freedom of navigation and fishing in the Pacific
Ocean, set up procedures for trade with natives along the Northwest
Coast, and set Russia's southern boundary in North America at
fifty-four degrees and forty minutes.

The 1824 Convention encouraged the United States to press for a
full commercial treaty with Russia. After several years of intermit-

tent negotiations, a Treaty of Commerce and Navigation was signed in 1832. The treaty served as a foundation for a steady development of Russian-American trade during the ensuing eighty years.

## A Proliferation of Links, 1832–1890

During the half century between the 1840s and the 1890s, Russian-American relations were characterized in the main by cooperation and goodwill. The sources of such harmony were many, but among the more important were two that bore directly upon the Pacific: common problems with Great Britain and Russian accommodation of American expansion.

Since the 1780s, Russia and the United States had shared a commitment to the freedom of the seas, which British naval supremacy appeared at times to jeopardize. This commitment was jointly affirmed for the first time in 1854 in a Russian-American declaration on neutral rights. The timing of the 1854 declaration was significant. American sympathy for Russia during the Crimean War (1854–1856) was no secret. Rumors abounded of Americans being enlisted to man privateers against British commerce. The Royal Navy suspected that American ships and crews were supplying Russia's exposed Pacific settlements. While these suspicions proved exaggerated, they do not appear to be unfounded. There is some evidence that an American official provided Russia with one piece of valuable information in the Pacific. In June 1854 the American consul in Honolulu is said to have warned visiting Russian officers about a projected Anglo-French assault against Petropavlovsk on Kamchatka, thereby enabling the defenders to take measures that ultimately contributed to the repulse of the attackers.[15]

Russia displayed similar goodwill to the Union during the American Civil War. Visits by the Russian Fleet to San Francisco and New York in 1863 boosted the morale of the North at a time when both England and France openly favored the Confederacy. Some years later Oliver Wendell Holmes referred to this moral support in a poem praising Russia, "our friend when the world was our foe."[16]

Russia's accommodation of American expansion in the Pacific constitutes an important theme of the two countries' relations between 1840 and 1867. St. Petersburg's willingness to contemplate an enlarged American political and economic presence in the Pacific Basin stemmed from three principal reasons. First, the American acquisition of California in the war with Mexico (1848) portended American moves toward the Northwest Coast, multiplying possibilities for friction with Russia. Second, the Crimean War alerted St. Petersburg to the strategic vulnerability of Russian America. Together with the unprofitability of the Russian-American Company, this recognition contributed to an inclination in government circles in the 1850s to withdraw from Russian America. Third, some officials perceived that if Russian America were to be sold, it would better serve St. Petersburg's interests to sell it to the United States rather than to Britain.

Signs of these calculations manifested themselves in official and unofficial pronouncements and policies during the 1850s and 1860s. On the eve of the Crimean War, St. Petersburg expressed its approval of American economic penetration of the southwestern Pacific.[17] On November 4 (16) 1854, Foreign Minister Count Nesselrode indicated that His Imperial Majesty Tsar Nicholas I would not look upon an American annexation of the Hawaiian Islands with a *"mauvais oeil."*[18] In 1867, Russia sold its North American possessions (Alaska, and the Aleutian, Pribiloff, and Komandorskii islands) to the United States for $7,200,000.

While St. Petersburg accommodated, American enterprise in the North Pacific extended to the Siberian littoral. In 1848, New England whalers began appearing off the Kurile Islands, Kamchatka, and the Chukchi Peninsula. By the 1860s American whalers were making regular landings on Siberian shores for hunting and trading. Some mariners set up living quarters along the coast and spent the winter in Siberia rather than returning to Honolulu to wait for the spring whaling season.[19] In an 1862 report, Capt. P. N. Golovin disapprovingly noted that whalers from Hawaii were making a profitable business supplying Kamchatka and Chukchi natives with rum, cheap cognac, tobacco, gunpowder, and firearms.[20] Lest one assume that whalers sold only arms and alcohol to Siberia's natives, it is useful to recall that when George Kennan (1845–1924) surveyed Kamchatka and the Chukchi Peninsula for a possible telegraph line in 1865–1866, he came across American cooking utensils, linen, magazines, lithographs, and heard American songs in the remotest hamlets.[21]

The extent to which American enterprise had established itself in Eastern Siberia in the 1850s can be gauged from an eyewitness account of A. V. Vysheslavtsev, a physician who in 1858 visited Nikolaevsk, a port founded in 1850 sixteen miles from the mouth of the Amur River. Vysheslavtsev noted the presence there of an American club, American stores, and an American river steamer. A good part of the settlement's supplies came from San Francisco. Local opinion about Americans was divided. Some welcomed the Yankees for stimulating competition, while others preferred that Siberia's commerce be in Russian hands.[22]

American interest in the Amur derived from the river's strategic location between Siberia and China as well as its proximity to Japan. As early as 1848 a New York businessman named Aaron Haight Palmer offered President Polk a plan to develop Sakhalin, turning the island into an emporium for trade with Japan.[23] Less than ten years later a Virginian named Bernard Peyton traveled to Irkutsk and tried to convince Nikolai Muraviev, governor-general of Eastern Siberia, to endorse a proposal for American commercial dominance in the Amur region.[24] In 1856 Perry McDonough Collins, a California entrepreneur, persuaded President Pierce to appoint him "Commercial Agent of the United States for the Amoor River." In 1860, following an inspection of the area, Collins publicized the Amur Basin as a channel for American enterprise to penetrate Northeast Asia.[25] During the Civil War Collins received charters from the Russian and American governments and raised $3 million through the Western Union Company to lay a telegraph line across Alaska, under the Bering Strait, and across Siberia to connect the United States with Europe.[26] Work had begun on both sides of the Bering Strait when the telegraph project was cancelled in 1867 in the wake of the successful installation of the Atlantic cable. Other businessmen talked of connecting the Union Pacific and projected Trans-Siberian railroad systems by tunneling under the Bering Strait and opening service from Chicago to Paris via Irkutsk.

Like the citizens of Nikolaevsk, St. Petersburg adopted an ambivalent attitude toward American economic penetration of Eastern Siberia during the last half of the nineteenth century. American enterprise promised to supply remote areas, to raise living standards, and to promote the economic development of Russia's Pacific territories. Yet there was an undercurrent of concern about a foreign presence on Russian soil.

Sensitivity to a foreign economic presence in Eastern Siberia derived from the area's remoteness from European Russia, its small Russian population, the proximity of China and Japan, and the perceived danger of British encroachment. Moreover, from a Russian perspective, American whalers along Siberia's Pacific coast were having a deleterious effect on the aboriginal population. When in 1879 Konstantin Pobedonostsev urged the heir apparent and future Tsar Alexander III to have the navy send a cruiser to the Far East, he gave the following justification: "If we do not send Russian vessels to those shores, the non-Russian natives of the coast will altogether forget that they belong to Russia. Already many Chukchi speak English."[27]

St. Petersburg eventually took steps to restrict the Americans in Eastern Siberia. In the late 1860s the navy mounted patrols to keep a watch for whalers. American offers to develop Sakhalin's coal reserves in the 1870s were politely declined. At the same time, however, St. Petersburg showed a generally understanding attitude toward American commercial enterprise along the Amur. In 1856 Foreign Minister Prince Gorchakov instructed his minister in Washington, Eduard Stoeckl, that for the time being no U.S. consul could be admitted to the Amur Basin but that American merchants should be told in confidence that they would find a warm welcome there.[28]

Meanwhile, new developments in Russian-American economic relations were occurring along the Northwest Coast. The flow of goods was temporarily reversed in 1848 when the Russian-American Company, taking advantage of shortages caused by the California gold rush, shipped provisions to San Francisco.[29] In 1854 a San Francisco businessman named Beverley C. Sanders signed a contract in St. Petersburg with the Russian-American Company granting his firm a twenty-year monopoly on Alaskan ice, lumber, coal, and fish. The contract was concluded during the Crimean War when Russian ships were subject to interception by the British navy. Sanders took it upon himself to ship supplies in American vessels to Russian settlements in Alaska and Kamchatka. His contract was cancelled in 1860, but Russian ice from Sitka and Wood Island (near Kodiak) continued to turn up in San Francisco bars, stores, and homes until the sale of Alaska in 1867.[30]

Russian-American trade across the Pacific expanded steadily in the 1870s and 1880s. The establishment of Vladivostok in 1860 gave Russia a new gateway to the Pacific which soon replaced Nikolaevsk as an entrepôt for trade with the American West Coast. The dollar volume of Russian-American trade in the Pacific as reported in official American statistics for 1866–1881 was not great. But the growth is clear, as Table 1 indicates.

Official statistics, however, did not account for all the trade between Russians and Americans on the Pacific during this period.

TABLE I
**Russian-American Trade in the Pacific**
(In Dollars)

|       | U.S. Exports | U.S. Imports |
| ----- | ------------ | ------------ |
| 1866  | 3,300        | —            |
| 1868  | 59,341       | 15,849       |
| 1874  | 134,583      | —            |
| 1881  | 207,061      | 89,727       |

*Source:* Bureau of the Census, *Statistical Abstract of the United States, 1907* (Washington: GPO, 1907), p. 357.

There were unreported exchanges along the Siberian coast. Moreover, Americans doing business in the Kingdom of Hawaii had dealings with Russians. According to records of Russian consular representatives in Honolulu, an average of four Russian ships visited the islands annually between 1859 and 1884.[31] The Russian-American Company obtained supplies there and in exchange exported salted fish to the islands in the 1860s. In 1887 the illustrious navigator and naval commander Capt. Stepan O. Makarov stopped in Honolulu on the *Vityaz.* Makarov was approached by local businessmen interested in establishing trade between Hawaii and Russian Pacific ports.[32] The results of these negotiations are unfortunately not clear, but the fact that they took place is in itself significant.

## Apogee, 1890–1916

Russian-American relations in the Pacific underwent a fundamental change in magnitude and structure during the 1890s. The volume and value of bilateral trade increased dramatically. Americans came to have major trade and investment interests in Siberia, whose proximity to the U.S. West Coast gave American firms an advantage over their European competitors for the Pacific part of the Russian market. When Henry Adams wrote Henry Cabot Lodge on 4 August 1891 that it might be possible to "Americanise Siberia," he was not indulging in idle speculation.[33]

American interest in the Russian market had been rising in the 1880s as a result of Russia's quickening pace of industrialization and because of Russian-American competition as exporters of petroleum products. English and German firms had been active in Russia for years and had a commanding lead over their relatively inexperienced American competitors. American traders also faced an obstacle in the imperial tariff system, which placed high duties (collected in gold) on products that the United States was then exporting, namely, grain, cotton, petroleum, and agricultural machinery.

Some of these obstacles began to be removed in the 1890s when the influence of Finance Minister Sergei Witte made itself felt in imperial economic policies. Meanwhile, the Siberian market was assuming major proportions because of heavy influxes of peasant settlers and by the construction of the Trans-Siberian Railroad, which began with a ground-breaking ceremony in 1891 at Vladivostok.

Taking advantage of the propitious economic climate, Ambassador Ethan Allen Hitchcock, a St. Louis industrialist, energetically championed the cause of American-Russian trade during his tenure in St. Petersburg (1897–1899). Hitchcock was instrumental in having a U.S. consulate opened in Vladivostok in 1898 and sought the establishment of American consulates throughout Siberia.* His efforts to boost commerce were assisted by an imperial ukase in 1898 which temporarily lifted duties on imported agricultural machinery.[34] American imports entering Vladivostok jumped from $566,512 in 1896 to $1,543,127 in 1899 and reached $3,050,902 in 1900.[35]

In view of mounting peasant migration into Siberia and the Far East (4 million from 1890 to 1914), it is not surprising that agricultural machinery stood out among American products entering Vladivostok. One traveler reported in 1902 that McCormick and Deering advertisements could be seen in every Siberian village.[36] The International Harvester Company had a lion's share of agricultural equipment being sold in Siberia, and after 1900 it was the largest U.S. firm operating in Russia. Whatever the brand name, most of the agricultural machinery in Siberian warehouses was of American origin.[37] American harvesters were highly esteemed among cultivators along the Amur River and in the Maritime Territory. "Such is the demand," wrote the U.S. commercial agent in Vladivostok in 1903, "that private firms cannot fill orders."[38]

Construction of the Trans-Siberian and Chinese-Eastern railroads created strong demand for rails and rolling stock, the bulk of which was supplied by American firms. The Americans beat out their English and German rivals in this market by superior quality, competitive prices, and speed of delivery. The latter two factors to some extent resulted from the geographical advantages enjoyed by Ameri-

---

*At this time Russia had consulates or consular representatives on the U.S. West Coast in Seattle, Portland, and San Francisco.

can exporters, who could ship rail equipment directly to the Russian Far East from the U.S. West Coast. Indeed, Vladivostok was the place of delivery for supplies connected with the construction of the Trans-Siberian line's eastern sections. Russia placed contracts for 40,000 tons of steel rails with the Pennsylvania & Maryland Steel Company in 1898 and for 180,000 tons of steel rails with the Carnegie Steel Company in 1899. American firms also constructed bridges along the Trans-Siberian route. In 1899 the Phoenix Bridge Company of Pennsylvania received a contract for twelve bridges. American rolling stock played an important role on Russian railways. The Baldwin Locomotive Works of Philadelphia sold over five hundred locomotives (about 60 percent of all Russia's locomotive imports) to Russia between 1892 and 1900.[39] One historian has gone so far as to assert that the Trans-Siberian and Chinese-Eastern railroads were "in all essentials" run on American equipment.[40]

Among consumer products imported from the United States into Vladivostok, mention should be made of Singer sewing machines. Such was the popularity of this brand that "Singer" entered the Russian language as the word for sewing machine. "Singers" were distributed throughout the Russian Far East. In 1898 during his travels around Kamchatka and the Kolyma Basin, an American gold prospector named Washington B. Vanderlip reported that a Singer was the most prized possession of a Koryak housewife in the Okhotsk seaboard hamlet of Gizhiga.[41]

By the turn of the century, Siberia was being called the "land of the future" and "a new California" in American journals.[42] The Klondike gold rush attracted Americans not only to Alaska but to the Chukchi Peninsula, Kamchatka, and the Kolyma region in 1898–1903, as prospectors such as Vanderlip or as investors such as Seattle's John Rosene, major stockholder in the Russian prospecting firm Northeastern Siberian Company.[43] It is interesting to note that a number of Americans in Eastern Siberia at this time were Russian Jews who had emigrated to the United States and, having become naturalized American citizens, returned to Russia to work as commercial agents without being subject to Russian laws pertaining to Jews.

The most successful American merchant in Siberia during the last half of the nineteenth century was Enoch Emery. Born in Massachusetts, Emery came to the Amur region as a boy on an American steamer in the 1860s. He remained there for forty years, living first in Nikolaevsk and then in Vladivostok. Emery made a fortune importing and selling American products from sewing machines to harvesters. He owned warehouses throughout Siberia and maintained offices in Moscow and Hamburg. In 1895 he founded the Amur Navigation Company, which operated a fleet of Detroit-built river barges and steamers.[44]

American enterprise in Eastern Siberia received a jolt in 1901 when authorities closed Vladivostok to free trade. For the next four years German products enjoyed a competitive edge over American goods coming across the Pacific. With the end of the Russo-Japanese War, however, Vladivostok reopened as a free port and American imports regained their preeminence.[45]

Consumer durables imported from the United States into Vladivostok between 1906 and 1916 included clothing, sewing machines, stoves, bicycles, automobiles, and motorboats.[46] Such was the reputation of Milwaukee beer that in 1909 a brewery in Blagoveshchensk was lucratively bottling lager under the Schlitz label.[47] Not all American products met a favorable local reception, however. U.S. tableware included knives that tapered at the tip, whereas Siberians like knives with broad blades permitting their use also as spoons.[48]

Siberia's demand for fruits and vegetables was strong, for these could not all be locally grown, and those that could be grown (apples, pears) were seasonal. During the 1880s and 1890s oranges and nuts were imported from China. Figs, honey, olives, olive oil, oranges, lemons, and nuts were also brought by steamer from Genoa, Marseilles, and Odessa. Around 1890, Russian merchants in Vladivostok became interested in California fruit, which was abundant, accessible, and of high quality.[49] By 1900 California apples, apricots, peaches, prunes, lemons, and raisins were enjoying a fine reputation among Siberians. Nevertheless, shipping costs, delivery delays, and poor packing hurt their competitiveness with European and Chinese produce. In the opinion of Richard T. Greener, U.S. commercial agent in Vladivostok: "No fruit from China, Japan, or Manchuria compares with that cultivated in the United States, and if it were possible to put our leading fruits into this market, I believe it would prove to be not only a blessing to the people, but a commercial success. But all depends on low rates of freight, quick transit, and proper packing."[50]

Thanks perhaps to Greener's advice, American fruit and other foodstuffs exports mounted after 1901 until by 1913 they comprised $600,000 or just over 20 percent of total U.S. exports to Eastern

Siberia.[51] Foodstuffs retained their importance in Russian-American trade in the Pacific through the vicissitudes of war, revolution, and civil war.

Siberian exports, largely furs, did not keep pace with imports. Consequently, the United States had a favorable balance of trade in every year from 1866 until 1933 in both the Atlantic and Pacific areas. Trade imbalances did not, however, dampen official enthusiasm for foreign commerce, judging from Amur Governor N. L. Gondatti's sustained support of international economic ties.[52]

For all its impressive growth, Russian-American trade across the Pacific did not match Russian-American trade in the Atlantic. On the basis of official statistics, Pacific bilateral trade amounted in 1900–1914 to about 10 percent of Atlantic trade between the two countries. The percentage may, in fact, have been even lower, because these statistics do not reflect that portion of the Atlantic trade that passed through English and German ports.

Historians have devoted considerable attention to Russian-American rivalry in Manchuria during the first decade of the twentieth century. Often overlooked, however, is the fact that American capital investment in Russia increased significantly after 1905. Before the end of the Russo-Japanese War, St. Petersburg circles considered drawing American capital into the Russian Far East as a means to forestall a Japanese invasion. After the battle of Mukden in March of 1905, the imperial court became the scene of discussions about selling Sakhalin to the United States before the island fell into Japanese hands. The Russian ambassador in Washington proposed at least granting Americans extensive concessions on the island. The idea won some support but was eventually turned down by the tsar, who conjectured that President Roosevelt's pro-Japanese sympathies would lead to Japanese control of Sakhalin.[53]

After the Portsmouth Peace Conference, St. Petersburg continued its efforts to reach economic agreements with Washington involving, among other things, American capital investment in Russia's eastern territories. During 1905 and 1906 Finance Minister V. N. Kokovtsev corresponded with J. P. Morgan on Siberian investment possibilities. He discussed the Ussuri Railroad (joining Khabarovsk and Vladivostok) with Judge Charles Mayer and several American financiers who were thinking of bidding on construction contracts. Although American participation did not materialize, American capital investments in Russia, led by the House of Morgan, grew steadily until the First World War.

The outbreak of war in 1914 precipitated a surge of shipments to Siberia from the U.S. West Coast. With maritime approaches to the Baltic and Black seas blocked by the Central Powers, Vladivostok emerged as one of Russia's principal gateways. American exports to the Russian Far East leapt from $5.7 million in 1914 to $44.2 million in 1915 to $160.7 million in 1916. Sixty-five percent of cargoes consisted of war matériel, but foodstuffs were also well represented. Russian-American trade in the Pacific peaked in 1916. Thereafter political and social upheavals reduced but did not halt bilateral commerce.

## Turbulent Interim, 1917–1922

The American reaction to the February and October revolutions and American participation in foreign intervention in the Russian civil war are subjects fraught with controversy. Without delving into the motives of the Wilson administration, the State Department, Congress, business, the press, and other forces in the United States, it can be said that the presence of the American Expeditionary Force in the Russian Far East from August 1918 until April 1920 has colored Soviet perceptions of U.S. policies in the Pacific.

The economic aspects of "America's Siberian adventure" (as Expeditionary Force commander Maj. Gen. William S. Graves called it)[54] were nearly as tangled as the political aspects. For four years the United States found itself doing business with at least three sets of Russian authorities. The American business community split over what attitude to take toward the new Soviet regime. The Morgan interests, which had lent $182 million to the imperial government, supported the State Department policy of withholding credits to Moscow. Other firms, including International Harvester, General Electric, and Baldwin Locomotive, opened negotiations with Moscow and by the late 1920s had concluded trade and construction contracts. A pioneer in this area was Armand J. Hammer, whose Allied American Company served from 1923 as an agent for more than thirty U.S. firms conducting trade with the USSR. Interestingly, one Soviet historian has noted that attitudes toward trade relations with the Soviet Union were generally more favorable in U.S. Pacific states than along the Eastern seaboard.[55]

American exports to the Russian Far East continued to reach Vladivostok, a city which for the most part between 1917 and 1922 was under a confusing succession of White (anti-Bolshevik) administrations buttressed by the presence of Japanese troops. In 1917, American exports to the Russian Far East fell by over 30 percent to $109.3 million as a result of unstable conditions inside the country following the collapse of the tsarist regime in March and the overthrow of the Provisional Government in November.

The spread of civil war to Siberia and the Far East in 1918 caused a further decline of American exports to Vladivostok. Many American goods which reached Vladivostok in 1917–1918 could not be shipped inland because of disrupted rail services. In his memoirs, General Graves recalled large quantities of cotton, rubber, and a thousand automobiles lying idle and exposed to the elements on the wharves.[56]

Unsettled conditions did not discourage plans for future economic cooperation between local authorities in the Russian Far East and American businessmen. On 4 December 1917 the Russian-American Committee for the Far East was founded in Vladivostok with the purpose of encouraging trade and investment. The committee held trade exhibitions, published a journal, and maintained an office in San Francisco during its five-year existence. The National City Bank opened a branch in Vladivostok in October 1918 at the invitation of August Heid, former representative of International Harvester in Russia and member of the War Trade Board's Russian bureau, which granted licenses to Americans engaged in commercial ventures in Siberia.[57]

By upsetting harvests and sending waves of refugees across Siberia, the civil war eventually generated heavy demands for imported foodstuffs. American exports to Vladivostok rebounded from $8.4 million in 1918 to $52 million in 1919.[58] Among these were sizeable quantities of dried fruit, powdered milk, and canned meat.

After the creation of the Far Eastern Republic (FER) following the evacuation of the last echelons of American troops from Vladivostok,* a small amount of trade took place between the FER government in Chita and American merchants. This continued until 1922 through the port of Okhotsk fifteen hundred miles north of Vladivostok.[59]

A third level of economic interaction during this interim existed in the form of negotiations between the Soviet regime and American

---

*The FER was a buffer state created on 6 April 1920 and absorbed into the Soviet Union in November of 1922.

businessmen seeking concessions in the Far East. Two of these deserve mention: Washington Vanderlip's bid for a concession in Northeastern Siberia (1920) and the Sinclair Oil Company's concession on northern Sakhalin (1922–1925).

The Vanderlip concession never got further than words. As announced on 22 October 1920 by Foreign Affairs Commissar Georgii Chicherin, the concession consisted of a sixty-year grant of exclusive rights to develop coal, oil, and fisheries east of the 160th meridian, an area of four hundred thousand square miles including all of Kamchatka, the Chukchi Peninsula, and the Kolyma Basin.[60] The concessionaire claimed to represent a consortium of wealthy West Coast luminaries and to possess a letter of endorsement from a U.S. presidential hopeful, Ohio senator Warren G. Harding.

Vanderlip was none other than the onetime prospector who marveled at a Singer sewing machine on the Okhotsk seacoast while looking for a Siberian Klondike in 1898–1902. Two decades later, as a middle-aged Hollywood engineer, Vanderlip's Siberian visions revived when a Far Eastern Republic delegation visited Los Angeles to promote American investment in the FER. Vanderlip's claims of ties with U.S high finance and politics, coupled with his sharing a surname with Frank A. Vanderlip (former president of the National City Bank of New York), led Soviet officials to receive him when the Californian showed up in Moscow late in 1920.

Vanderlip was accorded the privilege of a meeting with Lenin, who had his own ideas about Vanderlip's political utility as an irritant in Japanese-American relations. As Lenin told a group of Moscow party workers on 26 November:

> An intense hostility is now developing between America and Japan. We are making use of this and are offering a lease of Kamchatka instead of giving it away gratis; after all, Japan has taken a huge expanse of our territory in the Far East, this by force of arms. It is far more to our advantage to run no risk, grant a lease of Kamchatka, and receive part of its products, the more so for our being unable, in any case, to run or exploit it. The treaty has not been signed, but it is already being spoken of in Japan with the utmost anger. Through this treaty we have aggravated the differences between our enemies.[61]

In the Sinclair Oil Company's Sakhalin concession, Soviet motives were analogous: to utilize American investors as a counterfoil to Japan's occupation of Soviet territory. On 7 January 1922 the Sinclair Consolidated Oil Company signed a 36-year contract with the FER, providing for oil exploration rights along Sakhalin's northeastern coast. The contract was formally ratified by the Russian Republic (RSFSR) on 23 January 1923. But when Sinclair officials attempted to land on Sakhalin that autumn, they were interned by Japanese troops and escorted off the island. Unable to secure diplomatic support from the State Department, the Sinclair Company could not fulfill the contract, which the Soviet Supreme Court subsequently nullified in May 1925.[62]

## A New Beginning, 1923–1941

On 16 January 1920 the Supreme Allied Economic Council lifted the trade embargo against the Soviet regime. Nevertheless, the State and Treasury departments, mindful of claims on prerevolution financial obligations, instituted credit restrictions and did not accept Soviet bullion payments. Such obstacles constrained but did not preclude Soviet-American trade, which began in the early 1920s notwithstanding the absence of diplomatic relations between Washington and Moscow.

Soviet-American trade in the Pacific seems to have started in 1924 with a total exchange of $813,000. By 1930 the figure had reached $5,460,000. Industrial products rather than foodstuffs predominated among American exports to Vladivostok. Agricultural machinery led American exports to the USSR in general during the 1920s. In 1930 the Soviet Union was buying 36 percent of all agricultural implements and 50 percent of all tractors sent abroad from American factories.[63] In the Far East, Sakhalin and Kamchatka canneries used American equipment. In 1940 wide-diameter steel pipes were imported from the United States and used for a pipeline under the Tartary Strait from Sakhalin oil fields to Komsomolsk, the newly established industrial center on the lower Amur.[64]

Soviet exports from the Far East across the Pacific to the American West Coast during the late 1920s and 1930s consisted largely of foodstuffs, notably marine products. In 1933, 27 percent of American crabmeat imports were from Kamchatka.[65]

Political as well as economic factors appear to have constrained the growth of Soviet-American trade in the Pacific during the 1930s. The rising level of international tension after Japan's occupation of

Manchuria in 1931–1932, coupled with Soviet policy reassessments following the lack of success in a common front against Japan, seems to have cooled Moscow's interest in developing the foreign trade ties of Soviet Far Eastern ports. Concurrently, a balance of payments problem led to a sharp curtailment of Soviet imports from the United States after 1931. American exports to the USSR did not regain 1931 levels until a decade later. Exports from the Soviet Union, on the other hand, climbed steadily after 1932, but they did not exceed import levels except in 1933.

## Lend-Lease in the Pacific

West Coast ties with the Soviet Far East strengthened after the outbreak of the Second World War as a result of the Lend-Lease Act, passed by Congress in March of 1941 and extended to the USSR in November of that year. The first lend-lease convoy reached Vladivostok in May 1942. These convoys helped to boost the share of the USSR in American exports from 2.1 percent in 1941 to 17.6 percent in 1942.[66] By 1945, 6.7 million tons of supplies had reached the USSR along North Pacific sea lanes.[67] In addition, several thousand tons were flown from Alaska to Yakutsk.

Fully 75 percent of all lend-lease tonnage sent to the USSR during World War II came across the Pacific.[68] Cargoes included tanks, airplanes, trucks, machine guns, ammunition, and foodstuffs. The ships were mostly American built, of Soviet registry, and manned by Soviet crews.

Lend-lease shipments across the Pacific faced multiple obstacles. Vladivostok's port capacity in 1941 was still limited. Installation of American cranes and imports of American rolling stock alleviated trans-shipment bottlenecks.[69] Yet closure of Seattle to Soviet ships in 1942 provoked complaints. Throughout the war, Portland, Oregon, remained the main lend-lease port on the West Coast.

Lend-lease convoys were obliged to pass through the Japanese-held Kurile Islands in order to reach the Sea of Okhotsk. Although Tokyo and Moscow had concluded a Neutrality Pact in 1941, the Imperial Navy not infrequently interfered with the convoys, especially during the war's early years. Twenty-five transports were sunk, two of them erroneously by U.S. submarines.[70]

Lend-lease in the Pacific involved more than shipments of cargoes. From May until September 1945, the U.S. Navy trained some fifteen thousand sailors of the Soviet Pacific Fleet at Cold Harbor, Alaska, in the operation of 138 surface vessels handed over to the USSR under the lend-lease agreement.[71] Meanwhile, although not related to lend-lease, it should be recalled that American fliers in combat missions over Japan who were forced to make emergency landings in the Soviet Far East were discreetly cared for in Kamchatka, Vladivostok, and Khabarovsk before their eventual repatriation.

## Conclusion

For a quarter of a century after the end of World War II, Soviet-American trade remained insignificant in general and virtually non-existent in the Pacific. Starting in the early 1970s, however, economic ties between the American Far West and the Soviet Far East revived. This occurred despite nonimplementation of the 1972 Soviet-American Trade Agreement.

One important stimulus for trade expansion in the Pacific has been Soviet purchases of American grain. In 1972 some two hundred thousand tons of maize, barley, and oats were shipped to Nakhodka. There have also been sales of California citrus fruits such as Sunkist and Pure Gold lemons in 1973 and 1975 respectively. Cooperation in fisheries has been achieved by the joint activities of the Far Eastern Fisheries Administration and the Seattle-based US-USSR Marine Resources Company described by Elisa Miller later in this volume.

Historical experience shows that the American Far West and the Russian Far East have a proven record of mutually beneficial economic interaction. The current development of both regions increases the goods and services that each region can offer the other. Geographical propinquity to an economically dynamic Japan suggests trilateral options for economic cooperation that would redound to the advantage of each country.

### NOTES

1. Norman E. Saul, "Beginnings of American-Russian Trade, 1763–1766," *William and Mary Quarterly* 26, no. 4 (October 1969): 596–600.

2. James Duncan Phillips, "Salem Opens American Trade with Russia," *New England Quarterly* 14 (December 1941): 686.

3. Nikolai N. Bolkhovitinov, *The Beginnings of Russian-American Relations, 1775–1815,* trans. Elena Levin (Cambridge: Harvard University Press, 1975), pp. 153–154.

4. James R. Gibson, *Feeding the Russian Fur Trade* (Madison: University of Wisconsin Press, 1969), p. 220.

5. James R. Gibson, *Imperial Russia in Frontier America* (New York: Oxford University Press, 1976), pp. 154–155.

6. N. N. Bolkhovitinov, "Vydvizhenie i proval proektov P. Dobella, 1812–1821," *Amerikanskii ezhegodnik 1976* (Moscow: Nauka, 1976), pp. 264–282.

7. N. N. Bolkhovitinov, "Avantiura Doktora Sheffera na Gavaiiakh v 1815–1819 godakh," *Novaia i noveishaia istoriia* 1 (1972): 121–137. Richard A. Pierce, *Russia's Hawaiian Adventure, 1815–1817* (Berkeley and Los Angeles: University of California Press, 1965).

8. Glynn Barratt, *Russia in Pacific Waters, 1715–1825* (Vancouver: University of British Columbia Press, 1981), pp. 100–189.

9. Mary E. Wheeler, "Empires in Conflict and Cooperation: The 'Bostonians' and the Russian-American Company," *Pacific Historical Review* 40, no. 4 (November 1971): 422–427.

10. Bolkhovitinov, *Beginnings of Russian-American Relations,* p. 182.

11. William Appleman Williams, *American-Russian Relations, 1781–1947* (New York: Rinehart & Co., 1952), p. 7.

12. Capt. John Dundas Cochrane, R. N., *A Pedestrian Journey through Russia and Siberian Tartary* (Edinburgh: Constable, 1829), pp. 323–324.

13. N. N. Bolkhovitinov, *Russko-amerikanskie otnosheniia, 1815–1832* (Moscow: Nauka, 1975), pp. 377–378.

14. Howard I. Kushner, *Conflict on the Northwest Coast: American-Russian Rivalry in the Pacific Northwest, 1790–1867* (Westport, Conn.: Greenwood Press, 1975), pp. 25–42, 59.

15. E. A. Adamov, "Russia and the United States at the Time of the Civil War," *Journal of Modern History* 2, no. 4 (December 1930): 592.

16. Foster Rhea Dulles, *The Road to Teheran: The Story of Russia and America, 1781–1943* (Princeton: Princeton University Press, 1944), p. 62.

17. Williams, *American-Russian Relations,* p. 18.

18. Frank A. Golder, "Russian-American Relations during the Crimean War," *American Historical Review* 31, no. 2 (January 1926): 467.

19. Albert Parry, "Yankee Whalers in Siberia," *Russian Review* 5, no. 2 (Spring 1946): 40.

20. P. N. Golovin, *The End of Russian America: Captain P. N. Golovin's Last Report,* translated with an introduction and notes by Basil Dmytryshyn and E. A. P. Crownhart-Vaughan (Portland: Oregon Historical Society, 1979), p. 93.

21. George Kennan, *Tent Life in Siberia* (New York: G. P. Putnam & Sons, 1870), pp. 81–82, 104, 329–330.

22. A. V. Vysheslavtsev, *Ocherki perom i karandashem iz krugosvetnago plavania v 1857, 1858, i 1860 godakh* (St. Petersburg: M. O. Vol'f, 1867), pp. 272–276.

23. John J. Stephan, *Sakhalin: A History* (Oxford: The Clarendon Press, 1971), p. 50.

24. Norman Saul, "An American's Siberian Dream," *Russian Review* 37, no. 4 (October 1978): 410–417.

25. Perry McDonough Collins, *A Voyage Down the Amoor* (New York: D. Appleton, 1860), p. 2.

26. Richard L. Neuberger, "The Telegraph Trail," *Harper's Magazine,* October 1946, pp. 363–370.

27. *Pis'ma Pobedonostseva k Aleksandru III,* vol. 1 (Moscow: Novaia Moskva, 1925), p. 184, cited by Parry, "Yankee Whalers," p. 36.

28. Gorchakov to Stoeckl, 21 September 1856, cited by Golder, "Russian-American Relations during the Crimean War," p. 475.

29. Golovin, *The End of Russian America,* p. 101.

30. Norman E. Saul, "Beverley C. Sanders and the Expansion of American Trade with Russia, 1853–1855," *Maryland Historical Magazine* 67, no. 2 (Summer 1972): 156–169.

31. Russian Consular Papers, Honolulu, Record Group 261, Box Aj 2, Archives Division, Washington National Records Center, Suitland, Maryland.

32. John F. Hackfeld to Capt. Stepan Makarov, 4 March 1887, Russian Consular Papers, Honolulu, RG 261, Box Aj 2.

33. *Letters of Henry Adams (1858–1891),* ed. Worthington Chauncey Ford, vol. 1 (Boston: Houghton Mifflin, 1930), p. 511.

34. George Sherman Queen, "The United States and the Material Advance of Russia, 1881–1906," Ph.D. diss., University of Illinois, Urbana, 1941, pp. 65, 123.

35. Bureau of the Census, *Statistical Abstract of the United States, 1907,* (Washington: GPO, 1907) p. 377. Bureau of the Census, *Statistical Abstract of the United States, 1920,* p. 418.

36. H. Norman, *All the Russias* (New York: William Heinemann, 1902), p. 154.

37. John Foster Fraser, *The Real Siberia* (London: Cassell, 1902), p. 202.

38. Richard T. Greener, "American Interests and Oppotunities in Siberia," Department of Commerce, Bureau of Statistics, *Monthly Consular Reports,* no. 276 (September 1903), p. 35.

39. Queen, "The United States and the Material Advance of Russia," pp. 79–83, 167–169.

40. Williams, *American-Russian Relations,* p. 83.

41. W. B. Vanderlip, *In Search of a Siberian Klondike* (New York: Century & Co., 1903), p. 64.

42. S. M. Williams, "A New California," *Munsey's Magazine* 26 (1902): 761. *The Nation* 61 (1895): 165, 203, 238.

43. Queen, "The United States and the Material Advance of Russia," pp. 205–206.

44. Ibid., pp. 170, 201–202.

45. Ibid., p. 108.

46. Department of State, Division of Commercial Affairs, Register of Consular Trade Reports, Vladivostok (1906–1923), Washington National Records Center, Suitland, Maryland.

47. Lester Maynard, U.S. consul in Vladivostok, to Secretary of State John Hay, 22 October 1909, Microfilm 862, roll 1131, item 22363, State Department Archives, National Archives.

48. Vanderlip, *In Search of a Siberian Klondike,* p. 33.

49. Platon Chikhachev, "Kaliforniia i Ussuriiskii krai," *Vestnik Evropy* 25, no. 6 (June 1890): 550.

50. Richard T. Greener, "Fruit Market in Siberia," Bureau of Foreign Commerce, *Consular Reports* 64 no. 243 (December 1900): 483.

51. Bureau of Foreign Commerce, *Commerce and Navigation of the United States, 1901–1914* (Washington: GPO, 1915).

52. Lester Maynard to Secretary of State, 22 March 1911, Department of State, Consular Reports (Vladivostok), 861c., p. 461, Microfilm 316, roll 175, State Department Archives, National Archives.

53. Williams, *American-Russian Relations,* pp. 52–53, 55.

54. William S. Graves, *America's Siberian Adventure* (New York: Peter Smith, 1941).

55. E. I. Popov, *Politika SSHA na Dal'nem Vostoke, 1918–1922* (Moscow: Nauka, 1967), p. 201.

56. Graves, *America's Siberian Adventure,* p. 80.

57. John A. White, *The Siberian Intervention* (Princeton: Princeton University Press, 1950), pp. 320–321.

58. Bureau of the Census, *Statistical Abstract of the United States, 1920,* p. 418.

59. "Closing of Okhotsk as a Free Port," 17 August 1922, Division of Commercial Affairs, Register of Consular Trade Reports (Vladivostok), File no. 70954, Department of State Archives, National Archives.

60. Albert Parry, "Washington B. Vanderlip, the 'Khan of Kamchatka,' " *Pacific Historical Review* 17, no. 3 (August 1948): 312.

61. V. I. Lenin, *Collected Works,* 4th ed., vol. 31 (Moscow: Progress Publishers, 1968), p. 431.

62. Floyd J. Fithian, "Dollars Without the Flag: The Case of Sinclair and Sakhalin Oil," *Pacific Historical Review* 39, no. 2 (May 1970): 205–222.

63. Williams, *American-Russian Relations,* p. 218.

64. N. M. Pegov, *Dalekoe-blizkoe: vospominaniia* (Moscow: Polit. izdat., 1982), p. 95.

65. *Handbook of the Soviet Union* (New York, 1934), p. 309. Bureau of the Census, *Statistical Abstract of the United States, 1934,* pp. 428–429.

66. Mikhail V. Condoide, *Russian-American Trade* (Columbus, Ohio: Ohio State University, College of Commerce and Administration, 1947), pp. 91, 104.

67. Robert Huhn Jones, *The Roads to Russia: United States Lend-Lease to the Soviet Union* (Norman, Okla.: University of Oklahoma Press, 1969), p. 214.

68. V. P. Lomakin, *Primor'e* (Moscow: Polit. izdat., 1981), p. 24.

69. Richard E. Lauterback, *Through Russia's Back Door* (New York: Harper & Bros., 1946), p. 22. Pegov, *Dalekoe-blizkoe,* p. 177.

70. N. A. Kolotov, *Okean v ogne: moriaki transportnogo flota Dal'nego Vostoka v Velikoi Otechestvennoi voine 1941–1945* (Vladivostok: Dal'nevostoch. knizh. izdat., 1972), pp. 5, 11.

71. Edward Pinkowski, "Soviet Trainees in the USA in World War II," *Russian Review* 5, no. 1 (Autumn 1945): 15–16.

# Changing Economy
# of the American West

WILLIAM B. BEYERS

IN DISTINCTION from other authors of this book, I define the geographic boundaries of my discussion to include all of the American West. Although there is no universally accepted definition of the "American West" (hereafter the West), for present purposes the designation will refer to the area encompassing the eight Rocky Mountain states as well as the five Pacific coast states. As diverse as the region might appear, these thirteen states nevertheless share certain important characteristics. For one, they share common environmental features. Furthermore, they contain today most of the publicly owned land in the United States. Finally, their industrial characteristics set these states apart from the rest of the country.

This chapter begins with an overview of the demographic trends in the West over the past century. Current employment patterns are discussed. The economies of the Western states are then examined as an internally interdependent system with external ties to the national and international economies. Finally, levels of per capita income and sources of income are compared to those found in other parts of the United States.

## Overview

Exploration of the Pacific littoral and American West in the eighteenth and early nineteenth centuries revealed opportunities for exploiting the area's natural wealth. Construction of transcontinental railroads in the second half of the nineteenth century provided access to resources and laid the foundation for integrating Western natural resources into the national market.[1] The economies of the Western states are still oriented toward resource-based industries, but in recent years new forces have been at work reducing dependence on them. Southern California, for example, developed a highly diversified industrial base in the early twentieth century and is today a major manufacturing center. Since the Second World War the West has become an important center for high-technology industry. The region's natural beauty and generally hospitable climate have attracted millions to the West, many to find work, others to retire. In the process new communities have been created, indirectly inducing shifts in the West's economic structure.

The thirteen Western states account for half of the nation's land area but only 18.2 percent of national employment in 1978.[2] Table 1 shows the magnitude of employment in the region on a state-by-state basis from 1969 until 1978 with projections until 1990. California alone accounts for more than half of the region's employment, a striking testimony to the dominance of a single state in the West's economy.

While the West's share of the nation's economy is small compared with its share of the nation's area, its population is growing faster

TABLE I
**Employment Change by State**

| | 1969–1978 | | 1978–1990 | |
|---|---|---|---|---|
| | Change in Jobs (in Thousands) | % Change | Change in Jobs (in Thousands) | % Change |
| Alaska | 70.2 | 50.2 | 86.9 | 41.3 |
| Arizona | 385.6 | 57.4 | 353.5 | 33.4 |
| California | 2,338.2 | 27.6 | 3,572.2 | 33.1 |
| Colorado | 428.8 | 46.0 | 545.3 | 40.1 |
| Hawaii | 98.7 | 26.0 | 126.6 | 26.5 |
| Idaho | 130.0 | 45.1 | 109.8 | 26.2 |
| Montana | 86.1 | 31.3 | 65.0 | 18.0 |
| Nevada | 163.1 | 70.4 | 221.8 | 56.1 |
| New Mexico | 151.2 | 40.9 | 138.8 | 26.6 |
| Oregon | 321.0 | 37.6 | 413.1 | 35.1 |
| Utah | 176.6 | 43.3 | 233.0 | 40.0 |
| Washington | 331.9 | 23.2 | 533.4 | 30.0 |
| Wyoming | 79.9 | 54.1 | 101.3 | 44.5 |
| WEST TOTAL | 4,761.3 | 32.6 | 6,500.7 | 33.6 |
| Other States | 10,941.1 | 15.4 | 14,367.0 | 17.6 |
| U.S. TOTAL | 15,702.4 | 18.4 | 20,867.7 | 20.6 |

*Source:* Department of Commerce, Bureau of Economic Analysis, *BEA Regional Projections,* vol. 1 (July 1981).

than that of the rest of the country. This westward redistribution of people is expected to continue in the foreseeable future.[3] The region underwent particularly rapid demographic growth between 1870 and 1910, a phenomenon reflecting the development of resource-based industry and construction of the transcontinental railroads. From 1910 to 1940, however, the growth rate slowed in most Western states and actually declined in Montana. Arizona, New Mexico, and Hawaii exhibited a more continuous path of expansion up to 1940, with Arizona and Nevada displaying very rapid rates of growth in the years since World War II.[4]

The increasing proportion of the West's population as a share of the national total is explained by relatively rapid growth of the regional economic base.[5] A state's economic base can be defined here as that portion of economic activity which is tied to external markets. It is widely argued that the level of activity in the industries composing a region's economic base determines, through "multiplier" relationships, the total level of economic activity in the region.

For example, let us assume that oil or natural gas is discovered in a region. As these resources are developed, investments in facilities generate local employment in construction and related industries. Sources of capital for this investment will likely be external. From a regional perspective such investment is an infusion of outside funds, or conversely an export of services. Workers in the construction industry spend their income to buy goods and services, leading to additional employment in the local service sector. The cumulative effect of these expenditures is a general rise in employment. The ratio of the overall employment level to employment directly related to oil/gas construction constitutes a multiplier. Once the oil/gas field is in operation, new structural relationships in the region will ensue. Workers involved in extracting oil and gas would be export-tied employees, assuming that most or all of the petroleum is exported from the region. Multiplier relationships between export and locally tied employment would also exist in the extraction process.

The West has been able to sustain a relatively rapid population growth because its industries have grown more quickly than those of the nation as a whole. Table 1 indicates employment patterns in the Western states relative to the entire United States during the years 1969–1978. Employment is used here as a representative measure of economic activity. It can be seen that every Western state experienced more rapid employment growth in this period than the national average. Although California's growth rate fell short of all other Western states except Washington, its increase in absolute terms nonetheless accounted for more than half of the regional total. Underlying these figures is the fact that a net migration of 5 million people to the West occurred during the 1970s.[6] Thus, the surge of employment in the West came at the expense of employment growth in other parts of the United States.

The federal government projects employment levels by region. Table 1 contains growth estimates for the years 1978–1990. These forecasts anticipate a slightly larger percentage gain than between 1969 and 1978. At the same time there will probably be some convergence of Western states' growth rates as extreme variations between individual states narrow.

Some 2.5 million jobs will be redistributed to the West between 1978 and 1990. Influxes from other parts of the country and from Mexico will continue to meet employment needs for the rapidly expanding regional economy. Table 2 shows levels of net migration to Western states during 1970–1980. Comparison of data in Tables 1 and 2 reveals a correspondence between net migration and employment levels.

Settlement of retirees has also stimulated the growth of employment. Hawaii, Arizona, and southern California have attracted large numbers of retired Americans seeking sunny skies and mild winters. Retirement communities generate income which in turn

TABLE 2
**Net Migration to Western States, 1970–1980**

|  | Net Migration | Net Migration as a % of 1970 Population |
|---|---|---|
| Alaska | 76,000 | 25% |
| Arizona | 712,000 | 40 |
| California | 2,078,000 | 10 |
| Colorado | 446,000 | 20 |
| Hawaii | 76,000 | 10 |
| Idaho | 130,000 | 18 |
| Nevada | 257,000 | 52 |
| New Mexico | 141,000 | 14 |
| Oregon | 396,000 | 19 |
| Utah | 149,000 | 14 |
| Washington | 474,000 | 14 |
| Wyoming | 96,000 | 29 |

*Source: Statistical Abstract of the United States, 1982–1983,* 103d ed. (Washington: Department of Commerce, 1982), p. 13.

has multiplier effects in state economies, notably in the service sector.

Some have argued that as the structure of employment in the United States has shifted from primary (agriculture, mining) and secondary (manufacturing) to services (including information processing), people exercise significantly more freedom in selecting their workplace. If this is the case, westward migration is both a symptom of and a stimulus to an economic restructuring of the country.

## Patterns of Employment

Table 3 affords a more detailed view of the economic structure of the West by providing data on employment in each state in 1978. Each row of this table shows the percentage of total employment associated with seven industrial groupings for each Western state and for the United States as a whole.

If we compare the structure of Westen state economies to the nation as a whole, it is apparent that they have a larger than national

TABLE 3
**Employment by Sector, 1978**
(Percentage of Total)

| | Agriculture, Fisheries, Forestry | Mining | Construction | Durable Mfg. | Non-durable Mfg. | Services | Government |
|---|---|---|---|---|---|---|---|
| Alaska | 1.2 | 3.5 | 6.4 | 4.1 | 1.5 | 48.8 | 34.5 |
| Arizona | 3.2 | 1.8 | 7.6 | 3.1 | 9.3 | 53.3 | 21.6 |
| California | 3.7 | 0.4 | 4.6 | 5.9 | 11.9 | 54.6 | 18.9 |
| Colorado | 3.5 | 2.1 | 6.7 | 4.8 | 7.9 | 54.2 | 20.8 |
| Hawaii | 3.4 | * | 4.7 | 4.1 | 1.1 | 56.2 | 30.5 |
| Idaho | 10.8 | 1.0 | 6.6 | 6.3 | 8.0 | 47.9 | 19.4 |
| Montana | 8.1 | 2.0 | 6.3 | 2.6 | 5.1 | 52.3 | 23.6 |
| Nevada | 1.4 | 1.1 | 7.2 | 1.6 | 3.1 | 68.5 | 17.1 |
| New Mexico | 3.4 | 4.7 | 7.6 | 2.8 | 3.9 | 51.1 | 26.5 |
| Oregon | 5.2 | 0.2 | 5.5 | 4.8 | 14.4 | 52.3 | 17.6 |
| Utah | 2.7 | 2.7 | 7.3 | 4.9 | 9.0 | 50.7 | 22.7 |
| Washington | 4.5 | 0.2 | 6.4 | 4.8 | 11.7 | 52.2 | 20.2 |
| Wyoming | 5.9 | 12.8 | 10.0 | 2.5 | 2.1 | 46.3 | 20.4 |
| U.S. | 3.4 | 0.9 | 5.3 | 8.3 | 12.4 | 51.8 | 17.9 |

*Source:* Department of Commerce, Bureau of Economic Analysis, *BEA Regional Projections,* vol. 1 (July 1981).

* = less than .1%

average employment in agriculture, forestry, fisheries, mining, construction, government, and a somewhat larger proportion of employment within the service sectors. In general, they have a smaller
share of employment in manufacturing sectors than the nation as a
whole. Rocky Mountain states tend to show relatively high dependence on agriculture, forestry, and mining, while Alaska and Hawaii
show unusual dependence on the federal government. The proportion of workers in Western states employed by the government and
service sectors—75 percent—is striking.

Table 3 also demonstrates the orientation of Western state economies toward natural resources. Agriculture and the food industry
are important in Arizona, California, Hawaii, Idaho, Montana,
Oregon, Washington, and Wyoming. Fisheries and fish products are
of notable significance in Alaska. Mining and chemicals, petroleum
refining, and associated transportation services (pipelines, railroads)
are prominent in Alaska, Arizona, Colorado, Idaho, Montana,
Nevada, New Mexico, Utah, and Wyoming. Forest products assume an important position in the economies of Idaho, Montana,
Oregon, and Washington.

While the Western states are heavily involved in the extraction
and processing of natural resources, they also have developed industrial specializations. The manufacture of transportation equipment,
especially aerospace products, is significant in Washington and California and to a lesser extent in Arizona. Instruments are produced
on a large scale in Oregon, California, and Colorado. Electrical
machinery plays an important role in the economies of Arizona and
California.

Industries serving civilian and military government agencies figure prominently in the economies of all Western states except Oregon. Significant levels of military employment exist in Alaska,
Hawaii, New Mexico, Colorado, and Washington, while federal
civilian employment reaches relatively high levels in Hawaii, Alaska, and New Mexico.

An attractive environment has encouraged the development of
burgeoning recreation and tourist industries in much of the West.
Nevada's high level of employment in hotels and amusement facilities is tied to that state's gambling and entertainment industry.
Hawaii's economy is to a notable degree (roughly 35 percent) dependent on tourism. California has seen the production of motion pic-
tures become a major state industry; "Hollywood" is a word that
enjoys international currency. Tourism and entertainment figure

importantly, if less dramatically, in the economies of Arizona, Alaska, Colorado, Montana, and New Mexico.

During the 1970s, industrial specializations in the Western states changed only marginally. Agriculture in Hawaii gradually lost its former preeminence with the closing of sugar mills and curtailment of pineapple production. Metal mining declined in Arizona, Idaho, Montana, Nevada, and Utah. On the other hand, coal mining grew in Colorado, New Mexico, Montana, Utah, and Wyoming. Non-metal mining showed dramatic increases in Wyoming.

The 1970s witnessed an increase in the Western states' share of the nation's manufacturing industry, notably in high technology, transport equipment, and instruments. Indeed, the West achieved during this decade an above-average concentration in the instruments sector. The West's rise to prominence in the high-technology field in this period is even more impressive. Western state governments began to actively attract high-tech corporations to locate their research and production facilities in the San Francisco Bay area, Los Angeles, Phoenix, Denver, Seattle, and Portland. Universities and research institutes in the West continue to generate high-tech ideas, which in some cases find their way into industrial production. The internationalization of production in electronics opened the way to a proliferation of corporate and scientific ties between the Western states and countries in East and Southeast Asia, notably Japan, South Korea, Taiwan, Hong Kong, and Singapore.[7]

Certain sectors in the Western states stand out as being particularly dynamic, the service sector having outpaced all others. Relatively rapid growth has occurred in retail trade (except in Hawaii), state and local government employment (except in California, Washington, Wyoming), wholesale trade, and personal and business services. The development of petroleum resources has set the economic tempo in Alaska. California's food industry has displayed dynamic growth, although the state's agricultural resources are already heavily utilized. Federal military expenditures has risen sharply in Hawaii and New Mexico. Nevada's hotels and amusement centers have benefitted from an unprecedented influx of tourists. Idaho and Oregon have continued to show gains in agriculture, while instruments manufacture have made strides in Oregon. Wyoming's economy has been boosted by strong activity in mining. On the other hand, transportation equipment employment in the state of Washington, symbolized by the Boeing Aircraft Corporation, has fallen off in recent years.

It has been widely argued that the Western states were, in an earlier era, colonial dependencies of the Eastern U.S. industrial complex,[8] supplying resources and importing manufactured goods. This situation is much less the case today. The economies of California and Washington show little structural difference from the industrialized Northeast or Midwest. Moreover, industrialization patterns of California and Washington are spreading to other Western states.

The growth of "Silicon Valley" in California vividly illustrates the formation and diffusion of new patterns of industrialization in the West. Silicon Valley is not a geographic region defined by natural physiographic boundaries. It is, rather, an assemblage of electronics manufacturers clustered south of San Francisco Bay, directly and indirectly tied to institutions of higher learning such as Stanford University and the University of California at San Jose. Silicon Valley represents a new type of industrial complex. In recent years there has been a diffusion of industrial activity of this type to other regions of the West. Similar high-tech complexes have appeared in Oregon's Willamette Valley, in the Seattle area, and near Phoenix and Denver. Many smaller communities have also become dependent on high-tech electronics production, hosting branches and production plants of major corporations.

In addition to the sectors mentioned above, textiles and apparel, fabricated metals, machinery, transportation equipment, and instruments are also experiencing geographical diffusion throughout the Western states. Until a decade ago such developments were confined to major cities. More recently, however, high-tech industries can be found in moderate-size communities, most of which are within commuting range of metropoli.

## The West as an Interdependent System

The Western states are interdependent with one another and form part of a complex national and international system involving the flows of goods, services, and income.[9] These relationships are not well documented, but recent research throws light on some patterns of intraregional interaction.[10]

The relative importance of intrastate and interstate ties varies according to each Western state. It may be said in general that intrastate linkages are stronger than any single interstate tie; however, the cumulative magnitude of economic relations with other regions

=""

tends to be greater than internal linkages. For example, about 25 percent of Montana's intermediate requirements are met by Montana production. About 35 percent by other Western states and another 35 percent by the rest of the United States. No American state supplies Montana with more than Montana produces for itself. Yet Montana is more dependent upon other regions than it is upon its own economy. This structure is typical among Western states.

## The West's Income: Magnitude and Structure

Income payments are sources of funds for consumers, investors, and govenments; they come in the form of wages and salaries, taxes, profits and dividends, and allowances for depreciation. Within a federal system such as that of the United States, it is not necessary for the income earned in a region to be equal to the income spent in that region. Consumers may have sources of income which include not only wages and salaries earned locally but also "transfer payments" from the central government (Social Security checks, for example), interest, dividends, royalties, and rents. State governments may receive funds from the federal government. Some regions "export" more funds than they receive. Other regions are in a deficit position. On a national scale, of course, these internal balances are neutralized.

Two circumstances tend to divert income toward the West. The first is the relatively large presence of the federal government, leading to heavy transfers of tax revenue from Washington, D.C., to the Western states in order to maintain civilian and military government agencies located there. Second, many retirees have settled in the West. These people tend to be dependent on income from the federal treasury or from dividends, royalties, or rents from investments which they hold in corporations located primarily outside of the West.

As in the nation as a whole, personal income in the West has risen over the past decade and is anticipated to show gains in the next decade. Concurrently, income from wages has tended to decline as a fraction of total income as Americans have become relatively more dependent on transfer payments such as Social Security and returns from investments. Some parts of the West have become particularly dependent upon nonwage sources of income. Regions with major concentrations of agriculture such as the Central Valley in California together with areas such as San Diego and Tucson that have a high proportion of retired people have almost 30 percent of personal income derived from nonwage sources. There are, to be sure, sharp variations within individual states. For example, the Seattle area has an overall percentage of wage income roughly equal to the national average, but in San Juan County (a region north of Seattle favored by retirees) only 45 percent of personal income comes from wages.

The Pacific coastal states and Hawaii have income levels above the national average. In 1970 all of the interior states of the West except Nevada had per capita income levels below the national average, but in 1983 Wyoming and Colorado were above the national average thanks to a mining boom. The North Shore oil bonanza gave Alaska the lead in the United States in per capital income. Indeed, in 1984 every Alaska resident was eligible to receive a $331.29 dividend check from oil revenues.[11]

## Conclusion

The economy of the Western states is distinctive in structure, rapidly growing compared to the rest of the nation, and relatively wealthy in per capita income. It is also increasingly diversified. This diversification has occurred most significantly in high technology and tourism, adding new dimensions to a regional economy traditionally based on the exploitation of natural resources. Moreover, the West has experienced the growth of all types of service sectors.

The international trade of the Western states is dealt with in Dr. Parkanskii's chapter. Suffice it to say here that the West has extensive trade and investment linkages with other parts of the world economy and particularly with nations of the Pacific Basin. In my recent survey of Washington State businesses, I estimated that Japan formed a market approximately equal in significance to that of the adjacent state of Oregon.

It is clear that the historical vision of the Western states as an appendage of the industrialized Northeast needs to be modified. The state economies of the West today are still linked to the larger national economy, but they are also becoming increasingly "autonomous" as new manufacturing and export service industries emerge. The spectacular rise of Nevada as an entertainment center constitutes a dramatic example of the West's new "independence." Disneyland in Los Angeles is another example of a nontraditional

industrial innovation. Western innovations are even being adopted
in other parts of the country (Nevada-style gambling and entertainment in New Jersey, a branch of Disneyland in Florida) and in East
Asia (Tokyo's newly constructed Disneyland).

The West is now the center of the nation's high-technology electronics industry. At the same time, resource-based sectors of the
West's economy continue to prosper under increasing capital-inten-
sive development. The recent mining boom in the Rocky Mountain
states and Alaska, continuing developments in irrigation technology,
intensification of the exploitation of coastal fisheries, and diversification of the forest products industry all suggest that the West's economy will be characterized by dynamism for many years to come.

## NOTES

1. Ray A. Billington, *The Westward Movement in the United States* (New York:
Van Nostrand, 1959), pp. 73–86.

2. Department of Commerce, Bureau of Economic Analysis, *BEA Regional
Projections* 1 (July 1981): 5, 11, 14, 20, 23, 41, 44, 86, 92, 101, 119, 140,
149, 158.

3. Bureau of the Census, *Historical Statistics of the United States,* vol. 1 (Washington: GPO, 1975), pp. 24–37. Bureau of the Census, *Statistical Abstract of the
United States, 1982–1983,* 103d ed. (Washington: Department of Commerce,
1982), pp. 10–11.

4. For historical overviews of the growth of the U.S. economy, see Harvey S.
Perloff et al., *Regions, Resources and Economic Growth* (Baltimore: Johns Hopkins
University Press, 1960).

5. A good general treatment of the economic base concept may be found in
C. M. Tiebout, "The Community Economic Base Study," Committee for Economic Development, Supplementary Paper No. 16 (December 1962).

6. Bureau of the Census, *Statistical Abstract of the United States, 1982–1983,*
p. 13.

7. The process of internationalization is described in B. Bluestone and
B. Harrison, *Capital and Communities: The Causes and Consequences of Private Disin-
vestment* (Washington, D.C.: The Progressive Alliance, 1980), pp. 33–63, 217–
223.

8. Perloff et al., *Regions, Resources, and Economic Growth,* pp. 284–292.

9. A comprehensive discussion of the concept of interdependent regional
economies may be developed by adapting the city-focused arguments of Pred
into a state level of regionalization. See Allan Pred, *City-Systems in Advanced
Economies* (New York: Wiley, 1977).

10. William B. Beyers, "The Interregional Structure of the U.S. Economy,"
*International Regional Science Review* 8, no. 3 (1983): 213–231.

11. *Honolulu Advertiser,* 29 September 1984.

# Economic Development
# of the Soviet Far East

V. P. Chichkanov

P. A. Minakir

The Soviet Far East is one of the most exotic and least-known regions of the Soviet Union. Until the twentieth century events swirled around but seemingly did not touch this territory. The economic power of Russia increased; political and economic upheavals shook Japan and China. Meanwhile, the Far Eastern Russia appeared to doze, as if waiting for its hour to strike.

Several factors explain this situation. The Far East is geographically and psychologically remote. Development of productive capacities was very expensive because the region lacked an internal market and reliable communications with the rest of Russia. Natural conditions are severe. Agriculture developed to an extent in the south, but the northern expanses remained untouched. What riches lay undiscovered in the earth could only be conjectured. Only gradually did the economic developments in European Russia before the Revolution move eastward across the Urals. Toward the end of the nineteenth century, industry was just beginning to penetrate Western Siberia. Construction of the Trans-Siberian Railroad (1891–1916) finally broke the Far East's insularity and breathed life into the region, quickening the rhythm of growth and restructuring the area's economy.

The Trans-Siberian Railroad made Russia a Pacific power, transforming its presence in the Far East from a geographical fact into an economic and political problem for all countries of the region. The railroad formed an artery which nourished the Far East's fledgling economy, opening new possibilities for a large-scale, systematic exploitation of regional natural wealth.

Industrial development in the Far East began at the outset of this century. To be sure, the fur industry was already well established and continued to function. New industries included fisheries, gold mining, and forestry. In 1913 the Far East provided the country with 40 percent of its gold supply. Yet on the eve of the October Revolution only 9 percent of the Far East's population was engaged in industry. Moreover, such industrial concerns as did exist were for the most part rudimentary and small-scale.

Before the Revolution the Far East's economy was basically agrarian. Starting in the 1880s the tsarist government took active measures to promote peasant migration from European Russia to Siberia and the Far East. It is estimated that 4 million migrants crossed the Urals between 1890 and 1914, a significant proportion of whom settled in the Far East, strengthening the area's agricultural coloration.

Both agricultural and industrial development concentrated in the southern part of the region along the Trans-Siberian Railroad, an area enjoying comparatively favorable climatic conditions and having arable land. The northern expanses, although resource rich, remained largely inaccessible. Here and there sparsely populated oases existed in isolation from the rest of the territory. There was neither the means nor the will to make a major investment in what was generally considered a barren wilderness.

World War I put a strain on the fragile filaments that linked the Far East with the rest of Russia. This strain increased in the aftermath of the October Revolution when the Far East became the scene of civil war and foreign intervention, both of which endured longer here than in other sections of the country. During this difficult interim the Far East was forced to rely on its own resources. Disruption of ties with the interior interrupted the flow of vital supplies and capital. Years of fighting and foreign occupation left a wake of destruction.

Extraordinary measures were required in the 1920s to reconstruct the Far East's shattered economy. Yet reconstruction constituted but the first step toward a long-term objective. The ultimate goal of the Soviet leadership was the integration of the Far Eastern economy into that of the rest of the nation and the building of a new regional industrial base capable of serving international as well as domestic markets.

## Regional Integration into the National Economy, 1922–1945

With the establishment of Soviet rule in the Far East in 1922, a search was begun for the most effective means to bring about a general recovery from the ravages of war and intervention. The task was formidable. Even achievement of prewar production levels required herculean efforts. Gross output had fallen in 1922 to half of that of 1913. Gold production, an important source of income, had come to a virtual standstill.

The Far East's economic prospects were tied to the area's natural resources: gold, timber, and fish. Both historical experience and prevailing circumstances pointed to their intensive exploitation. Extractive industries can be a catalyst for comprehensive economic development. But for this catalyst to start working, enormous amounts of capital and labor must be mobilized. Activation of extractive industries was a matter of critical importance in the 1920s because of the country's acute need for raw materials and foreign currency. Yet at this juncture, planners in Moscow were not in a position to release capital to the Far East. The region had no choice but to rely on its own resources in building a new economic base.[1]

A combination of central planning and local initiatives tackled this problem. During the early and middle 1920s the Far East concentrated on repairing the prerevolutionary productive structure. The region thus remained essentially agrarian with but a modicum of extractive industries. Manufacturing accounted for only a third of regional gross output and employed less than 10 percent of the population.

By 1928 the region's economy was well on the way to recovery. Gross output had almost reached that of 1913, and in certain areas such as coal, timber, and freight haulage it had exceeded 1913 levels. Japanese concessions promoted the development of northern Sakhalin oil and Kamchatka fisheries, but they were not regarded as a permanent factor in the economy.

It was now necessary to link the development of the Far East with all-Union economic plans, specifically with the First Five-Year Plan (1928–1933). Until 1928, regional recovery had been carried out with minimal capital inputs from Moscow. After 1928, such inputs increased and came to lend a vital impetus to regional growth. During the 1930s, 6.3 percent of national capital investments were allocated to the Far East, which ranked fifth behind the Ukraine, the Urals, the Moscow region, and the Northwest.[2] These capital transfers were no gift. Every ruble invested in the Far East carried with it the expectation of a productive payoff from the regional economy.

Several factors explain the relatively high priority accorded the Far Eastern economy during the 1930s. The country's attention in general was drawn eastward. Grandiose construction projects were transforming the face of the Urals and Siberia. International tensions were mounting in East Asia and assumed a threatening character. Strengthening the USSR's eastern frontiers economically and militarily became a national priority. Consequently, the regional capital construction program increased five times between 1930 and 1931 and doubled again in 1932.

During 1922–1941 the Far Eastern economy grew faster than that of the country as a whole. Between 1913 and 1940 the region's heavy industry increased 17 times (11.7 times for the USSR as a whole). While such rapid growth can be partially attributed to the low regional industrial level of 1913, nevertheless, heavy capital inputs from Moscow, an influx of labor, and improved knowledge of local natural resources also played significant roles.

By the beginning of World War II the Far East's economic profile had been transformed. Not only extractive but manufacturing industries had appeared: petroleum, metallurgy, machine construction, and ship construction.[3] The city of Komsomolsk had been built, joining Khabarovsk and Vladivostok as industrial centers.

The Far East gradually assumed the character of an economic complex relying increasingly on its own resources. Yet capital inputs from outside were still important, particularly for heavy industry (ferrous and nonferrous metallurgy, coal, petroleum, chemicals, machine building, construction materials). As a result of these inputs, by the end of the 1930s the manufacturing sector acquired preeminence in the region's economy and more than half of manufacturing fell into the category of heavy industry.

The approach of war confirmed the correctness of plans emphasizing the development of a broad range of largely self-reliant productive facilities in the Far East capable of satisfying needs of the local population. No one could predict whether the Far East would turn out to be a rear area supporting a distant western front or whether the region itself would be a military front. In either eventuality the Far East would have to support itself.

World War II both retarded and stimulated the Far East's development. The war made security considerations a top priority. The Far East in this situation was faced with a double challenge. It had to support not only itself but to produce for the western front, and this at a time when the rest of the country could no longer afford to provide capital inputs to the Far Eastern economy. The region's economic development was thus subordinated to the requirements imposed by a national emergency.

The Far East met these twin challenges. Economic capabilities acquired during the 1930s enabled the Far East to expand production in basic industries. The Amur Steel Works and petroleum refineries were constructed at Komsomolsk, supplied by an oil pipeline from northern Sakhalin fields. These projects were carried out under extraordinarily difficult conditions.

The war years witnessed a culmination of trends characteristic of the 1930s, namely, coordination of regional economic activities with national needs. Under peaceful conditions an optimal balance between the internal and export dimensions of the Far East's economy might have been worked out. As it turned out, however, the wartime transformation of the region's economic structure in favor of manufacturing industries left a deep and lasting impression on this correlation.

## Postwar Adjustments

The Far East faced a complex situation with the end of World War II. Its economic potential surpassed that of the early 1920s, yet maintaining the region's economy required even greater efforts than previously. As has been indicated, the Far East's development had been sustained during the 1930s by all-Union rather than local sources of capital. Wartime centralization of the allocation and utilization of resources reinforced the Far East's dependence upon national economic politics.

In the postwar five-year plans, the Far Eastern economy continued to be oriented almost exclusively toward the fulfillment of all-Union needs. The region took an active part in the national recovery, sending timber, ores, machines, fish, and other local products to European Russia.

Moscow's giving priority to the recovery and reconstruction of war-wasted European parts of the USSR could not help but have consequences for capital investment levels in the Far East. In the late 1940s and early 1950s, production growth in the Far East was respectable in absolute terms (averaging 9 percent annually) but fell below the national rate of 12.3 percent.[4] By 1960, even though the Far East had increased production by 302 percent in comparison with 1940, the increase for the USSR as a whole was 424 percent.[5]

During the 1950s, in contrast to the 1930s, development in the Far East did not evolve within a framework of a massive centralized effort aimed at rapid, comprehensive construction. Rather, capital investment levels and planned growth rates were worked out within the administrations of individual industrial sectors. It would appear that in the 1950s, our country had not yet found an effective organization for the economies of its eastern areas.

This interim did not last long. By the beginning of the 1960s national attention again focused on the Far East, partially as a consequence of deteriorating relations with China. At this time the country's productive forces were again moving eastward as they had during the 1930s, and the Far East's natural wealth loomed large once more as a source of raw materials for industry. The tempo of the region's growth picked up, averaging 9.5 percent during the 1960s, which exceeded the national rate of 8.5 percent.[6]

It is important to note that this growth occurred on a qualitative as well as a quantitative basis. The Far East transformed itself from a primarily agrarian to an industrial region. Industrial production comprised nearly two-thirds of gross output, compared to one-third in the late 1920s. Agriculture's share plummeted from 70 percent to 8 percent over the same period. The absolute volume of agricultural production, however, grew (40 percent in the 1960s alone).

Three decades of extensive exploration of local natural resources gave the Far East the reputation of one of the most promising repositories of mineral and biological wealth in the USSR. It was extractive industries, in fact, that propelled the region's comparatively rapid growth in the 1960s and 1970s.

In the 1980s the Far East's development has become more dynamic, its economic infrastructure more complex, and its prospects more exciting. Certain sectors of the regional economy have developed to a high level and now exercise a discernable influence on the national economy.

Planning the Far East's economic future involves the resolution of mind-boggling problems, the grappling with imponderables, and the search for new ways to achieve the balanced development of what is still a frontier area. This search has its share of disappointments. But in the last analysis it more often than not finds ways to promote stable growth, achieve a higher return on capital investments, and attain a satisfactory equilibrium in the delicate balance between economic development, protection of the natural environment, and social needs.

Let us take a look at the Far East's contemporary profile, examining the salient characteristics of its major areas of economic activity: industry, transport, construction, and agriculture.

# Industry

Industry today constitutes the core of the Far East's economy. Three branches account for more than 50 percent of the region's industrial production: nonferrous metals, fishing, and forestry. Because raw materials are comparatively cheap in the Far East, regional specialization on extractive industries is beneficial for the country as a whole. But for the Far East itself, this emphasis upon extractive industries is in a certain sense an annoying circumstance.

One source of the problem is that different regions of the USSR compete with each other for capital investment. That region which demonstrates the highest growth of productivity gets the most capital investment. Applied to the Far East, this formula artificially lowers the return on capital investment because the Far East has a high share of extractive industries whose products (raw materials) are processed in other regions which receive a sizeable part of the value-added (increased value of raw material after processing). If the Far East were to process its own raw materials, the region would show greater productivity increases and as a result would receive a larger share of national capital investments.

Emphasis on extractive industries creates yet another problem for the Far Eastern economy. Because Far Eastern extractive industries supply a significant share of all-Union raw materials needs, these industries get an abnormally high level of regional investment funds. This leaves auxiliary sectors in the Far East (energetics, construction materials, transport) undercapitalized.

Price information and economic planning reforms are correcting such dysfunctions. First, wholesale prices of raw materials were raised relative to those of manufacturing in 1982. Second, economic planning now takes into account the role of separate regions in the framework of overall national development, and plans of corresponding sectors are coordinated so as to promote balanced regional growth. This is achieved by working out a system of synchronized projects and programs at the level of each sector, region, and finally the country as a whole. The Far East has become a proving ground for testing the effectiveness of this experimental system of planning and management.

Industrial development depends on the size, education, and stability of the labor force. Climatic conditions in the Far East pose problems for recruiting and retaining skilled industrial workers. Even in the southern, climatically favorable parts of the region, the

comforts of life do not match those of the rest of the country. Consequently, measures are taken to find labor-saving devices and to concentrate available resources in the most important parts of the
regional economy—priority and key auxiliary sectors.

This strategy has enabled the Far East to provide the rest of the
USSR with a broader variety of products. The region is supplying
the country with 8 percent of all production (in terms of value) of
nonferrous metals. Certain raw materials from the Far East, such as
gold, tin, boron, diamonds, and tungsten, constitute the main
source of supply for the USSR. About 40 percent of the nation's fish
catch comes from the Far East, as does 10 percent of the USSR's forest products. Locally produced bridge cranes, giant transformers,
casting equipment, and gas turbines are of particularly high quality.

During the 1970s, major efforts were made to build up auxiliary
industries in the region. Since 1981 the growth of capital investment
in fisheries and forestry has fallen relative to that of coal and oil in
order to increase local supplies of energy. In 1981–1985 considerable
capital was invested in the reconstruction of oil refineries in Khabarovsk and Komsomolsk as well as in coal extraction in the Khabarovsk Territory, southern Yakutia, and the Maritime and Amur
districts. Capital investment is also increasing in the construction
industry, machine manufacturing, and ferrous metallurgy.

## Transport

Of all nonindustrial sectors, transport has the largest significance for
the Far East. Transport comprises more than 17 percent of regional
gross output, compared to 11 percent for the USSR as a whole. Geographical factors underlie transport's preeminence. The Far East
encompasses a territory equivalent in area to Western Europe. Unit-
ing far-flung enterprises and a scattered population is a struggle with
space that must be won if the region is to be a functioning economy
effectively linked with other parts of the Soviet Union.

In 1980 the Far East accounted for 8 percent of all-Union freight
haulage and 3 percent of passenger traffic. The correlation of these
figures reflects that priority is given to economic rather than to
demographic growth.

Rail and marine transport handles most freight going in or out of
the Far East. Most products (by weight) sent to European Russia are
hauled by the Trans-Siberian Railroad, now reinforced by the

recently completed Baikal-Amur Railroad. Products from the Far East's extreme north are carried by ships along the Northern Sea Route. The Far Eastern merchant fleet services the bulk of regional exports abroad. Vostochnyi, a port near Nakhodka, has become a major terminal for trans-Siberian container shipments between East Asia and Europe.

Vehicular and river transport play a significant role in supplying northern parts of the Far East. River boats bring provisions to Yakut towns during the summer months. The Amur is a vital freight and passenger artery connecting interior and maritime regions. In winter special lorries *(avtozimniki)* ply the frozen roads of Yakutia and the Magadan District. Air transport also plays a vital role in the Far East. Some remote communities are accessible only by planes or helicopters, particularly during the winter season when rivers and coastal areas are frozen.

It has become increasingly apparent that river, vehicular, and air transport cannot solve the problems inhibiting further development of the Far East. At best these forms of transport can help to maintain established levels of economic activity. As the economist Murad Adzhiev has noted, "The mass cargoes remain for trains which form the skeletal basis of the region's transport framework."[7] The American economic geographers Victor Mote and Theodore Shabad are correct when they assert the obvious need for transportation alternatives. "Air transport, with the possible exception of dirigibles . . . is restricted to high-value, low-bulk freight, is inhibited by vagaries of the weather, and is too expensive a solution. Truck transport is economically feasible only over short distances because of high costs of fuel and maintenance."[8] For a genuine breakthrough in opening up the Far North's natural wealth, a rail network with year-round capabilities must be constructed.

## Construction

Construction occupies a central position in the Far Eastern economic complex. During the 1970s more than 70 percent of all capital investment in the region went into new construction. Construction's share of the Far Eastern gross product is more than 14 percent, compared with 10 percent for the USSR as a whole. The share for the building materials industry is 18 percent (12 percent for the USSR as a whole). Current emphasis on the machine industry, ferrous metallurgy, and building materials should strengthen the construction sector of the Far East's economy. Bases to support capital construction are rapidly forming in Vladivostok (for maritime areas and the Far North) and in Khabarovsk (for the Baikal-Amur Railroad zone and the interior).

## Agriculture

For many years the Far East remained a mainly agrarian region. Now, however, agriculture accounts for merely 8 percent of the area's gross output. In a national context Far Eastern agriculture looks quite modest: utilizing 1.5 percent of arable land, accounting for 1.3 percent of land under cultivation, and providing 1.1 percent of all-Union agricultural output.

Difficult climatic conditions limit the potential of Far Eastern agriculture. Severe cold and short growing seasons in the north and capricious weather conditions in the south hinder cultivation. In 1981, for example, heavy rains inundated the Khabarovsk, Sakhalin, and Maritime regions, destroying a large proportion of crops.

Consequently, the Far East is still unable to provide itself with adequate foodstuffs. The most important of these are grains, meat, and dairy products. The available land has the potential to supply local needs for milk, meat, eggs, vegetables, and potatoes, but for the time being this task remains unfulfilled. Except for potatoes and eggs, basic foods must be imported from other parts of the USSR.

Severe natural conditions and limited arable land underline the logic of emphasizing livestock raising. Grain can be brought to the Far East from Siberia, whereas the importation of meat and dairy products pose logistic complications. Thus capital investment in regional agriculture now focuses on four areas: (1) the construction of livestock complexes (notably chicken and pork); (2) the modernization of agricultural equipment; (3) the creation of "agro-belts" around cities; and (4) concentrated cultivation of the relatively rich soils in the Maritime Territory and Amur District.

## Economic Growth

During the 1960s and 1970s the Far East maintained, in economic sectors of regional specialization, growth rates above those of corresponding all-Union indices. During the 1960s, average annual rates were (all-Union figures in parentheses): 14 percent (7.8 percent) for nonferrous metallurgy; 7.5 percent (6.2 percent) for forestry; and 11 percent (8.4 percent) for fisheries.

Growth rates in these three sectors declined during the 1970s both regionally and nationally. This decline was an unwelcome phenomenon for the Far East because it signaled a general slowdown of the regional economy. Whereas the three sectors accounted for only 10 percent of all-Union industrial growth, they constituted 40 percent of such growth in the Far East. Thus, during the 1970s, the Far Eastern economy as a whole developed more slowly than that of the USSR (5.3 percent compared to the 5.9 percent all-Union annual average).

At the same time, the 1970s witnessed a significant refinement of the region's general economic structure. If one analyzes various indices showing the Far East's proportion of all-Union production, the region's share has in general not changed over the course of two decades, although there has been a modest increase in certain nonindustrial sectors. This process should eventually lead to the formation of a fully balanced Far Eastern economic complex. Another sign of refinement is the comparatively high degree of interaction among the Far East's economic sectors.

Effective utilization of natural resources is an acute issue in the Far East. Declines in growth rates of the region's leading sectors, all of which depend on the value of exploited natural resources, have led to general declines in regional productivity. In the 1960s and early 1970s regional productivity surpassed that of the country as a whole. Since the late 1970s it has fallen below all-Union levels.

At present, heavy inputs of capital are invigorating almost all branches of the Far Eastern economy. Investment is especially intensive in leading sectors where equipment modernization and new technologies can, by opening up hitherto inaccessible raw materials deposits, halt the general slowdown of production growth rates.

Not surprisingly in view of selectively heavy capital investments in the Far East, the growth rate of labor capitalization exceeds that of labor productivity. During the past fifteen years, labor capitalization in Far Eastern industries has grown 58 percent more than has labor productivity, except in the machine-building industry. The differential between capitalization and productivity is highest in the Far East's leading sectors: 217 percent for nonferrous metallurgy, over 100 percent for fisheries, and 75 percent for forestry.

Perhaps the most encouraging trend in the Far East's economy during the 1970s was experimentation with new approaches to planning regional development. Piecemeal attempts to coordinate separate sector plans gave way to an integrated system of programs for extrapolating growth patterns. This method, involving extensive use of computers, has allowed planners not only to predict possible imbalances but to "play out" beforehand various development options in order to assess their repercussions.

Implementing these programs involves high costs and requires fresh technical and organizational practices. Experience convincingly shows that what works in the western (European) parts of the country does not always work in the Far East. A recognition of these differences has led to the Far East and Siberia being accorded priority in experimenting with new approaches to planning economic development. Siberia and the Far East have consequently become the scene of major complex projects involving this type of sophisticated planning. Best known are West Siberian oil and gas projects and the Baikal-Amur Railroad. There are others which also deserve our attention. Projects aimed at exploring and exploiting the region's mineral wealth, forest reserves, and ocean resources are but a sample of the programs being developed.

## The Nedra Program

Proven deposits of minerals in the Far East are so great and prognoses for yet undiscovered natural wealth so sanguine that the word "Eldorado" comes to mind. The Far East's Eldorado, however, is well hidden. Access to it is littered with obstacles and risks. The Nedra (Mineral Wealth) Program is designed to expedite the productive exploitation of the Far Eastern Eldorado. In general the program centers around the study and evaluation of mineral deposits, the perfection of special extractive and processing techniques, and the modernization of the production structure.

Far Eastern minerals are noteworthy for their complex material composition. In addition to their basic metal, ores contain a variety of often valuable components. As long as all of the elements are cheap and easily available, this complex character of Far Eastern ores can be ignored and the additional components discarded. But when the additional components assume a value comparable to the main element, traditional methods of ore extraction and processing become economically unsound.

One of the main problems faced by the Nedra Program is restructuring the mining industry so as to extract all valuable ore components, to avoid waste, and to conserve existing ore deposits. One innovation has been the recycling of mine wastes into auxiliary industries. At present, recycled wastes supply several industries with material for the production of useful commodities, thus cutting production for these commodities in half.

While raw materials are being more intensively utilized in southern parts of the Far East, new mineral deposits are being uncovered in the Far North. Northern resources, hitherto largely inaccessible, constitute a reserve for the nonferrous metallurgical industry which is a motor propelling regional economic development.

Energy resources are also of major importance. Coal has traditionally figured prominently in the Far East and today satisfies nearly half of all regional energy demands. As a major source for electric energy, coal acts as a driving shaft of regional industry. Exploration and extraction of coal underlie the momentum of all economic sectors. At present, the coal industry is being intensively modernized. Exploitation of rich deposits in southern Yakutia has begun, and mining in the Khabarovsk and Maritime territories is being expanded.

It is a common assumption that Far Eastern petroleum falls into the category of "little oil," oil which, even if of high quality, nonetheless does not exist in sufficient quantities to justify a local refining industry. Fossil fuels have not loomed prominently in past images of the Far East's endowments—gold, furs, timber, and fish, yes, but not oil. Improved knowledge of the area's geology and more sophisticated extraction technology, however, have led to a re-evaluation of this assumption. While it still may be premature to talk about "big oil" (such as in Western Siberia), preliminary exploration of the Sakhalin shelf and prognoses of offshore deposits along the Okhotsk and Pacific seacoasts are opening new perspectives for a regional petroleum industry. As the American scholar Allen S. Whiting has noted in a 1981 study, "Yet assuming the ultimate technological feasibility of extracting such oil and gas as may be discovered in East Asian Siberia, the economic benefit for the region could be considerable."[9]

To summarize, modernization of the mining industry has created an array of auxiliary industries which collectively form territorial production complexes. Taken in conjunction with the growth of a regional petroleum industry, we can see that Far Eastern extractive industries have made a transformation from being single-resource enterprises to being part of a dynamic interconnected network of productive activities.

## Forestry Programs

The Far Eastern forestry industry, based on enormous local supplies of timber, has grown steadily, increasing annual output tenfold since the 1920s. Logging has traditionally played a leading role in the Far East, accounting for about 40 percent of valued output. Another 40 percent falls into the category of processing of wood products: chips and cellulose, paper, cartons, building materials, and furniture.

Logging has until recently been concentrated in the southern part of the Far East, where the availability of labor, the rail and road networks, and the proximity of ports offer logistic advantages. However, from the late 1970s, exploitation levels of the southern coniferous forests reached its limits. Today the industry's center of gravity is shifting northward.

Wood processing in the Soviet Far North is a challenging enterprise. Now that the Baikal-Amur Railroad is completed, it will help solve the problem of cost-effective transport of forest products to consumers. But other problems await solutions. For example the composition of northern forests differs from southern forests, yet wood-processing technology and user preferences are attuned mainly to trees found in the south. Southern trees are coniferous and deciduous while northern forests consist largely of larch. Both production and marketing practices need to be adapted to suit new species of wood. Another difficulty is the location of northern forests, which are as a rule located in mountain areas. This situation poses special logistic problems.

Wood-processing industries in the Far East embrace a broad spectrum of activities, from sawmills to furniture factories. Constant efforts are being made to upgrade the quality of these products for external as well as internal markets.

Foreign economic ties have played a significant role in the development of the Far East's forestry industry. Timber and wood products have for many years figured prominently in regional exports, particularly to Japan, whose physical proximity and demand for wood as a construction material create favorable market opportunities.

Nature has generously endowed the Far East with a variety of medicinal plants and edible condiments: nuts, honey, mushrooms, ginseng, and a galaxy of useful herbs and berries. Far Eastern fern tips enjoy a reputation as a delicacy in Japan. The export of ferns to Japan has influenced local tastes, and ferns today occupy an honored position in the region's cuisine.

## Ocean Resources

For years the high seas have animated the imaginations of writers of romantic tales and adventures. Recently the oceans have also become a source of hope for humanity. We already know that the oceans contain a major portion of the earth's natural resources, 60 percent of its oil and gas, for example. As our knowledge of the oceans grows, so no doubt will these proportions. Scientists and economic planners are increasingly turning their attention toward the oceans. New marine-based industries are appearing. The Far East, more than any other region of the USSR, is drawn to the oceans, bordering as it does on the world's greatest expanse of waters, the Pacific.

Marine-related industries in the Far East are at present centered around the exploitation of biological resources. The Pacific shelf zone contains about 80 percent of the ocean's fish, and nearly 17 percent of this zone lies along the Soviet Far Eastern littoral. The fishing industry is and will probably remain one of the most important areas of economic specialization in the Far East, which currently supplies the USSR with 40 percent of its total catch, 60 percent of fish products for industrial uses, 99.5 percent of its salmon, and 100 percent of crabs.

The Far Eastern fishing fleet operated almost exclusively in nearby waters during the 1960s, but in the 1970s its range expanded to include the North and South Pacific. North Pacific fisheries provide 90 percent of the Far Eastern catch. However, the deterioration of the natural resource base noticeable in other sectors has also affected the fisheries industry. The problem is not that there are less fish. In fact, there are probably more, but of different kinds. Overexploitation and lack of control have led to appalling declines in hauls of certain traditional favorites: herring, flounder, and perch. Naturally, scarcity has increased market prices of these favored fish.

Increasing the size and range of operations of the fishing fleet cannot compensate for the deteriorating natural resource base. Building bigger fleets and expanding the geographical scope of operations will only increase costs. A fundamental solution to the problem of how to catch more fish can only be found by a scientific search for a new approach to exploiting marine resources. The fishing industry as it is presently constituted is essentially maritime hunting. Eventually maritime hunting must give way to maritime production, where a restructured fishing industry rationally plans and develops renewable ocean resources.

Several research institutes and planning organizations are working out scenarios for possible solutions to these problems. Some of the scenarios fall into a traditional mold: enlarge the fishing fleets; develop untapped parts of the Pacific (Antarctica, oceanic plateaus, seamounts, ocean trenches); emphasize different species (squid, tuna, anchovies); and more intensively exploit the 200-mile economic zone along the Pacific and Okhotsk littorals. One scenario, aquaculture, has the potential to open a completely new chapter in marine resources development.

Aquaculture promises in the near future to emerge as a profitable and reliable source of marine products. At present, work is focusing on certain high-value species such as salmon, trout, scallops, trepang, oysters, and kelp. In the end of the 1970s about one hundred fish farms and other aquaculture enterprises were established in the Far East, mainly in the Maritime Territory and on Sakhalin. The area of these enterprises will soon be increased tenfold. In time this form of marine production should make high-value fish more widely available.

The development of new approaches to utilizing marine life has been accompanied by the modernization of shore-based processing facilities and the introduction of new marine products in vitamins, medicinal preparations, and animal feed. The Far East is likely to consolidate its leadership in marine-related industries.

Development of nonbiological oceanic resources within the Far Eastern economic complex is also moving ahead. Offshore oil and gas resources will soon generate additional energy for regional nonferrous metallurgical and building-materials industries. Manganese nodules in the Pacific Ocean depths are also attracting our attention.

## Baikal-Amur Railroad

The decision to construct the Baikal-Amur Railroad, or BAM, (completed on 1 October 1984) determined the main outlines of development strategy for the entire Far East for the rest of this century. The BAM development zone embraces over 260,000 square miles, or more than 10 percent of the Far East's territory. As Allen Whiting has written, "It is clear . . . that the Baikal-Amur Railroad is essential to any significant development of East Asian Siberia or exploitation of its natural resources."[10]

A series of new industrial complexes utilizing local mineral and timber resources are planned in the BAM zone. Development is taking place practically from scratch. Aside from the Komsomolsk and Urgalsk (Khabarovsk Territory) industrial complexes, the region has virtually no centrally coordinated economic activity. On the one hand, this complicates the task of development. On the other, it creates opportunities for testing a general development plan.

Four fundamental considerations underlie the BAM zone development strategy. First, a new economic base for opening up the Northeast (Yakutia, the Khabarovsk Territory, and the Magadan District) will be established. Second, the zone will provide the regional and national economy with natural resources. Third, new labor opportunities will change the living conditions of the aboriginal peoples of the Northeast. Fourth, the BAM zone's opening will generate international repercussions. Theodore Shabad and Victor Mote have noted that a fully operational BAM "may have a significant impact not only on the further domestic development of the Soviet economy, but also on the Soviet Union's economic relations with the rest of the world."[11]

The process of developing the BAM zone raises complex questions about how to organize production, apply new technologies, resolve inevitable social problems. Current practices and policies are naturally based upon present-day conceptions of development. The implementation of such conceptions creates an undesirable inertia within the development zone, an inertia that in the future can only be overcome with considerable difficulty, both material and psychological. Therefore, developing the BAM zone is not only an economic but a social experiment. During its course methods will have to be worked out to help managers cope with new and unfamiliar production techniques. This experiment has not only regional but global significance.

## The North

The northern part of the Far East holds the most interesting development prospects for the region. Here are concentrated the main proven and unproven reserves of valuable raw materials. Analysis of optimal models for regional development shows that while unit costs of production are cheaper in the south, production effectiveness (i.e., the contribution to the regional and national economy) is greater in the north thanks to the high value of resources.

The Soviet Union has already addressed the problem of developing its northern areas. A system of territorial-production complexes is taking shape in the northern reaches of European Russia. It took several years to open up the rich hydrocarbon deposits in Western Siberia. Next on the agenda are the Eastern Siberian and Far Eastern north, which promise to yield great amounts of gold, diamonds, and tin among other minerals.

In the northern areas, energy is a problem of problems. It is far more complicated and expensive to set up an electric power system in the north than in other parts of the country. Wide expanses separate individual industrial sites, obliging planners to find new solutions for providing the region with heat and electric energy. Whereas the southern part of the Far East has a unified energy system, the north is supplied by isolated and small electric power stations using liquid fuels. This situation is being rectified by several major projects such as the Bilibinsk Nuclear Power Plant and the North Kolyma Hydroelectric Station, both located in the Magadan District.

The task of developing northern regions is not limited to purely economic questions. It encompasses a complex process of planned socioeconomic change. Fortunately the USSR has extensive experience in opening northern regions. Current plans call for the construction of a network of "socioeconomic complexes" that will bring together productive and human resources into new communities, communities which will offer attractive living conditions and will exist in harmony with the Far East's still-unspoiled natural environment.

## Conclusion

Contemporary development of the Soviet Far East is characterized by an interaction of potentials and constraints affecting an economy whose scale, structure, and growth rates are constantly changing. The foreseeable future is likely to bring the following developments. In industry the share of processing and marine sectors will increase. The region's center of economic activity will move northward. New areas will be opened by territorial-industrial complexes. Capital investment in infrastructural consolidation and in geological exploration will grow. New technologies will increasingly be applied to each sector of the regional economy. The Far East's role in the Soviet economy and its position in international commerce in the Pacific will expand.

## NOTES

1. *Na novom puti: zhizn i khoziaistvo Dal'ne-Vostochnoi oblasti v 1924 g.* (Vladivostok, 1925), p. 11.

2. M. B. Mazanova, *Territorial'nie proportsii narodnogo khoziaistva SSSR* (Moscow: Nauka, 1974), p. 118.

3. A. B. Margolin, "Sovetskii Dal'nii Vostok," in *Geograficheskie problemy kompleksnogo razvitiia proizvoditel'nykh sil i osvoeniia estestvennykh resursov SSSR* (Irkutsk: Institut Geografii Sibiri i Dal'nego Vostoka, 1968), p. 55.

4. *Ekonomicheskie problemy razvitiia Sibiri: metodologicheskie problemy razvitiia i razmeshcheniia proizvoditel'nykh sil,* ed. B. P. Orlov (Novosibirsk: Nauka, 1974), p. 34.

5. Margolin, "Sovetskii Dal'nii Vostok," p. 34.

6. *Ekonomicheskie problemy razvitiia Sibiri,* p. 64.

7. Murad Adzhiev, *Sibir': XX vek* (Moscow: Mysl', 1983), p. 222.

8. Theodore Shabad and Victor L. Mote, *Gateway to Siberian Resources (the BAM)* (New York: John Wiley & Sons, 1977), p. 65.

9. Allen S. Whiting, *Siberian Development and East Asia: Threat or Promise?* (Stanford: Stanford University Press, 1981), p. 51.

10. Ibid., p. 57.

11. Shabad and Mote, *Gateway to Siberian Resources,* p. vii.

# The Soviet Far East and the International Economy

## N. L. Shlyk

THE SOVIET FAR EAST's involvement in the international economy is making an increasingly significant contribution to the development of the region. By promoting an international division of labor, external economic ties raise productivity, accelerate scientific and technological progress, and improve the efficiency of allocations of human and material resources.

Several factors determine to what extent a region participates in the international division of labor: the region's level of economic development, its economic structure, and the type and accessibility of natural resources. Conversely, the character and growth rates of discrete regions may depend on the degree of their involvement in the international division of labor. This interrelationship is found in maritime and frontier regions of the USSR, notably in the Far East, where geography strongly influences the regional economy. Whereas the Far East's remoteness from production and consumption centers of the USSR reduces the relative significance of internal economic ties, the region's proximity to Asian and Pacific countries creates objective conditions for extensive economic ties.

The scale and character of the Far East's external economic ties depend among other things on the development of the region and on supplies coming from central parts of the country. During the initial stages of the Far East's settlement, both internal and external trade were constrained by the small size of the area's population, its dispersal over a wide area, and poor communications. With the development of the fishing, forestry, and mining industries in the late nineteenth century, together with increases in population arising from peasant migration from European Russia, the Far East established a network of trading relations with foreign countries.

The prerevolutionary Russian Far Eastern economy exhibited a heavy dependence on foreign commerce. Remoteness from European Russia, the unreliability and high cost of transport, the absence of local manufacturing industries, and chronic neglect by St. Petersburg all reinforced a tendency in the Far East to rely on external markets and foreign capital. In 1885, European Russia accounted for only 23 percent of imports entering Vladivostok. The remainder came from Western Europe, the United States, China, and Japan.[1]

Foreign companies penetrated both commerce and industry in the Far East. State Council member V. I. Denisov wrote apropos of this in 1913, "From that mass of impressions which I carried back from a journey around the Far East, the strongest was made by the utter indifference, indeed the criminal neglect of our ruling circles toward those countless riches hidden in the earth, in the forests, rivers, and seas of the Far East, riches which foreigners are successfully beginning to snatch from us.[2]

The Far East had a chronic deficit in its foreign trade balance in the sixty years before 1917. From 1906 to 1915, imports exceeded exports from three to nineteen times. Exports accounted for 45 percent of total trade in 1905 but dropped to only 5 percent in 1915.*[3]

After the October Revolution, development of the Far East became an indivisible part of socialist construction in the USSR. Soviet authorities addressed the complex task of utilizing the region's natural wealth by adapting a comprehensive program of planned development.

The 1920s witnessed a development of economic ties between the Far East and foreign partners. As a result of destruction caused by the civil war (1918–1922), Soviet Russia had only limited resources to divert to the Far East. Consequently, recovery and development during this decade were pursued within a framework of regional self-sufficiency supplemented by foreign trade. Much of what had formerly been brought from central Russia had to be imported from abroad. This policy was not without its negative side effects. Attempts of foreign capital to gain control over internal commerce in the Soviet Far East persisted even after the end of the Siberian Intervention. As late as 1923 some 87 percent of trade turnover in the region was in the hands of foreign firms.

During the remainder of the 1920s, regional commerce gradually shed its dependence on foreign capital. The institution of a state monopoly over external commerce constituted a decisive step in this

---

*The dramatic rise of imports into the Far East after 1914 is explained by the outbreak of World War I, which made Vladivostok one of Russia's few gateways. —AMERICAN EDITOR

Table i
**Foreign Trade of the Soviet Far East**
(In Thousands of Rubles)

|         | 1913    | 1923–1924 | 1924–1925 | 1925–1926 | 1927–1928 | 1928–1929 | 1929–1930 |
|---------|---------|-----------|-----------|-----------|-----------|-----------|-----------|
| Total   | 56,417  | 30,500    | 28,446    | 30,470    | 56,126    | 79,887    | 74,168    |
| Export  | 9,675   | 19,000    | 18,646    | 18,380    | 35,800    | 50,005    | 37,800    |
| Import  | 46,742  | 11,500    | 9,800     | 12,090    | 20,326    | 29,882    | 36,368    |
| Balance | –37,067 | +7,500    | +8,846    | +6,290    | +15,474   | +20,123   | +1,423    |

*Sources:* Compiled from *Otchet Dal'kraiispolkoma za 1925–1926 gg.* (Khabarovsk, 1927) and I. G. Leshchinskii, *Respubliki i kraia v sovetskom eksporte* (Moscow, 1935).

direction. In 1923 a Bureau of Licenses was established in Vladivostok, regulating local organs of the People's Commissariat of Foreign Trade. Under this new regulatory system, regional foreign trade showed its first positive balance (see Table 1).

Recovery of the Far East's fishing, forestry, and mining industries in the late 1920s propelled a surge in exports coupled with a structural change in the region's foreign trade. Exports came to consist largely of forest materials, fish, foodstuffs, and furs, with their proportions changing over time. Forestry, fish, agricultural commodities, and furs accounted respectively for 38 percent, 17 percent, 12 percent, and 11 percent of total exports in 1923–1924. In 1927–1928 these percentages had shifted to 32 percent, 34 percent, 5 percent, and 17 percent respectively.[4]

Priority was accorded at this time to improving the quality of exported products in order to increase their competitiveness in the world market. Canned fish and other processed marine products (crab, seaweed, trepang) enjoyed considerable overseas demand. Canned fish exports, for example, grew by five times between 1927 and 1930.

Diversification accompanied growth. Fourteen categories of exports in 1924 had multiplied to more than thirty by 1930. New exports included coal (which until 1923 had been imported into the Far East) and oil. At a 1927 meeting of the Far Eastern Regional Commission, the export of linen, berries, mushrooms, nuts, honey, jam, and mineral water received endorsement. Hard currency earnings from these exports were deposited in the bank accounts of relevant producers, who could then draw on the funds for purchase of imported equipment needed by these enterprises. This type of exchange, implemented with Japan, China, and Manchuria, anticipated the "border" or "coastal" trade which is conducted by Soviet Far Eastern enterprises and neighboring Asian countries today. The success of this arrangement in the late 1920s can be adduced from the fact that secondary exports tripled between 1926–1927 and 1929–1930.[5]

The growing volume of primary and secondary exports created favorable financial conditions for increasing imports in accordance with the needs of the country. Purchases of foodstuffs dominated the period of recovery (1923–1925). Thereafter emphasis was placed on imports of equipment, a reflection of priority accorded to national and regional industrialization in the First Five-Year Plan (1928–1933). Whereas imports of machinery amounted to only 2 percent of total regional imports in 1923, they had reached 41 percent by 1929. In that year, Rub 1,277,000 worth of agricultural machinery, Rub 7,390,000 worth of fishing equipment, Rub 1,014,000 worth of forestry equipment, and Rub 613,000 of machinery for the metal-processing industry were imported into the Far East.[6]

During the 1920s, China and Japan were the Far East's main trading partners. However, commerce was also developed with Mongolia, the United States, Great Britain, Germany, France, and other countries.

Economic relations between the Russian Far East and the United States have a long and vicissitudinous history. Trade between the two countries remained relatively modest until the First World War. Between 1909 and 1913, American goods constituted an average of 7 percent of Russia's total imports. The United States absorbed a mere .9 percent of Russia's exports.[7] Far Eastern furs were one of the empire's main export items. A considerable quantity of furs left Russia as contraband taken from the shores of Kamchatka, the Chukchi Peninsula, the Kurile Islands, and Sakhalin.

Toward the end of the nineteenth century, American companies displayed an energetic interest in exploiting Far Eastern deposits of coal, oil, and gold. Underlying a number of propositions to develop these resources was the idea of opening the entire Far East to American capital penetration. Among other projects, plans were formulated for acquiring monopoly rights to export coal from Vladivostok and for organizing surveys of East Siberian mineral deposits by American specialists.[8] Not one of these proposals, however, was accepted by the imperial Russian government.

World War I stimulated Russian-American trade. Russian imports tripled between 1914 and 1916. Exports increased 1.6 times during the same period. By 1916 the United States accounted for a remarkable 32.2 percent of Russia's imports (but only 2.8 percent of Russia's exports).[9] The war offered American enterprise new opportunities to strengthen its position in the Russian economy. With this goal in mind, American bankers floated $86 million of loans to the tsarist government in 1916, purchased stock in Russian companies, and conducted surveys of Russia's natural wealth, among other places in the Far East.

After the October Revolution, the Wilson administration did not extend diplomatic recognition to the Soviet state; moreover, it discouraged American businessmen from establishing trade relations. The potential for trade was further complicated by the dispatch of an American Expeditionary Force to Vladivostok in July of 1918, resulting in the presence of American troops in the Far East until April of 1920.

Withdrawal of military forces opened the way for contacts between the United States and the Far Eastern Republic (FER). An American mission reached the FER capital of Chita in Trans-Baikalia in May of 1921 and was received by the chairman of the FER Council of Ministers, N. N. Nikiforov. The mission collected information about the FER and explored prospects for establishing trade relations.[10] The FER showed a serious interest in economic cooperation with the United States. In the fall of 1921 a FER delegation visited Washington to promote trade and capital investment.

The 1921 exchanges of missions between the United States and the FER catalyzed renewed American interest in the Far East. Representatives of business circles from various states visited the region. A special Department of Commerce emissary spent several months during 1921–1922 in Vladivostok studying investment opportunities.[11] In January of 1923 an American formerly attached to the Inter-Allied Committee for the Chinese-Eastern Railroad visited Chita for negotiations with FER representatives. Despite the lack of diplomatic recognition, Soviet-American economic ties had been established and were becoming stronger.

American business circles could not help but take note of the economic implications attending the unification of the FER with Soviet Russia in 1922. The event brought substantial changes in the Far East's economic structure and external ties. A barometer of interest was a speech by businessman Henry Hunt on 30 September 1923 at a meeting of trade and manufacturing enterprises in New York City. Recently returned from Russia, Hunt noted that the economy there was quickly returning to normal. He cited stabilization of its foreign currency, increases in industrial production, and growing foreign trade. Hunt's speech precipitated a resolution calling for the formation of a special committee to study the question of Russian-American trade. The resolution noted that Russian-American trade was an issue which deserved inclusion in the agenda of the upcoming Congress.

Three months later President Coolidge clarified his administration's position on the question of trade with the USSR. In a statement delivered before Congress, the president affirmed that the American government had nothing against American citizens entering into trade deals with Soviet Russia. Nonetheless, he added, a restoration of diplomatic relations would have to await a settlement of outstanding debts owed to the United States by the tsarist regime, debts which the Soviet government had refused to honor.

The absence of diplomatic recognition constrained the expansion of Soviet-American trade during the 1920s. Nonetheless, business circles in the United States displayed growing interest in economic cooperation, notably in developing the Far East's natural wealth. An illuminating example of the complexities of such cooperation was a 36-year agreement concluded in 1922 between the Council of People's Commissars and the Sinclair Oil Company for the exploitation of four hundred square miles of oil, natural gas, and mineral pitch on northern Sakhalin.* The company was given access, under Soviet supervision, to two ports on Sakhalin's eastern coast. The government of the Russian Republic (RSFSR) retained the right to abrogate the agreement in the event of hostile action by the United States against the RSFSR or in the event of Washington's failure to recognize the Soviet government within five years. The Soviet government assumed neither judicial nor moral responsibility to compensate the company for any losses incurred by the agreement's abrogation.

The Sinclair concession was politically as well as economically significant, for it served to remind Japan of the merits of clarifying policy toward the Soviet Union. Japan, it will be recalled, was at this time a leading foreign concessionaire in the Soviet Far East. Moreover, investment prospects in the region figured among international issues in the early 1920s. American firms alone made sixteen

---

*The southern half of Sakhalin (Karafuto) was under Japanese rule from 1905 until 1945. The Imperial Japanese Army occupied northern Sakhalin from 1920 to 1925.—AMERICAN EDITOR

requests for concessions in 1926–1927 and thirty-four requests in 1927–1928. While it is true that a number of these requests were not accepted (largely as a result of the unfeasibility of the project or as a result of the applicant's unsuitability), still a number of concessions were put into practice, notably in the gold-mining industry of the Okhotsk region.[12]

Trade formed a second avenue of economic interaction between the Soviet Far East and the United States during the 1920s. The most important contracts were concluded with U.S. fur importers. In addition, Far Eastern foodstuffs and semiprocessed goods made their way to the American market: wood for construction and furniture, scrap material, oil cakes, and soybeans. The American share of the Far East's foreign commerce fluctuated from 6.1 percent (1923–1924), to 19 percent (1925–1926), to 13 percent (1927–1928).[13] In 1929 the volume of U.S.-Soviet Far East trade reached $4.2 million. According to U.S. customs data, over two-fifths of all exports to the Soviet Far East consisted of various types of machines (threshers, tractors, canning and transport equipment).[14] American salt, leather shoes, cloth, linen, clothing, foodstuffs, hunting gear, and tobacco ranked prominently among imports, especially in Kamchatka. Considerable quantities of American raw cotton and textile equipment destined for European Russia passed through Far Eastern ports.

As the Soviet Far East developed in the interwar years, it assumed increasing significance as a base for exports to Asian and Pacific countries. In 1932 the Far East accounted for 10.6 percent of the USSR's exports. In some categories this share was higher, notably in coal and fish (24 percent) and lumber (38 percent).[15]

Deterioration of the international climate during the 1930s, however, brought about a sharp reduction of the Far East's foreign trade. Japan, a traditional trade partner, pursued policies which resulted in an aggravation of relations with the USSR. China, preoccupied by an escalating war of resistance against Japan and torn by internal political divisions, was not in a position to maintain stable levels of foreign commerce. China's northeastern three provinces (Manchuria), which had had strong economic ties with the Soviet Far East during the 1920s, were occupied by Japanese forces in 1931–1932 and ceased to be a significant trade partner.

The outbreak of the Second World War terminated "normal" trade relations of the Soviet Far East. This heralded, however, a new form of economic interaction with the United States, lend-lease. Congress passed the Lend-Lease Act on 11 March 1941. The act provided for American financial loans, arms, ammunition, strategic materials, foodstuffs, and other resources to countries participating in the war against the Axis powers. The Lend-Lease Act was not applied to the Soviet Union until 7 November 1941 and the first lend-lease convoys from the U.S. West Coast did not reach Vladivostok until 1942. From 1941 until 1945 the USSR received $10.8 billion, or just over 23 percent of total lend-lease aid disbursed during that period.[16]

The end of World War II signaled a new stage in the development of the Far East's external commercial ties. The postwar period has been characterized by the active use of new forms of international economic cooperation. Since 1968, Japan has become a major partner in so-called compensation agreements with the USSR. Projects both completed and ongoing on a compensation basis include the joint exploitation of forestry resources, wood chip production, construction of Vostochnyi Port, and the exploration and development of Sakhalin offshore petroleum and Yakutia coking coal.

The export of transport services in the Soviet Far East has become an important form of international cooperation. Two types of services are offered: the carrying of foreign cargoes throughout the Pacific Basin, and the carrying of containers from Japan, Hong Kong, the Philippines, and Australia to Europe across Siberia. The trans-Siberian "land bridge" went into operation in 1967 and has since steadily increased its capacity. From 1971 until 1982, volume grew seventy-five times.*[17] Since 1977, eastward bound containers have been trans-shipped through the specially equipped port of Vostochnyi. With the completion of Vostochnyi's second phase, the "land bridge" will be able to accommodate much more traffic. With full operation of the Baikal-Amur Railroad, trans-continental shipments should now be reduced to twenty days.

Since the inauguration of coastal trade with Japan in 1963, the Soviet Far East has expanded the list of "coastal trade" partners to include North Korea (1968), Australia (1978), and the People's Republic of China (1982). All regions of Siberia and the Far East take part in this trade, which is administered by a specially created all-Union organization called Dalintorg.

Coastal trade involves the export of resources and products which

---

*In 1982, however, land bridge shipments declined by 12 percent (Allen S. Whiting and Victor L. Mote, *Pacific Basin Transportation Prospects* [Washington: Wharton Econometric Forecasting Associates, 1984], p. 27).—AMERICAN EDITOR are either unusable in the Soviet Far East or which, for a variety of reasons, enjoy only limited internal demand. Imported articles received in exchange are distributed to enterprises in proportion to each enterprise's export earnings. This arrangement calls to mind the "secondary exports" of the 1920s alluded to earlier in this chapter.

The stable growth of regional exports has promoted the Far East's active participation in an international division of labor in the Pacific region. During the 1970s, Far Eastern exports increased one and a half times. Certain regional products occupy significant proportions of all-Union exports: lumber (over 40 percent), cellulose (8 percent), ship winches (over 24 percent), grain harvesters (8 percent), fish (23 percent), and canned fish (70 percent).[18] Three-quarters of Far Eastern exports pass through the Khabarovsk and Maritime territories.

With the exception of forest products, which are shipped from all Soviet Far Eastern ports, exports reveal subregional patterns and emphases. The Khabarovsk Territory and Amur District account for a major proportion of machine exports. Sakhalin is the only exporter of Far Eastern oil and is also a major supplier of cellulose and paper products. The Maritime Territory ships out large quantities of sea products and equipment for the chemical and mining industries.

Although the list of Far Eastern exports encompasses hundreds of different items, forest products account for over half (by value) of all regional goods shipped abroad. The prominence of forestry exports has been reinforced by the expanding proportion of relatively high-value finished and semifinished wood products: cellulose, paper, wood-fiber panels, saw timber, and chips. Marine products occupy the second position in regional exports. Canned fish exports are growing particularly fast.

The Far Eastern machine industry is making advances in international markets. Ship engines and winches, metal-cutting machines, steam turbines and compressors, and casting equipment enjoy a favorable reputation abroad. Although these regional machine products are sent to over thirty countries, only about 6 percent of machine exports go to Pacific region nations. These industries are now studying how to increase the proportion of Pacific Basin customers.

Far Eastern exports reach more than fifty countries. Japan accounts for a major share, followed by North Korea and Vietnam.

Overseas customers also include Australia, Singapore, Hong Kong, and Thailand, but their share of the total remains modest.

In recent years only 20 percent of Soviet exports to Pacific Basin countries have been produced in the Far East.[19] This relatively modest percentage suggests that there is a potential for activating the Far East's role in Soviet foreign trade in the Pacific. For the time being the Far East's limited export base constrains tendencies for the region to assume a larger share in the USSR's exports to Asia and the Pacific. Although regional exports are growing faster than general production, their share of total valued production remains small. The structure of regional exports has hardly changed in the past few decades. Lumber and fish still account for 70 percent to 80 percent of the volume of regional exports. Despite qualitative changes in these two categories, the Far East remains primarily a supplier of raw materials.

This situation can be explained by the Far Eastern economy's accelerated growth strategy, which has resulted in a concentrated exploitation of natural resources at the expense of infrastructural investments. To some extent this imbalance has been reinforced by strong Japanese demand for raw materials which the Soviet Far East is, for geographical reasons, in an advantageous position to supply.

The experience of economic cooperation with Japan demonstrates how international trade influences the Far East's economic structure. Five of the seven major joint projects concluded with Japanese firms involve intensive exploitation of natural resources, imparting a resource-oriented complexion to Far Eastern exports. This state of affairs is likely to endure because plans to the year 2000 envision the formation of regional export bases emphasizing the shipment of raw materials and semiprocessed goods. These shipments will be maintained at the cost of developing new territories in the BAM zone and along the Far East's Pacific littoral.

Preparation of a long-term stable export base requires the organization of production complexes. Most promising in this area are prospects for timber and fish processing, chemical fertilizers, and machine industries. Careful attention will be given to deepening cooperation with Asian and Pacific countries.

In view of the above, there appear to exist favorable conditions for the development of economic ties between the Soviet Far East and the American Far West. In addition to their geographical propinquity, the two regions share an extensive Pacific coastline, have major oceanic ports, and enjoy relatively dynamic regional growth rates.

On the basis of projected economic trends and potentials, one can asssume that the Soviet Far East could well become a customer for American products and a supplier of manufactured goods and essential raw materials for U.S. industries. Using existing resources in the Far East, a share of production could be geared for U.S. West Coast markets. In the early stages, trade would be conducted on a barter basis. In the longer run, assuming that trade ties had reached a suitable magnitude and had demonstrated stability, other forms of cooperation could be implemented, such as compensation agreements, cooperative production in specialized, joint companies (such as the US-USSR Marine Resources Company of Seattle and Nakhodka), tourism, and systematic coordination of scientific research.

Far Easterners reacted with deep interest to the industrial exhibition mounted by Washington State firms in Khabarovsk in May of 1975, a pioneer event of its kind.[20] On display were a wide variety of industrial goods showing the technological "state of the art" in wood processing, construction, drilling and petroleum machinery, transport equipment, electronics, and food-processing equipment. The Washington State Industrial Exhibition in Khabarovsk graphically demonstrated the attractiveness of businesslike cooperation between the Soviet Far East and the American Far West, including the inauguration of coastal trade arrangements such as are currently in effect between the Soviet Far East and Japan, Australia, North Korea, and China. Former Alaska governor Walter Hickel stressed these points during his August 1980 visit to Khabarovsk.

There are also attractive possibilities for broadening academic cooperation between the Far East Science Center's constituent institutes and institutions of research and higher learning in the U.S. Pacific States. Joint oceanological and geological research in the Pacific and cooperative measures to protect the environment are just some of the potential spheres of scholarly cooperation. The realization of such cooperative efforts would not only strengthen economic ties between our two countries, but would make a genuine contribution toward building a stable peace in the Pacific Basin.

## NOTES

1. A. V. Dattan, *Istoricheskii ocherk razvitiia Priamurskoi torgovli* (Moscow, 1897), p. 31.

2. V. I. Denisov, *Rossiia na Dal'nem Vostoke* (St. Petersburg, 1913), p. 144.

3. *Ekonomicheskaia zhizn' Dal'nego Vostoka* (Chita), no. 5 (1924), p. 1.

4. *Kon'iunkturnyi obzor narodnogo khoziaistva Dal'nego Vostoka za 1927–1928 gg.* (Khabarovsk, 1929).

5. *Otchët o rabote Dal'nevostochnogo kraevogo eksportnogo soveshchaniia* (Khabarovsk, 1929).

6. *Ekonomicheskaia zhizn' Dal'nego Vostoka,* no. 4 (1929).

7. *Vneshniaia torgovlia Sovetskogo Soiuza* (Moscow: Mezhdunarodnaia kniga, 1938), p. 110.

8. Zhukov, E. M., ed., *Mezhdunarodnye otnosheniia na Dal'nem Vostoke (1870–1945)* (Moscow: Gospolitizdat, 1951), p. 108.

9. *Dokumenty vneshnetorgovoi politiki SSSR* (Moscow: Gospolizdat, 1957), p. 289.

10. *Dal'nevostochnaia respublika* (Chita), no. 98 (1921).

11. *Ekonomicheskaia zhizn' Dal'nego Vostoka,* nos. 5–6 (1922).

12. *Otchëty Dal'nevostochnoi kontsessionnoi komissii i Upravleniia Dal'nevostochnogo gornogo okruga* (Khabarovsk, 1929), p. 115.

13. *Kon'iunkturnyi obzor.*

14. *Problemy sovetskogo Dal'nego Vostoka s SSHA* (New York: Amtorg, 1930), pp. 63–69.

15. *Materialy k plany razvitiia narodnogo khoziaistva i sotsial'nokul'turnogo stroitel'stva DBK vo vtoroi piatiletke (1933–1937 gg.)* (Khabarovsk, 1932), p. 7.

16. V. A. Val'kov, *SSSR i SSHA: ikh politicheskie i ekonomicheskie otnosheniia* (Moscow: Nauka, 1965), pp. 329–343.

17. *Ekonomicheskaia gazeta* (Moscow), no. 52 (1982), p. 16.

18. Special Novosti Press Release no. 117 (2140), 30 June 1981.

19. *Isvestiia Sibirskogo otdeleniia AN SSSR* (Novosibirsk), vyp. 2 (1981), p. 35.

20. *Tikhookeanskaia zvezda* (Khabarovsk), 20 May 1975.

# American Far West-
# Soviet Far East Trade

## Elisa B. Miller

THERE IS NO SHORTAGE of opportunities for businesses in the American Far West to develop mutually beneficial economic relationships with state enterprises in the Soviet Far East. Take, for example, the potential for industrial goods and technology. West Coast corporations produce specialized tunnel-boring equipment which the USSR needs for such projects as the recently completed Baikal-Amur Railroad (BAM). Oregon and Washington have a forest products machinery industry whose products would be suitable for forestry operations in the Soviet Far East. Technology and thermal products developed for the Alaskan market would also be suitable for Siberia. Machinery for the food-processing industry would have wide applications in the Soviet Far East. These products and technologies fall into the very areas which Soviet planners are stressing in the Far East: developing the BAM zone, forestry, mining, petroleum, and fisheries.

In addition, foodstuffs and consumer products from the U.S. Pacific states could play a positive role in the Soviet Far Eastern economy by attracting and retaining skilled labor from other parts of the USSR. The American Far West produces a wide variety of exportable agricultural goods which could diversify and improve regional food supplies in the Far East. Far Easterners could enjoy lemons, oranges, and nuts from California, apples from Washington and Oregon, and papaya and pineapple from Hawaii. For its part, the Soviet Far East has products that would find a ready market in the United States: salmon, caviar, furs, diamonds, gold, oil and natural gas, and certain types of timber (such as a log species similar to the Western red cedar no longer available in the United States).

In view of the potential for trade between the two regions, what has been the record in recent years? Since the early seventies when détente stimulated Soviet-American economic relations, Far Western businesses have made a number of attempts to enter Soviet Far Eastern markets. Tables 1 and 2, which show major categories of goods traded between the West Coast and the Soviet Far East from 1974 to 1983, suggest that as of 1983 their efforts have met with only mixed success.

With these statistics as background, this chapter will examine and evaluate the experiences of selected West Coast firms during the past

TABLE 1
**Exports from West Coast to Soviet Far East Ports**
(In Thousands of Dollars)

|  | Grain | Petroleum Products | Fruit | Machinery & Equipment | Other | TOTAL |
|---|---|---|---|---|---|---|
| 1974 | 2,154 | 0 | 0 | 1,605 | 0 | 3,759 |
| 1975 | 34,759 | 0 | 139 | 3,855 | 6 | 38,759 |
| 1976 | 15,825 | 5,945 | 164 | 14,864 | 0 | 36,798 |
| 1977 | 15,859 | 14,380 | 609 | 2,063 | 54 | 32,965 |
| 1978 | 22,743 | 16,091 | 408 | 454 | 0 | 39,696 |
| 1979 | 150,183 | 12,655 | 531 | 13,044 | 219 | 176,632 |
| 1980 | 58,176 | 19,719 | 0 | 6,625 | 12 | 84,532 |
| 1981 | 61,743 | 33,312 | 0 | 165 | 52 | 95,272 |
| 1982 | 40,836 | 32,319 | 0 | 14 | 21 | 73,190 |
| 1983 | 33,447 | 2,375 | 0 | 0 | 0 | 35,822 |

*Source:* Bureau of the Census, Foreign Trade Statistics, Census Bureau Tapes 305/705.

TABLE 2
**Exports from Soviet Far East to West Coast Ports**
(In Thousands of Dollars)

|  | Wood & Wood Products | Fish | Machinery & Equipment | Other | TOTAL |
|---|---|---|---|---|---|
| 1974 | 0 | 0 | 0 | 10 | 10 |
| 1975 | 0 | 0 | 0 | 157 | 157 |
| 1976 | 290 | 0 | 0 | 15 | 305 |
| 1977 | 493 | 0 | 23 | 0 | 516 |
| 1978 | 1,188 | 26 | 46 | 50 | 1,310 |
| 1979 | 634 | 45 | 0 | 0 | 679 |
| 1980 | 206 | 0 | 2 | 20 | 228 |
| 1981 | 0 | 0 | 0 | 19 | 19 |
| 1982 | 0 | 0 | 15 | 47 | 62 |
| 1983 | 0 | 5,416 | 0 | 0 | 5,416 |

*Source:* Bureau of the Census, Foreign Trade Statistics, Census Bureau Tapes 305/705.

decade. The problems encountered by these companies appear to have certain common characteristics which reveal structural asymmetries that need to be recognized and dealt with if the trans-Pacific economic relationship is to reach its potential.

## Efforts to Increase Trade, 1972–1976

Dana McBarron is a retired lumberman who in the 1970s was raising Scottish Highland cattle, a breed well suited for Siberian climates. As part of a global marketing effort, he wrote the Soviet Embassy in Washington, D.C., hoping to interest trade officials in the prospects of using his expertise in cattle breeding and raising to improve meat supplies in the USSR. He was encouraged when in 1972 Soviet agricultural officials responded that they were interested. This notification occurred on the eve of Leonid Brezhnev's visit to the United States.

During the course of Brezhnev's visit, Mr. McBarron invited the Soviet leader to his farm on Lopez Island in the state of Washington, adding that he would like to present a bull as a gift to the people of Siberia as an expression of "friendship between our two nations." Mr. Brezhnev declined the invitation, but the Soviet government showed its appreciation by inviting Mr. McBarron to visit the Soviet Union to present his Scottish Highland bull. This invitation was accepted. Amid considerable press coverage, Mr. McBarron's bull Bonnie Boy was transported across the Pacific to Vladivostok and from there across Siberia to Moscow for the presentation ceremony.

Bonnie Boy, however, had no successors. In 1982 Mr. McBarron told me that while a great deal of interest was shown in his cattle by Soviet buying agents, he made not a single sale. They could obtain, he said, Scottish cattle from England for a cheaper price. He nevertheless still sees a need for cattle-raising expertise in the Soviet Far East, especially in the area of breeding and feedlot technologies.[1]

Mr. McBarron's case is in some ways symptomatic of a pattern: hopes and encouragement followed by lack of results. During 1972 and 1973 the U.S. Department of Commerce sponsored trade conferences in all West Coast states on how to do business with the USSR. Large and small firms in several sectors showed interest in both import and export aspects of trade. Considerable attention focused on the Soviet Far East. It was assumed that geographical propinquity and efficient maritime transport would give West Coast firms advantages over European competitors in making sales in the Far East.*

This interest soon expressed itself in trade fairs, trade missions, and friendship exchanges. Oregon and Washington states showed the highest degree of activity in this respect. In 1975 the Washington State International Trade Fair Exhibition was held in Khabarovsk, featuring forest products machinery, concrete-making machinery, insulation technology, and doughnut machines.[2] In that same year, trade missions were exchanged between the two Pacific Northwest states (led by the Washington State governor Daniel Evans) and the Soviet Ministry of Woodworking and Forest Products.[3] Also in 1975, Oregon and Washington businesses, citizens, and state officials cooperated in erecting a monument in Vancouver, Washington (on the Columbia River opposite Portland, Oregon), honoring the Soviet pilot Valerii Chkalov (1904–1938), commander of a 1937 transpolar flight originating in Moscow.[4]

California also participated in similar activities in the mid-1970s. In 1975, Oakland and Nakhodka were formally designated "sister cities and sister ports" in a Soviet-American agreement which provided for exchanges of delegations and envisioned an increase in trade.[5] In 1976, Robert Gomperts, president of the California Council on International Trade, visited Moscow and lectured at the Institute of USA and Canada on trade relations between the United States and the Soviet Union with special reference to the American Far West-Soviet Far East trade potential.[6]

## Disappointed Expectations

How have West Coast companies fared since they seriously considered marketing their products to the USSR in the early 1970s? Most of the firms whose representatives I interviewed had sold one or two pieces of equipment to the USSR. Thereafter, experiences varied.

Stetson-Ross is a rather small company (about 150 employees) that sells sawmilling equipment and other wood-processing machinery.[7] The company has developed a machine that chips a log square.

---

*The assumption that cheaper freight costs would favor West Coast suppliers does not appear to be a deciding factor from a Soviet perspective. Purchased equipment is usually transported in Soviet vessels connecting with Soviet rail lines. This does not involve hard currency expenditures and thus makes transport costs less "visible" in Soviet calculations.

The machine has been used successfully on Canadian wood similar to that grown in the Soviet Far East. One of these chipper-edger machines was displayed and sold at an exhibition of forestry equipment in Moscow in 1973. Another was sold through a Japanese trading company overseeing the construction of a turnkey sawmill in the Soviet Far East. These sales prompted the company to pursue further marketing efforts in the USSR.

The company's efforts yielded results but did not generate sales of machines. The company was asked to bid on a turnkey plant but declined the request because the manager felt that putting together such a bid involved a greater integrative and engineering task than the company could afford without surer prospects of winning the bid. Since then the company has lost sales to the Finns (who are "better able to cope" with turnkey plant bids) and to Canadians (who sell a similar machine).

Nicholson Manufacturing is also a small company (about 150 employees and $15 million in annual sales) which produces debarking, chipping, and logging machinery that has been used successfully on Canadian wood similar to that grown in the Soviet Far East.[8] Early in the 1970s the firm sold eight debarker machines through a Japanese trading company and one machine at the 1973 Moscow exhibition of forestry equipment. In 1974 the USSR asked the company to provide a quotation for chip mills. The company responded with quotations. Though nothing came of this, the Soviets did invite the company to give a demonstration to potential users in the Soviet Far East. In 1976 the company sent a team and a machine to the Far East but again no sales resulted. A representative explained this lack of success as a result of high product price caused by product modifications, transportation costs, and inflation.

Nicholson Manufacturing continues to give quotations upon request to the USSR, investing company time and money in doing so. However, sales have been lost to the Finns. The company feels that Finnish firms have a competitive edge because Finland maintains a balanced trade with the USSR, giving the Soviets a hard currency credit balance with Finland that the USSR does not have with the United States.

The Robbins Company makes, among other things, tunnel-boring and vertical-drilling equipment. The company has sold such equipment to the USSR, produced to specification for the BAM Railroad. Recently the company was asked to quote prices for additional tunnel-boring equipment. The sale, however, went to a competing West German firm that ended up buying from Robbins part of the technology for specific features of the product.[9]

The reason Robbins lost the sale was, they were told, because their price was too high. But the company felt that other factors also played a role, namely, the U.S. embargoes imposed in the wake of events in Afghanistan and Poland. "The Soviets," remarked the company's president, "could not risk buying equipment from us for a critical project like the BAM, wait for eleven to twelve months while we built, only to have that shipment then embargoed." Buying from the West German firm avoided that risk. Moreover, the West German company won the contract at a time when the USSR-West European pipeline was being negotiated, a circumstance which may also have influenced the outcome of the competitive bidding.

Themes found in these examples also cropped up in interviews with other West Coast firms. First, active interest in selling to the USSR is still widespread. Second, West Coast companies are losing out on sales to Finnish, West German, and Canadian competitors.

If West Coast firms are experiencing difficulties selling the USSR what the USSR wants to buy, how are they faring in efforts to sell the USSR new products with an untested market? There are a number of "visionary" companies who regard as only a short-term problem the absence of a given product in the current or upcoming Soviet five-year plan. For these businessmen, the art of selling is to convince the customer to buy a new product whose effectiveness has yet to be fully demonstrated.

Columbia Machines produces machinery that makes concrete blocks for the construction of office and residential buildings, hospitals, and schools. The raw materials for these blocks are crushed stone and cement. The company has tried energetically to sell this machine in the USSR. They have given seminars in Moscow, hoping to reach construction planners. They have visited every foreign trade organization which handles materials for the construction industry. They participated in a trade fair in Khabarovsk and were instrumental in erecting the Chkalov monument. They feel that Soviet planners who define what materials to use in the construction industry do not adequately appreciate the company's technology. Nonetheless, the company remains optimistic about long-term prospects. As a representative remarked, "Someday the idea will take hold, and at that time we'll be there first."[10]

Dwyer Overseas makes machinery for sawmills and plywood plants. The company president has visited the USSR thirty-five times and participated in the first negotiating team to sell grain to the USSR. Recently he has concentrated his efforts on trying to convince Soviet planners of the benefits of producing plywood for the building industry. The USSR produces plywood but only in sizes large enough for crating and furniture. Dwyer Overseas has been trying to make plywood sales in the USSR for several years and is not slackening its efforts. The company president is "realistic" about present possibilities but is confident that someday the USSR will recognize the plywood potential in its abundant forests.[11]

## The Problem: Balanced Trade

For all their efforts, the above West Coast firms are not succeeding in selling their products to the USSR. At first glance, prices and financing may appear to be important reasons for the lack of sales. Yet company representatives discounted these factors. Financing did not seem to be relevant, as the dollar value of potential sales was too small to be eligible for U.S. government export credit subsidies. The companies felt that for the most part their prices were competitive. Wherein, then, lies the problem?

A larger set of issues not within the control of an individual company may be at work here, namely, the importance which the USSR attaches to balanced trade with its trading partners. Balanced trade programs have historically been important to the USSR and are especially emphasized during periods of foreign exchange shortages.

Balanced trade can be traced to the history and development of Soviet external economic relations. Since 1918 (1923 for the Far East), foreign trade in the USSR has been a state monopoly, a centrally administered instrument of national development. After World War II and the formation of the Council for Mutual Economic Assistance (COMECON) in 1949, the USSR conducted foreign trade primarily with socialist countries which also engaged in foreign commerce as a state monopoly closely tied to national economic and political goals.

Foreign trade planning in the USSR and other COMECON member nations operated so that exports corresponded in value to imports. Because the currencies of these countries were nonconvertible, there was no ready mechanism for instituting multilateral trade. Bilateral trade balancing—agreements between two countries to exchange one set of goods for another—became the easiest way to insure the equivalency of exports and imports.

Trade between the USSR and Western countries, on the other hand, involved Soviet payments for imports in "hard" currencies. Soviet planners were obliged to ensure that foreign exchange earned from exports would match foreign exchange required for purchasing imports. Since all hard currencies were and are by definition convertible, they served as a medium for multilateral trade relationships. The USSR could sell exports to one Western country and, using the hard currency proceeds, purchase imports from another Western country. The exchange of goods between the USSR and any particular Western trade partner did not have to balance as long as the overall trade with Western nations balanced.

Nonetheless, bilateral balancing is unofficially practiced in Soviet trade relations with a number of Western states as a means to insure that foreign exchange for imports will be earned by exports of equivalent value. Pressures to enact a form of bilateral balancing have been applied by some lobbyists in Western countries concerned about large Japanese imports, but the act of linking imports to exports on a bilateral basis is officially eschewed as harmful to a multilateral trading system.

A legacy of trade balancing and pressures to raise foreign exchange revenues for desired imports has given rise to the Soviet practice of "tied-trade" projects. The predominant form of tied-trade is the large-scale compensation, or product-payback, trade wherein machinery and equipment imported by the USSR are paid for by exports produced by this machinery and equipment. Exports are sold to the same country providing the imports, and in some cases to the same company.

Tied-trade is playing an increasingly prominent role in the international economic relations of the Soviet Far East. It lies at the basis of a growing list of joint projects with Japan which N. Shlyk discusses in this volume under the rubric "compensation agreements." These joint projects include exploitation of forest resources, wood chip production, construction of a container port (Vostochnyi), and exploration and development of Yakutia coal and Sakhalin offshore petroleum.[12]

Border or coastal trade is another visible form of tied-trade carried out between the Soviet Far East and, primarily, Japan. A local trade organization (Dalintorg) administers coastal trade so that exchanges between the Far East and Japan are balanced. To pay for imports from Japan, exports must first be sold to Japan. The volume of trade is limited to the amount of credits the region can obtain by selling its above-plan products as exports.[13]

Official U.S. policy does not endorse bilateral trade balancing. American policy toward the USSR constrains balanced bilateral trade in other ways. Withholding most-favored-nation status to the USSR limits Soviet imports into the United States. Severe limitations on export credits to the USSR for large-scale tied-trade projects in fuel exploration also inhibit balanced trade.

There is also resistance at the level of private business to linking sales with purchases. Most companies, large or small, have no experience in this area. When they make a sale, they expect letters of credit as a means of payment. American companies sometimes provide a credit package for their customers, but rarely does a company feel an obligation to find for the customer the wherewithal to pay for the product that is being sold to him.

Furthermore, the individualized, independent structure of American businesses (especially small businesses) and the absence of general trading companies means that the United States does not have an economic infrastructure conducive to tied-trade transactions. When faced with a demand to buy in order to sell, small American corporations balk, not knowing where to turn. Some observers feel that passage of the U.S. Trading Company Act will help create the infrastructure that is currently lacking. For the time being, however, government trade policies and private business practices reinforce a disregard for the bilateral trade challenge. Such inattention weakens U.S. competitiveness in trade with the USSR.

A few firms, however, are showing signs of developing new attitudes and a new expertise in order to compete in the international marketplace. The following two examples are illustrative and instructive of this tendency.

Premier Gear sells machinery that manufactures veneer for plywood, furniture, and other items. The company wants to sell its machinery to the USSR, where a potential for exporting veneer is perceived. The company feels that the Soviet Union has the ability to produce veneer at competitive prices on the world market. The USSR has the raw materials and only needs the machinery.

Premier Gear has designed a project for selling its veneer-making machinery to the Soviets. It has found a U.S. buyer for the subsequent veneer exports which the machines will produce. The foreign exchange the USSR needs to pay for the machine will be earned within eighteen months after production begins. The company feels that it has put together a tied-trade offer which the USSR cannot refuse.[14]

In 1977, Marine Resources of Seattle formed the first joint venture between an American and Russian company, with operations in the USSR. Capital was joined and profits are shared for an enterprise which harvests, processes, packages, and markets fish products all over the world. While it took years to develop, the project has succeeded because, among other reasons, it utilized productive capacity already existing in the two countries, adopted barter-type procedures in operations, and involved practically no foreign exchange. In 1982, Marine Resources expected to harvest 120,000 tons of fish with a gross value of $20 million.[15]

The above two examples demonstrate the feasibility of adapting to the practice of balanced trade. Yet Premier Gear and Marine Resources remain exceptions. Most individual businesses are still handicapped when trying to cope with this unfamiliar and somehow alien practice.

One step toward helping American firms working within a balanced-trade framework in the Pacific would be the establishment of an American Far West-Soviet Far East regional trade organization to oversee and coordinate trans-Pacific exchanges. With such a body in existence, each U.S. company would not have to commit itself to balanced trade, for the "balancing" would be accomplished at a regional level.

Creation of a Soviet-American regional organization of course must have the full cooperation from the Soviet side for it to succeed. As an umbrella for U.S. Pacific area businesses and Soviet Far East foreign trade production enterprises, it must have authority to commit resources. At present, foreign trade organizations and production enterprises in the Soviet Far East do not have adequate authority in these matters. This can lead to misunderstandings, as the following case illustrates.

A representative on an American company conducted negotiations in the Soviet Far East for the sale of machinery. Initial discussions appeared to be satisfactory for both parties. However, no contract materialized. The American company felt that it had expended time and money with out tangible results. Hindsight reveals that the American company's expectations would probably not have been disappointed had the company from the outset established contact with figures invested with more authority. Indeed, talking to the right person or persons is crucial in the USSR and underlies the importance of high-level Soviet input into any future regional trade body.

## Conclusion

American Far West-Soviet Far East economic relations have real potential; they are also fraught with difficulties. Some of the forces governing the potential of Soviet-American economic cooperation in the Pacific are beyond the control of individuals or organizations in either region. Other forces will depend upon the future development of the Soviet Far East and of the American Far West.

All of the constraints and imponderables notwithstanding, both sides can take a step forward by studying each other's regional economies and trade practices. The balanced-trade system, albeit unfamiliar and even rather alien to the American business tradition, deserves serious consideration as a mechanism that, properly understood, might be utilized to enhance the U.S. share of Soviet Far Eastern international trade and thereby strengthen mutually beneficial ties across the Pacific.

### NOTES

1. Interview with Dana McBarron, Sr., 30 October 1982.

2. "Washington State Plays Trade Show Footsies with USSR's Siberia," *Tradeshow Week*, 6 January 1975, p. 7.

3. "A Russian Trade Group Scouts Northwest Industry." *Seattle Post-Intelligencer*, 14 January 1975.

4. *Seattle Post-Intelligencer*, 21 June 1975. *Seattle Times*, 20 June 1975.

5. "Oakland/Nakhodka—Sister Cities and Ports," *Progress Magazine* (Oakland), May 1975.

6. Interview with Robert Gomperts, 18 November 1982.

7. Interview with Chandler Jones, retired sales and marketing manager, Stetson-Ross Company, 20 September 1982.

8. Interview with Bill Nicholson, president, Nicholson Manufacturing, Seattle, and Ed Brown, manager, Nicholson-Murdie Machines, Victoria, B.C., 8 November 1982.

9. Interview with Odd Askilsrud, sales department, and Richard Robbins, president, Robbins Company, 1 December 1982.

10. Interview with Norm Small, sales manager, Columbia Machines, 17 November 1982.

11. Interview with Robert Dwyer, Sr., president, Dwyer Overseas, 4 November 1982.

12. For details, see Richard Edmonds, "Siberian Resource Development and the Japanese Economy," in Robert Jensen, Theodore Shabad, and Arthur Wright, eds., *Soviet Natural Resources in the World Economy* (Chicago: University of Chicago Press, 1983), pp. 214–231.

13. Elisa B. Miller, "Soviet Participation in the Emerging Pacific Basin Economy: The Role of 'Border Trade,' " *Asian Survey* (May 1981), pp. 565–578.

14. Interview with Alan Cole, president, Premier Gear, 28 October 1982.

15. *Pacific News Service,* 18 September 1982.

# Soviet-American Trade
# in the Pacific

## A. B. Parkanskii

The Soviet Union and the United States belong to different social systems and occupy leading positions in the competition between these systems. Fundamental political and ideological differences exist and will continue to exist between them. Nonetheless, in certain vital areas both countries have an interest in large-scale and long-term cooperation.

The Soviet Union and the United States have developed modern economies, strong scientific and technological establishments, capacious internal markets, and a differentiated, complementary foreign trade structure, in short, those preconditions which in favorable circumstances open perspectives for businesslike, mutually beneficial ties. There is no question that a development of Soviet-American cooperation in solving energy problems, exploring outer space and the ocean depths, struggling against disease, and protecting the environment would not only improve the quality of life for Soviet and American peoples but would have salutary repercussions on the international climate.

In assessing prospects for foreign trade, the Twenty-sixth Party Congress (1981) raised the issue of activating economic relations not only with socialist states but with developing and developed capitalist countries. The Eleventh Five-Year Plan (1981–1985) anticipated a growth rate of foreign trade (22.5 percent) exceeding the growth rate of national income. These calculations were based on the experience of the previous five-year plan, during which foreign trade turnover increased 88 percent from Rub 50.1 billion in 1975 to Rub 94.1 billion in 1980.[1]

Although socialist countries have and will continue to have over half of the USSR's external commerce, "promotion of mutually beneficial trade with industrially developed capitalist countries constitutes a not insignificant part of the complex of external economic ties permitting us to utilize the international division of labor for the achievement of our economic goals."[2] The principles guiding Soviet economic policies toward the United States and other developed capitalist countries are equality, equitable distribution of benefits, mutuality of interests, and nondiscrimination. As is well known, these principles are enunciated in the Final Act of the Accord on Security and Cooperation in Europe, signed by European countries, the United States, and Canada at Helsinki in 1975.

## Soviet Trade with the West

At the outset of the 1980s, the Soviet Union ranked seventh (following the United States, Japan, the Federal Republic of Germany, Great Britain, and Italy) in the volume of foreign trade. As shown in Table 1, the USSR traded Rub 127.5 billion with 143 countries in 1983, a striking contrast to 1946 when barely Rub 1.3 billion worth of goods were exchanged with 39 states.

Economic relations between the USSR and 116 countries are regulated by intergovernmental agreements. Such agreements allow the Soviet Union to integrate trade more closely with its overall economic plans, guaranteeing in the process that the USSR's trade partners will have stable sources of supplies and market opportunities.

The 1970s in general were a period of intensive broadening of economic ties between the USSR and industrialized capitalist countries. From 1970 until 1983 Soviet commerce with these states grew eight times, as is shown in Table 2.

During the early 1980s, the volume of trade turnover between the USSR and a number of industrially developed capitalist countries (Sweden, Luxemburg, Spain, Portugal, Canada, and New Zealand, for example) has undergone dramatic increases. Trade with the United States, Great Britain, and Japan, on the other hand, has developed unevenly and in some cases actually decreased as a result of international strains. In 1983, for example, trade with Japan fell 23 percent, the largest single-year drop since the re-establishment of diplomatic relations in 1956.

Notwithstanding political complications, trade with capitalist countries in 1984 constituted nearly a third of our foreign commerce. Our leading trading countries in this category were (in descending order of magnitude) the Federal Republic of Germany,

TABLE 1
**Foreign Trade of the USSR, 1946–1983**
(In Billions of Rubles)

|         | 1946 | 1950 | 1955 | 1960 | 1965 | 1970 | 1975 | 1980 | 1981 | 1982 | 1983 |
|---------|------|------|------|------|------|------|------|------|------|------|------|
| Exports | 0.6  | 1.6  | 3.1  | 5.0  | 7.4  | 11.5 | 24.0 | 49.6 | 57.1 | 63.2 | 67.9 |
| Imports | 0.7  | 1.3  | 2.7  | 5.1  | 7.2  | 10.6 | 26.7 | 44.5 | 52.6 | 56.4 | 59.6 |
| TOTAL   | 1.3  | 2.9  | 5.8  | 10.1 | 14.6 | 22.1 | 50.7 | 94.1 | 109.7 | 119.6 | 127.5 |

*Source: Vneshniaia torgovlia SSSR v 1983 g.* (Moscow: Finansy i statistika, 1984).

TABLE 2
**Soviet Foreign Trade with Developed Capitalist Countries**
(In Millions of Rubles)

|         | 1970  | 1975   | 1980   | 1981   | 1982   | 1983   |
|---------|-------|--------|--------|--------|--------|--------|
| Exports | 2,154 | 6,140  | 15,862 | 17,247 | 18,849 | 19,653 |
| Imports | 2,540 | 9,702  | 15,721 | 18,112 | 18,892 | 18,719 |
| TOTAL   | 4,694 | 15,842 | 31,583 | 35,359 | 37,741 | 38,372 |

*Source: Vneshniaia torgovlia SSSR v 1983 g.* (Moscow: Finansy i statistika, 1984).

Finland, France, Italy, and Japan. The United States has ranked in sixth place, accounting for 1.5 percent of the USSR's foreign commerce.[3] This hierarchy of trade partners of course in no way reflects trading potentials. In a more favorable international political environment, the United States would almost certainly rank more highly on the list.

Trends in the USSR's trade with Western industrialized nations are not limited to quantitative indices. During the past ten years, Soviet-Western economic ties have deepened and assumed a more intricate form. Specifically, compensation agreements, scientific-technical cooperation, and joint productions projects are more commonly encountered. Contracts have increasingly reached a large scale and assumed an extended duration involving in some cases billions of dollars and running well into the next millennium.

For many Western firms such cooperation makes good business sense. The French concern Ron-Poulenc, which began business relations with the USSR in the 1960s, has for over twenty years supplied equipment to twenty-three Soviet factories.[4] In 1981 alone, Mitsui concluded $670 million worth of contracts with the USSR.[5]

The form, scale, and dynamics of cooperation between the USSR and any given capitalist country varies. As the economist M. M. Maksimova writes, the USSR's trade partners "differ from one another by the dimensions of their industrial and scientific-technical potential, by the structure of their economies, by the character of their specialization in the world economy, and by their experience in international cooperation. There are subtle differences in the foreign policies of capitalist states toward the Soviet Union, reflecting various degrees of interest in cooperation with our country on the part of their ruling and business circles."[6]

Our business contacts with foreign corporations do not constitute an end in themselves. Rather, such contacts are designed to expedite the solution of major national tasks, above all the intensification of economic development, the improvement of production quality, and the elevation of our living standards. Foreign economic ties form a not unimportant channel providing a supplementary source of capital investments. Using this channel, the country is accelerating the development of Siberia and the Far East.

At this stage it should be noted that for all its significance, foreign trade and other external economic ties are not of crucial importance for the Soviet economy. In 1981, for example, the Soviet gross national product was Rub 1.12 trillion. Of total imports (Rub 52.6 billion), Rub 18.1 billion, or 1.6 percent of the Soviet GNP, came from trade with developed countries with market economies. Imports from the United States represented just over one-tenth of one percent of the GNP.[7]

Up to one-third of Soviet imports consists of machines and equipment. Particularly well represented in this category are the chemical, transport, food, wood-processing, metallurgical, and construction industries. Capitalist countries accounted for Rub 5.9 billion, or 30.3 percent of 1982 equipment imports.[8] About Rub 186 million were spent on American machinery and other equipment, a drop from Rub 311 million in 1980.[9] Such modest levels are but a fraction of potential Soviet purchases from the United States. It is worth recalling that in the early 1970s, Soviet machine and technology imports from the United States grew impressively, reaching a record level of Rub 621 million in 1976. Subsequently, as a result of restrictions imposed by Washington, American corporations lost an estimated $4 billion in Soviet equipment orders.[10]

According to V. Molodtsov, general director of Soyuzkhimexport (a state trade organization dealing with chemicals), the number of different chemicals imported from the United States decreased by half, and their volume (excluding ammonia and superphosphates) dropped 80 percent, obliging Soviet foreign trade organizations to redirect orders of chemical products to other countries.[11] Molodtsov has nonetheless stressed that the USSR is prepared to resume trade in chemical products with the United States at previous, and eventually at increased, levels. Such prospects evidently interest a number of major American corporations (Allied Chemical, Monsanto, Kodak, American Cyanamid) who, notwithstanding current international complications, continue to maintain mutually rewarding links with Soviet trade organizations.

Consumer articles also offer opportunities for trade. Although the bulk of demand for consumer products is met by domestic production, the Soviet economy takes advantage of an international division of labor in this sphere. Demand for consumer articles and for consumer industries supplies accounts for 40 percent of the value of all Soviet imports, or slightly more than the combined value of machine and equipment purchases. The USSR buys clothing, shoes, cosmetics, and materials for light industries from France, West Germany, Italy, and other capitalist countries. The value of consumer product imports reached approximately 10 percent of general allocations of internal market funds, a proportion sharply higher in the case of specific articles such as clothing, leather shoes, furniture, fruit, and vegetables.[12]

In the second half of the 1970s the tempo of Soviet-American exchanges of consumer and food products accelerated. The growth can be ascribed to increased exports of Soviet furs, watches, hunting rifles, caviar, and fish, on one hand, and on the other, to larger Soviet orders for American synthetic fibers, animal skins, industrial fats, citrus fruits, and almonds. These exchanges sharply declined after 1980, however. Still, it is worth bearing in mind that consumer goods offer real possibilities not just for product exchanges but for more complex, long-term forms of cooperation between Soviet trade organizations and American corporations.

An instructive example of such cooperation is in the field of popular beverages. According to an agreement between the USSR and the Pepsi-Cola Company, ten Pepsi bottling plants were built in Moscow, Leningrad, Kiev, Tashkent, Tallinn, Novorossiisk, Evpatoriia, Novosibirsk, Alma Ata, and Sukhumi. An eleventh facility is reportedly now under construction at Vladivostok. Payment for bottling equipment and supplies of Pepsi concentrate is made in the form of earnings from sales of Stolichnaya Vodka in the U.S. market. Another example is an agreement with the Philip Morris Company, according to which Marlboro cigarettes are produced in the USSR from Virginia tobacco planted in the Moldavian and Azerbaijan republics.[13]

The USSR's import capacities depend directly on its export base, which is rapidly broadening in step with our country's growing industrial and technological potentials and with special measures designed to encourage export-oriented production.

Recently the Soviet machine industry has displayed a tendency toward specialization in its exports. Increasing emphasis has been placed on forge-pressing equipment, energy turbines, large generators, machine tools, electric engines, precision instruments, road-building and agricultural machines, aviation technology, tractors, automobiles, and household electric appliances.[14] Foreign markets absorb about 30 percent of Soviet camera and watch production, 20 percent of our bicycles, and 16 percent of our radio sets.

Richly endowed with natural resources and committed to the development of strong mining, forestry, and agricultural industries, the USSR has emerged as a major exporter of raw and semimanufactured materials. This aspect of our country's participation in the international divison of labor underlies the relatively high proportion (65 percent in 1983) of Soviet exports (by value) occupied by fuel and electric energy, ores, forest products, and textiles.

Oil and petroleum products lead Soviet exports of raw materials, accounting for 41.6 percent of them in 1983. Natural gas shipments abroad are increasing their share of total valued exports. Other major raw material exports include coal, methanol, chloride, ammonia, and chrome.[15] Among manufactured products, electric motors, metallurgical equipment, ships, automobiles and trucks, aluminum, lead, nickel, nitrate fertilizers, and petrochemical products are well represented. About a third of all Soviet exports go to developed capitalist countries.

The Soviet Union can offer the United States a variety of products. The modest volume of our current exports to the United States derives not from economic limitations but from political circumstances, among them Washington's denial of most-favored-nation (MFN) treatment to the USSR in the matter of tariffs. The accordance of MFN status to the USSR would probably double the market for Soviet goods in the United States. Under current conditions we are losing 22 percent and 30 percent of potential foreign currency earnings from exports of chemical goods and industrial equipment respectively.[16]

Even under these unfavorable conditions, Soviet exports to the United States grew six times from 1970 to 1979, from Rub 58 million to Rub 350 million. Unfortunately, exports fell sharply during the 1980s, plummeting by half in 1981 alone.[17] Vice-Minister of Foreign Trade V. Sushkov aptly summed up the situation when he remarked that "the volume of structure of Soviet-American trade in no way corresponds to its potential. . . . Under favorable conditions, Soviet-American trade could attain a remarkable magnitude."[18]

Recently production programs on a compensation basis have become increasingly common in economic cooperation between the USSR and capitalist countries. Whereas only three such programs existed in 1973, more than fifty were in force by 1980. Compensation agreements—wherein a part of production is sent overseas in payment for previously advanced credits—accounted in 1984 for 13 percent of total Soviet foreign commerce.

Several compensation agreements stand out because of their magnitude. West German firms are supplying equipment and technology for the construction of the Novo-Oskol Electro-Metallurgical Combine west of Moscow in exchange for a percentage of the combine's production over the course of fifteen years. The Finns are helping to build an ore-mining complex in the Karelian Autonomous Republic. Some 570 Western firms from ten countries participated in the recently completed gas pipeline from the USSR to Western Europe. Clearly, there is a real potential for new compensation agreements, particularly in resource-rich Siberia and along the Pacific continental shelf.

## The American Far West: A Soviet View

As Soviet and American specialists have repeatedly noted, it is difficult to overestimate the Soviet-American trade potential in the Pacific, specifically in the North Pacific, which is bounded by the Soviet Far East and the American Far West.[19] Geographical propinquity, convenient communications, and the complementary structure of Soviet and American foreign trade are all factors which open intriguing possibilities for economic interaction. Nor would such interaction be limited to the Soviet Far East and the American Pacific states. Soviet and U.S. Pacific ports could become gateways for exchanges of goods and services destined for internal markets in each country far removed from the Pacific Basin.

The Soviet Union presently imports from other countries many products which rank prominently among American exports: industrial equipment, consumer goods, and computers. Conversely, the United States imports products that the USSR exports: oil, forest materials, ores, furs, and many types of equipment and machines.

Statistics show that during the past decade East Asian-Pacific countries have assumed cardinal importance in American foreign trade. In 1970–1980, American capital investment in Asian-Pacific countries tripled, and trade with them increased almost sixfold, outpacing other sectors of American foreign commerce.[20] American technology is being disseminated in the Asia-Pacific region more actively than in any spot on earth.

The American Far West is one of the most economically developed and dynamic regions of the United States. The volume of foreign trade of the five Pacific states (California, Washington, Oregon, Alaska, and Hawaii) totaled more than $93 billion (equivalent to about 70 percent of total Soviet foreign trade at official exchange rates). Moreover, the share of U.S. foreign trade occupied by the five Pacific states has steadily grown since 1960 (see Table 3).

The export data cited in Table 3 refers to shipments through Pacific area customs. These shipments include not only goods produced within the region but in other parts of the country. However, the overwhelming share of Pacific states exports are of local origin.[21]

In general, manufacturing industries are more export oriented in the Pacific states than in the nation as a whole. In 1980, 13.8 percent of the region's production was sent abroad, compared with a U.S. average of 8.4 percent. Alaska and Washington export 37 percent

TABLE 3
**Growth of Pacific States' Percentage of U.S Foreign Trade**

|                | 1960 | 1965 | 1970 | 1975 | 1980 |
|----------------|------|------|------|------|------|
| Exports        | 12.7 | 13.2 | 16.9 | 15.7 | 21.0 |
| Imports        | 11.9 | 12.9 | 15.8 | 18.3 | 19.7 |
| Total Turnover | 12.4 | 13.1 | 16.4 | 16.9 | 20.3 |

*Sources: Historical Statistics of the United States,* pt. 2 (Washington, 1975), pp. 889, 896. *Highlights of U.S. Export and Import Trade,* July 1982.

and 30 percent respectively of their production, proportions unmatched by any other state in the Union. Exports in the Far West are growing faster than regional production and from 1966 to 1980 increased their share of the nation's manufacturing exports from 12 percent to 18 percent.

Regional exports draw upon a significant share of regional production in certain sectors of the economy, notably in metallurgy and chemicals. Moreover, a significant portion of plant capacity and the labor force is putting out goods for the export industries of other parts of the United States. In 1980 the number of employees indirectly involved in exports from the Pacific states reached 153,000, of whom over 122,000 worked in California.[22] According to the California Council for International Trade, an additional 80,000 were employed in international services such as engineering, insurance, trading companies, and banks.[23]

Selected branches of agriculture are also closely tied to foreign markets. Washington State, for example, sells 80–85 percent of its wheat abroad. In 1980, California exported 30 percent of its lemons and more than 75 percent of its rice and cotton crops. California cotton comprised 60 percent of all American exports of that commodity.[24]

The general character of statistical data occasionally obscures an orientation toward foreign markets found in other sectors of Pacific state economies. For example, the growth of California's transport equipment industry during the 1970s is partially attributable to strong overseas demand. Since the beginning of the last decade, Alaska's forestry and fishing industries have depended heavily on Japanese markets. About one-quarter of Washington's lumber is shipped to Japan.[25]

California dominates the foreign commerce of the five Pacific states, accounting for two-thirds of their total trade and one-eighth of the nation's foreign trade in 1980 ($56.2 billion).[26] More than half of the Pacific states' commerce with the outside world flows through fifteen ports and airports located largely in southern California.

California sends more manufactured goods abroad than does any other U.S. state ($16.5 billion in 1980, over double the 1976 figure). The state ranked first in the United States in exports of electronic products and second in overseas shipments of transport and nonelectronic equipment. Raw materials also figure prominently in California's external trade, especially textile fibers, iron and scrap iron, animal skins, paper pulp, and fertilizers. Over one-tenth of the state's exports (by value) consist of agricultural products, notably fruits, vegetables, grains, and meat.

Washington occupies the second position among the Pacific states in the volume of its foreign trade. Washington's international trade increased by eleven times between 1969 and 1979 in current prices. The state's exports are comparatively specialized. Some 60 percent of them are wheat, lumber, and aircraft. The Boeing Corporation, a major producer of civil and military aircraft, accounts for a third of the state's exports. With the exception of airplanes, Oregon exports similar products totaling $5.3 billion (1979), putting it in third place among the Pacific five.

Alaska's economy, as has been previously noted, is almost exclusively oriented toward foreign markets, with the exception of petroleum carried by the Alaska pipeline from the North Slope. Some 50 percent of Alaska's forest products and 30 percent of its natural gas is sent abroad. One-third of all American fish exports are from Alaska (and 90 percent of the nation's salmon exports). Hawaii's exports, on the other hand, are comparatively modest and consist largely of sugar, pineapple, prepared food, and trans-shipments of goods from other states. Tourism constitutes together with military allocations a major source of income for the islands.

The volume of imports into the Pacific states in recent years exceeds that of exports. In 1980 the regional deficit stood at just under a billion dollars. The unfavorable balance derives from heavy purchases by all five states of foreign raw materials, principally petroleum and petroleum products. Although the Far West is well endowed with energy resources, most corporations find it more convenient to rely on imports. Thus, even oil-rich Alaska satisfies local demand for petroleum products by imports, while exporting its own oil to other parts of the country. In addition to petroleum, California imports machines and equipment, notably for the electronic and transport industries. The state also brings in a wide variety of consumer goods and foodstuffs.

Washington has traditionally enjoyed a favorable balance of trade, although in the 1970s mounting costs of oil and natural gas began to cut into this surplus. Both Washington and Oregon import considerable quantities of manufactured goods for industrial and consumer uses. Alaska brings in from abroad construction materials and a wide range of accessories for the state's mining and petroleum industries.

In Hawaii's foreign trade, purchases of minerals, agricultural

goods, forestry products, and chemical materials occupy a relatively
larger position than they do in the imports of other Pacific states.
Even before the 1973 oil crisis, such commodities comprised two-
thirds of Hawaii's overseas purchases. Subsequent petroleum price
hikes have boosted this proportion as well as raised the absolute level
of the state's overall imports. The preponderance of petroleum
imports (which in the late 1970s represented more than half of all
imports by value) underlies the emergence of Indonesia as Hawaii's
main source of imports ($709 million out of $2 billion in 1981).

A significant share of foreign products entering West Coast ports
consists of components for manufacturing enterprises. Some of these
imports are destined for trans-shipment to other parts of the United
States, with or without processing on the West Coast. For example,
California ports are major gateways for motor vehicles and spare
parts imported from Japan and Western European countries.

Imports create jobs. According to the California Council for
International Trade, in 1980 some 145,000 residents of that state
were employed in import-related enterprises. Automobile imports
alone accounted for 20,000 jobs.[27]

Summarizing and assessing the above data, it is clear that since
World War II, and even more dramatically since 1960, the Pacific
states have assumed unprecedented significance in America's national and international commerce. It is also worth noting in this
context that the foreign trade of the Pacific states has consistently
concentrated in the Pacific Basin (75 percent for California and
Washington, 80 percent for Oregon and Hawaii, and nearly 100
percent for Alaska).

## New Patterns of Economic Cooperation

Trends analogous to those we have just looked at in the American
Far West are taking place in the Soviet Far East. The development
of regional industries, accelerated by the construction of the Baikal-
Amur Railroad, creates opportunities for business ties with coun-
tries of the Pacific Basin, including the United States. Not a few
American firms are expressing interest in such cooperation.

In the 1970s and early 1980s, delegations and individual representatives of West Coast corporations visited the Soviet Union. In 1973,
Washington became the first American state to organize a trade
exhibition in the USSR. Subsequently, twenty-one Washington

firms demonstrated their products at an international forestry exhibition held in Moscow. In 1975 a group of Washington businessmen visited a trade fair in Khabarovsk and successfully marketed a variety of American machines and equipment. During the 1970s, American businessmen and economists have not infrequently noted that there exist complementary trade interests between the Soviet Far East and the American Far West, based on exchanges of raw materials, industrial, and consumer goods across the North Pacific.

Current trade levels, however, fall far short of their potentials. In 1980, California and the Soviet Union exchanged $121 million worth of goods. The USSR's share of the state's exports barely reached .35 percent and of the state's imports, only .9 percent.[28] In comparison, about a third of the state's foreign commerce, or $17 billion, was with Japan. Soviet trade with other U.S. Pacific states remains at similarly modest levels.

References to one example of successful Soviet-American economic cooperation in the Pacific—the US-USSR Marine Resources Company—have been made elsewhere in this volume. For several years Soviet and American fishermen have been working together within the framework of this joint enterprise. Half of the company's stock is owned by Sovrybflot, commercial agency of the USSR Ministry of Fisheries. The remaining half is controlled by the Bellingham Cold Storage Company of Seattle. The company organizes the catching and processing of hake, perch, and cod in North Pacific waters. At the outset of the fishing season the company concludes contracts with American trawler owners, who subsequently hand over their catch to Soviet floating processing bases off the U.S. Pacific coast. Part of the catch is sent to the USSR and part is sold in third countries. The proceeds are divided equally between the Soviet and American partners.

Realistic prospects appear to exist for joint Soviet-American activity in Pacific Basin markets. The USSR has accumulated extensive experience in joint enterprises with developed capitalist countries. Our two countries might also study the feasibility of pooling resources for construction projects in developing countries, both within and outside of the Pacific Basin.

Tourism offers many possibilities for widening Soviet-American ties in the Pacific region. Eastern Siberia and the Far East, California, Hawaii, and the Pacific Northwest offer attractive destinations for Russians and Americans alike. The USSR has been making progress in the field of international tourism since the country revived tourist itineraries for foreign visitors in the 1950s. Between 1976 and 1980, 25 million travelers from 162 countries came to the USSR. More than 18 million Soviet citizens visited 142 countries.

Soviet authorities have taken pains to expedite the flow of foreign tourists into the USSR. Entry procedures have been simplified, and efforts are constantly being made to streamline visa and customs formalities. Since 1981, tourists from Scandinavian countries can, along certain routes, visit the USSR without obtaining visas. To facilitate financial transactions for foreign tourists within the USSR, Intourist hotels and a number of stores honor American and European credit cards.

The geographical scope of tourism is broadening. Soviet citizens can choose from among about 300 foreign itineraries. Within the USSR, foreigners can choose from some 500 itineraries in 150 cities and towns. In the Far East, Khabarovsk has become a popular international attraction, linked by air service to Niigata (Khabarovsk's sister city in Japan), Pyongyang, and Hanoi. Passenger service on modern liners connects Nakhodka and Yokohama.

The hotel business also provides opportunities for international economic cooperation. A series of new hotels in Moscow and Leningrad have been constructed with the participation of Swedish, Finnish, and French firms. There is no reason to assume that such ventures could not be successfully implemented in the Soviet Far East. Discussions are now under way with Japanese firms for a new hotel in Nakhodka.

There is no escaping the fact that Soviet-American economic ties in general and in the Pacific in particular remain underdeveloped. Fulfillment of the potential for Soviet-American economic cooperation depends on an improvement in the political climate. Fortunately, the past is rich in examples which demonstrate that such cooperation is not merely a rhetorical phrase. Today in Moscow the fact that the International Trade Center is popularly known as the "Hammer Center" (after the California industrialist and pioneer of Soviet-American trade Armand Hammer) testifies to the vitality of the idea of economic partnership between the two countries.

## NOTES

1. *Vneshniaia torgovlia,* no. 3 (1982), p. 2.
2. Foreign Minister N. Patolichev, quoted in ibid.

3. *Vneshniaia torgovlia SSSR v 1983 g.* (Moscow: Finansy i statistika, 1984), pp. 9, 15.

4. *Journal of the US-USSR Trade and Economic Council* 6, no. 5 (1981): p. 14.

5. Ibid. 7, no. 1 (1982): 16.

6. M. M. Maksimova, *SSSR i mezhdunarodnoe ekonomicheskoe sotrudnichestvo* (Moscow: Mysl', 1977), p. 149.

7. *Planovoe khoziaistvo,* no. 10 (1980), p. 82. *Moskovskie novosti,* 28 November 1982.

8. *Vneshniaia torgovlia SSSR v 1983 g.*

9. *Vneshniaia torgovlia SSSR v 1981 g.*

10. *SSHA,* no. 4 (1982), p. 61.

11. V. Molodtsov, quoted in *Journal of the US-USSR Trade and Economic Council* 7, no. 1 (1982): 25.

12. *Planovoe khoziaistvo,* no. 10 (1982), p. 83.

13. *Journal of the US-USSR Trade and Economic Council* 6, no. 1 (1981): 13; 7, no. 3 (1982): 32.

14. *Planovoe khoziaistvo,* no. 10 (1980), pp. 83–85.

15. *Vneshniaia torgovlia SSSR v 1983 g.*

16. *Moskovskie novosti,* 28 November 1982.

17. *Vneshniaia torgovlia SSSR v 1981 g.*

18. V. Sushkov, quoted in *Journal of the US-USSR Trade and Economic Council* 6, no. 2 (1981): 13.

19. *SSHA,* no. 8 (1980), pp. 76–87. M. Wolfson and G. Farrel, *The Prospects for Oregon-USSR Trade in the Forest Products Machinery Industries* (Corvallis: Oregon State University Press, 1974). *Journal of the US-USSR Trade and Economic Council* 3, no. 4 (1977): 32–34.

20. *Overseas Business Reports,* July 1980, pp. 22–28. Bureau of the Census, *Statistical Abstract of the United States, 1981* (Washington: GPO, 1982), pp. 846–849.

21. *Central Valley Counties of California,* 31 July 1981, p. 2.

22. *Business America,* 22 February 1982, p. 13.

23. *Who Needs Foreign Trade? California Does* (San Francisco: California Council for International Trade, 1979), pp. 2–3.

24. *Central Valley Counties of California,* 31 July 1981, pp. 1–2.

25. *The US-Japan Trade: Issues and Problems,* Report by the Comptroller-General of the United States (Washington: GPO, 1979), p. 136.

26. Calculated on the basis of *Caltrade Highlights* (San Francisco: California Council for International Trade, 1982), pp. 2–6.

27. *Who Needs Foreign Trade?* p. 3.

28. Calculated from *Caltrade Highlights,* tables 7 and 8.

# Soviet-American Scientific Cooperation in the Pacific

ROBERT RANDOLPH

JOHN BARDACH

WITH THE GROWING COMPLEXITY of problems facing humanity, the need for international scientific cooperation has become ever more urgent in recent decades. Such cooperation between the United States and the Soviet Union is especially important because of these two countries' great scientific potential, their overlapping research interests, and their responsibility to find ways to improve mutual understanding and to reduce international tension. Soviet-American scientific cooperation developed rapidly during the 1960s and 1970s. Although international events have recently reduced the level of cooperative activity, the long-term potential remains great. President Ronald Reagan acknowledged this fact in his 1982 report to Congress, stating that "potentially, American scientific cooperation with the Soviet Union could be highly beneficial to the whole world."[1]

Although Soviet-American relations have usually been thought of in the Atlantic context, the Pacific Basin's increasing importance in world affairs reminds us that the two countries are, after all, neighbors across the Pacific. In this concluding chapter of a Soviet-American joint monograph, we offer some reflections on past experience and future prospects for trans-Pacific cooperation between American and Soviet scientists. Based on selected examples of cooperative research involving scientists from the Soviet Far East and the American Far West, we derive conclusions about steps which might be taken to assist the future development of mutually beneficial scientific relations between these two regions.

## The Potential

The Soviet Far East and American Far West have compelling grounds for cooperative activity. Geographically they have much in common. The geographical commonalities imply a shared concern for problems relating to oceans, forests, energy resources, telecommunications, transportation, fragile ecology, seismic activity, and agriculture. The two regions also share historical and sociological features including a frontier heritage, aboriginal populations with special needs, and remoteness from the main centers of government.

Both regions possess important scientific capabilities. Of particular importance on the Soviet side is Vladivostok's Far East Science Center (established in 1970), a system of twenty-one research institutes (as of 1985) with special strengths in such areas as geography, geophysics, marine biology, and oceanography. On the U.S. side, the Pacific coast possesses some of the country's leading research institutions, such as the California Institute of Technology, Stanford University, the University of California's various campuses, the University of Washington, and the University of Oregon, not to mention a wide variety of private-sector research laboratories concerned with electronics, genetic engineering, and other areas of high technology. For specific fields such as Asian-Pacific studies and the marine sciences, the University of Hawaii is of special significance. The University of Alaska is the scene of important work on cold-climate technologies.

Despite the obvious factors which favor Soviet-American scientific cooperation, we must be frank in admitting that there are deterrents as well. Distance is one, affecting travel costs and making frequent contacts more difficult than would be the case, for instance, between the Soviet Far East and Japan or between the United States and Canada. Limitations on travel and information exchange are an even more serious obstacle. Language is also a problem. Translators and interpreters help, but they cannot provide the full mutual understanding on which the most fruitful collaboration depends. Differences in national experiences and therefore in assumptions and perceptions can sometimes also interfere with mutual understanding. Perceptions of unbalanced benefits can arise, reducing the motivation to cooperate. Finally, there is the unstable international climate, which not only can lead to abrupt changes in national policy regarding scientific cooperation but also can affect the time horizon of cooperation, thus discouraging long-term activities vulnerable to untimely termination.

## Marine Interests

Since the Pacific Ocean is both the bridge and the barrier between the two nations, a look at national marine interests of the United States and the Soviet Union (excepting those of a security nature) is illuminating. It is reasonable to assume that an examination of these interests will reveal some things about relative emphases in their ocean science endeavors and about incentives and constraints to cooperation.

An overriding consideration here is the place of fish in the diet of the Soviet people (as opposed to the American people) and the role of the USSR in world fisheries. As a result of concentrated efforts, the Soviet Union today vies with Japan for first place in the world fishing industry. There are geographic and climatic reasons for the Soviet emphasis on fisheries. In addition there are economic motivations, notably the lower cost in both capital investment and labor input required to produce a given amount of fish compared to the same amount of beef or other animal protein. By the same token, a case can be made that most fish production is less energy intensive on a unit-weight basis than production of grain-fed beef or other livestock.[2]

In both absolute and relative terms, fish are far more important in the diet of the average Soviet citizen than for the average American. The Pacific stands out as by far the most important Soviet fishing region. Moreover, the Pacific provides access to the Indian Ocean, where Soviet fishing efforts are increasing.

In contrast to Soviet-Japanese fishing relations, which are always competitive and sometimes strained, Soviet-American fishing relations are relatively free of elements that pose a potential for friction. The United States has some underused fishery resources, particularly in Alaskan waters, which the Soviets are exploiting in accordance with bilateral agreements, with Soviet vessels paying for fishing rights. In the tropical Pacific the two nations tend to fish for different species; the Americans (like the Japanese) fish for tuna, the Russians for white ground or "bottom fishes."

Scientific research on fishery biotechnologies is perhaps more strongly established in the Soviet Far East than in the American Pacific states, a gap underlined by the creation in 1984 in Vladivostok of a new major research institution to study problems of fishery economics. At present, institutes of marine science in the states of Washington and Alaska are in constant contact with their Soviet Far Eastern counterparts.

To Russians and Americans alike, the term "Pacific" evokes images of coconut palms and clear blue waters of coral reef lagoons. Soviet and American scientists share interests in reefs. American scientific interest in reefs is both geologic and environmental. The United States has coral reefs to "look after" both in the Atlantic and in the Pacific. Although the USSR has no coral reefs, a Soviet geologist has written that "reef complexes are the most common feature of the U.S.S.R. geological pattern."[3] There is, moreover, interest in the Soviet Union in reef organisms. The Pacific Institute of Bioorganic Chemistry in Vladivostok conducts research on biologically active substances in marine organisms. According to a 1981 report, foreign colleagues participate in the institute's expeditions.[4]

Turning to nonliving ocean resources, there has been considerable attention in both the United States and the Soviet Union devoted to the development of submarine hydrocarbons—petroleum and natural gas. Given present technology and market conditions, submarine hydrocarbons will be exploited on the continental shelf within 200-mile economic zones, where such deposits are national resources. This circumstance reduces the incentive for Soviet-American scientific cooperation in this domain; however, information exchanges in geological sciences do occur.

Other nonliving ocean resources of great current interest are deep-sea metallic deposits such as manganese nodules. The American government's stance in regard to their exploitation has led Washington to abstain from signing the Law of the Sea (LOS) Treaty. This may well place the United States in an awkward political position. The Soviet Union has signed the treaty and has established itself as one of the pioneer states within a future LOS seabed regime, this despite the fact that deep-sea minerals research so far appears to have been less vigorously pursued in the USSR than in the United States.

Another potential ocean resource is the generation of power from the thermal differential between the surface and deep waters of tropical seas. Both the Soviet Union and the United States have devoted theoretical and applied scientific efforts in this area and are exchanging information. Although involving costly initial investments, ocean thermal energy conversion promises, if successfully developed, to free many of the world's developing nations from the thraldom of their ties to Middle East oil.

Both the United States and the USSR engage in studies of the interaction of the ocean with the atmosphere. Climatology is an area of ocean sciences with serious implications for humanity's future.

After all, even a small warming of the atmosphere, conceivable if we continue to burn the world's fossil fuels at present rates, promises to change things fundamentally on the globe's surface. An understanding of air-ocean interface phenomena would permit long-range planning in such important areas as the northward extension of grain belts.

## Frameworks for Cooperation

Scientific cooperation between the United States and the USSR, like that between any two countries, can take place on various levels and by various means. At the most informal level, individual scientists can and do correspond, exchange publications, and interact at international conferences. It should be added that such interactions have often been the starting point for development of ongoing cooperation among individual scientists. These unofficial contacts are of course limited by financial and other constraints. They are perhaps most common among scientists who have already met and established a working relationship under other circumstances. However, such informal contacts deserve to be mentioned because they are often overlooked in discussions of scientific cooperation.

For some scientists, useful contacts may be facilitated by involvement in international conferences and seminars sponsored by academic or social organizations. One example of a forum that brings together (among others) Soviet and American students of Asia-Pacific issues is a series of international seminars held biennially at Nakhodka under the auspices of the Far East Science Center and other Soviet organizations concerned with international solidarity and cultural relations.[5] The Nakhodka seminars serve a useful purpose in that they enable American specialists on Asian and Pacific problems to meet, hold informal discussions, and establish good personal relations with a wide spectrum of Soviet economists, historians, and political scientists working on contemporary Asia-Pacific problems at research institutes in Vladivostok, Khabarovsk, and Moscow.

The Pacific Science Association also provides an important framework for Soviet-American scientific scholarly discussions of Pacific area topics and phenomena. Founded in Honolulu in 1920, the association holds congresses somewhere in the Pacific every four years (with smaller "intercongress" meetings also held every four years).

The association works through various national science bodies, academies, and national museums. The Fourteenth Pacific Science Congress was held in Khabarovsk in 1979. Several of the association's scientific committees have Soviet or American chairpersons. At present, Soviet scientists chair committees on marine sciences, public health and medicine, and solid earth science.

The Pacific Science Association's secretariat is in Hawaii, which underscores the islands' key role in building bridges across the ocean. The University of Hawaii is the home of the Law of the Sea Institute, which through annual conferences about questions of ocean governance brings together American and Soviet scientists.

Another mechanism for scientific contacts is the variety of multi-lateral intergovernmental agreements and organizations in which both the United States and the USSR are represented. Some of these, such as the Antarctic treaty system and various agreements concerned with wildlife conservation, serve to prove a legal and political framework for scientific cooperation. Others such as UNESCO, the United Nations Food and Agriculture Organization (FAO), the International Atomic Energy Agency, and the International Institute for Applied Systems Analysis provide opportunities for joint or at least coordinated research. Multilateral arrangements of this kind are the principal mechanism for American-Soviet cooperation in marine sciences.

Perhaps the most important single framework for American-Soviet scientific cooperation in the past two decades has been the official system of bilateral scientific exchange agreements which grew from modest beginnings in the 1950s into an impressive set of eleven formal agreements by 1974.*

As expressed in the main agreement on scientific and technical cooperation, the objective of this cooperation is "to provide broad opportunities for both parties and to combine the efforts of their scientists and specialists in working on major problems, whose solution

---

*(1) Science and Technology (1972–1982); (2) Exploration and Use of Outer Space for Peaceful Purposes (1972–1982); (3) Environmental Protection (1972–); (4) Medical Science and Public Health (1972–); (5) Transportation (1972–); (6) Agriculture (1973–1980, resumed in 1984); (7) Peaceful Uses of Atomic Energy (1973–); (8) Studies of the World Ocean (1973–); (9) Artificial Heart Research and Development (1974–); (10) Energy (1974–1982); (11) Housing and Other Construction (1974–). Other relevant agreements in forces include those on exchange of medical films; deep-sea drilling; economic, industrial, and technical cooperation; translation and publication of Soviet journals, articles, and books; and conservation of migratory birds and their environment.

will promote the progress of science and technology for the benefit of both countries and of mankind.''[6]

To implement each of the eleven cooperation agreements, an organizational structure was created consisting in nearly all cases of a Soviet-American joint committee. Each such committee consisted of co-chairpersons representing appropriate agencies or institutions in the two countries, a secretariat on each side, and a number of joint working groups composed of scientists. Activities undertaken under the agreements have included: exploratory visits, seminars, exchanges of scientists and research materials, joint research, and joint publication. From 1972 to 1978, 9,673 individuals took part in short-term visits, 5,125 from the United States and 4,548 from the USSR. In addition, eighty-two longer-term (up to nine months) visits took place. Of 301 publications resulting from joint research, 111 were jointly authored by U.S. and Soviet scientists.[7]

In 1979 the United States government sharply curtailed the level of activity under the agreements, and in 1982 three of the agreements (those on science and technology, outer space, and energy) were allowed to expire. The experience accumulated under the agreements, together with those agreements which still remain in force, constitute an important framework for future cooperative activities.

## Examples of Cooperation

The ideal data base for an analysis of the prospects for cooperative scientific relations between the Soviet Far East and the American Far West would be a broad set of historical cases of research cooperation between scientists in these two areas. Such cases, however, are difficult to locate except in a few specific areas such as the marine and atmospheric sciences. The examples of joint scientific research to be discussed here were chosen on the basis of involvement by scientists in the American Far West, on the assumption that insights gained from past cooperative efforts should be more or less applicable to future cooperation between the two regions themselves. It should be recognized, of course, that up to now there have been restrictions on travel by foreigners in the Soviet Far East, a situation that has affected the geographical distribution of cooperative activities.

The following examples of Soviet-American scientific cooperation illustrate types of obstacles as well as achievements in varying fields of knowledge. The activities range from exchanges of information to intensive joint research involving coordinated experiments and long-range inter-institutional agreements.

*Research and development planning and management.* This case involved the National Science Foundation, the Electric Power Research Institute, the Hoover Institution, Rand Corporation, Stanford Research International, and other American institutions. From the Soviet side, participants included the Ministry of Power and Electrification, the Ministry of the Electrotechnical Industry, the Ministry of Instrument Making, Automatic Equipment and Control, and other institutions. Data exchanged were used by two American authors to produce a two-volume report on science policy in the United States and the Soviet Union. More specialized reports were also prepared by U.S. study teams.

*Plastic pipe for irrigation and drainage.* Participants in this project included the U.S. Department of Interior, and the USSR Ministry for Reclamation and Water Management. Parallel experiments were conducted in Latvia and California, using plastic pipe and tubing provided by the United States. Field results were monitored, and detailed studies were prepared for publication.

*Study of Pacific seamounts.* The Hawaii Institute of Geophysics (HIG) of the University of Hawaii, and the Institute of Tectonics and Geophysics (part of the Far East Science Center) in Khabarovsk have a good record of cooperation. In 1982, for example, eight University of Hawaii graduate students, working in pairs, spent five months at sea on the Soviet research vessel *Pegas;* the HIG research vessel *Kana Keoki* performed some service functions in the mission. Although translators were supplied, the American students began to converse in Russian with their Soviet colleagues. Some Soviet scientists were quite fluent in English. Collaboration is reported to have been excellent. Data is being evaluated in both locations.

*Seismicity in the Kamchatka and Aleutian trenches.* The purpose of planned cooperation between HIG and the Sakhalin Complex Research Center (part of the Far East Science Center) is to obtain a better understanding of the tectonics of the intersection of these two trenches. Work will include determination of the acoustical characteristics of the region. Research is to be conducted cooperatively on the HIG vessel with predominantly U.S. equipment. It is expected that some fundamental problems of geology will be elucidated: the age and origin of the deep-sea floor, the origin of oceanic plateaus, and undersea vulcanism. HIG and Sakhalin scientists have already exchanged visits and have a proven record of fruitful cooperation in tsunami research. Both parties have high hopes for being able to undertake a significant joint project in basic ocean sciences.

*Gravitational wave detection.* This joint project began in 1979 with an agreement on joint research in gravitational wave detection between the California Institute of Technology and Moscow State University. The agreement grew out of a long-standing cooperative relationship between teams of scientists on each side. It called for exchanges of information on progress in gravitational wave detection, reciprocal research visits of one person for one month annually, and ultimately for the development of complex measuring devices for coordinated deployment in the United States and the Soviet Union. U.S. participants suggest that this program has been especially successful because it has been conducted on a person-to-person basis with institutional support.

*Deep underwater neutrino detection.* Proposed in 1960 by Academician M. A. Markov, this project began as a joint effort of the University of Hawaii and the USSR Academy of Sciences. It involves the operation, at a depth of 30,000 feet in the waters off Hawaii and 5,250 feet under the surface of Lake Baikal in Eastern Siberia, of sensitive optical detectors for neutrinos. Neutrinos are subatomic particles thought to be released by stellar explosions.

The project after 1974 developed as a collaborative effort between U.S. and Soviet scientists from several institutions. Work proceeded smoothly until 1980 when the United States government restricted collaboration with the USSR in certain federally supported projects. Thereafter, the Soviet scientists pursued research independently. Unofficial contact between Soviet and American scientists in this field continues.

*Chemical catalysis.* This project involved several Soviet and American institutions: California Institute of Technology, Stanford University, University of California (Berkeley), the Institute of Catalysis (Novosibirsk), Institute of Chemical Physics (Moscow), and the Institute of Theoretical Problems of Chemical Technology (Baku). Research fellows from each country spent several months in host laboratories, conducting research on selected topics in chemical catalysis, in some cases using special research facilities to test theories which had been formulated in their home country. Some of the research resulted in joint papers.

After the chemical catalysis cooperation program was phased out in 1980, its American chairman provided a postmortem. In it he indicated that the experience of the research fellows "ranged from disappointment to great satisfaction." Some of the problems encountered were: crowded laboratory conditions, occasional lack of proper equipment, limited access to top personnel, restricted access to work in related areas, difficulties in participating in scientific meetings in the host country, and difficulties regarding access to host country universities to observe how catalysis is taught.

But the program also yielded clear benefits. It helped to produce new scientific insights; it extended the range of problems that could be studied; it accelerated research in specific areas. Furthermore, because of unique instrumentation available in each country, it permitted research that could not have been done unilaterally. As the U.S. chairman noted:

> Many U.S. participants felt and experienced a very different, and refreshing, viewpoint on the pursuit of science and scientific methodology that prevail in the Soviet Union. The Soviet scientists seem to have a better grasp of the theoretical and conceptual side of science. On the whole, the participants in the program have felt a sense of real accomplishment not only with their contribution to the advancement of science, but also with their contribution to a better understanding between the scientists of the two countries.

## Options and Opportunities

In light of the experiences reviewed here, a number of conclusions can be suggested regarding steps which might usefully be taken to maximize the likelihood of success in future attempts at Soviet-American scientific cooperation, especially across the Pacific. The following elements would appear to deserve consideration:

1. High-level initiative—approval and preferably active support for cooperation at the level of each country's political leadership.
2. Working-level initiative—efforts by scientists themselves to identify counterparts with whom cooperative work might be fruitful and to develop initial scientific contacts.
3. Development of constituencies—informing and involving potentially interested sectors of industry and other groups and institutions for which the results of research might be directly or indirectly beneficial.

4. Avoidance of politically vulnerable topics—concentration on relatively noncontroversial topics including those of obvious humanitarian value such as health and environmental research.
5. Avoidance of false expectations—fuller understanding on the part of both scientists and sponsors about the complexities of cooperative research.
6. Avoidance of imbalance—conscientious efforts to meet the legitimate expectations of both parties.
7. Mutual respect for needs and constraints—recognition that there are limitations on what is possible in both countries.

Although these points apply equally to both sides, it should be recognized that there are inevitable differences in the way joint projects are initiated and carried out in the two countries. Science policy is centrally controlled in the USSR. As an organ planning and implementing scientific research, the USSR Academy of Sciences wields far more influence than do the U.S. National Academy of Sciences or the U.S. National Science Foundation.

It should also be noted that there have been many more joint projects planned than were executed. This disparity denotes the inhibiting influence of bureaucracy in both nations. It is acknowledged that travel permits, a sine qua non of joint projects, are more difficult to obtain in the USSR than in the United States. Similarly, marine research often requires permits for vessels to call in ports. The United States presently issues such permits on a quid pro quo basis. If a port call has clear evidence of value and importance to U.S. science, the Soviet desk of the State Department usually acts promptly and positively. Entry of U.S. vessels into Soviet sea space is more easily arranged if instruments not presently possessed by Soviet scientists are to be deployed in the joint work. Such is the case in the Kurile-Kamchatka seismicity projected alluded to earlier.

Certain subject matter areas are more important in one country than in the other. For example, the USSR tends to have a leading role in high-latitude research while the United States has shown leadership in tropical marine science. These differences notwithstanding, both nations recognize that much of scientific research has become team research and that joint undertakings make sense in many areas. But team research is often undertaken on a multilateral basis, as in the case of global atmospheric research programs coordinated by various United Nations agencies. Examination of Soviet research activities in recent years shows that Soviet science has inclined toward participation in international rather than in binational programs. Certain areas of science, nonetheless, are quite amenable to bilateral cooperation. Such projects should be fashioned in such a way that both sides can expect roughly equal payoffs. However carefully designed, it cannot be denied that the success of a joint project may depend upon political vicissitudes beyond the control of scientific participants.

In both nations there is a traditional emphasis on Europe and the Atlantic as arenas in East-West relations. Recent attention to the development of Far Eastern science in the USSR, however, suggests that the Soviet Union recognizes that the Pacific area is of increasing geopolitical importance. A similar process has been occurring in the United States since World War II.

The building of scientific bridges across the Pacific—the traditional "backdoors" of the United States and the Soviet Union—can be mutually beneficial. The success of such endeavors requires a sound basis of mutual understanding of each other's needs and constraints, of each other's ways of thinking and of conducting research, and of each other's languages. The effort is well worth making; experience shows that both the stakes and the benefits are high for science and for human life.

## NOTES

1. House Committee on Foreign Affairs, *Science, Technology and American Diplomacy, 1982* (Washington: GPO, 1982), p. vii.

2. For pertinent examples, see J. E. Bardach, "Economic Energy Use in Fish Production," in *Proceedings of the Fourteenth Pacific Science Congress,* Khabarovsk, August 1979.

3. B. V. Preobrazhensky, "Reef Studies in the U.S.S.R., A Review," in *Proceedings of the Fourth International Coral Reef Symposium,* vol. 1. Manila, 1981.

4. Ibid.

5. *Problemy Dal'nego Vostoka,* no. 1 (1980), 206–208.

6. Department of State, *Treaties and International Agreements Series,* no. 7346 (1972).

7. House Committee on Foreign Affairs, *Science, Technology and American Diplomacy, 1980* (Washington: GPO, 1980), p. 136.

# Appendix
## Cities of the Soviet Far East

V. G. Smoliak

This appendix consists of brief descriptions of ten Soviet Far Eastern cities, each of which is mentioned several times in the text of this work. It is hoped that the information provided will be helpful to American readers. All population figures are for the year 1984.

### Vladivostok (pop. 599,500)

Established in 1860, Vladivostok is the administrative center of the Maritime Territory. It is most recently remembered throughout the world as the venue for a summit meeting between General Secretary L. I. Brezhnev and President Gerald Ford in November 1974.

One of the Soviet Union's principal ice-free ports, Vladivostok is justifiably called a gateway to the Pacific. The city's picturesque natural setting amid deep coastal indentations etched into Peter the Great Bay, prompted the eminent polar explorer Fridtjof Nansen to write in 1913: "Vladivostok defers to no other city in beauty. Set along hillside terraces, it reminds one of Naples."

Vladivostok is a city of seafarers. Piers jut out along its capacious harbor, which is formed by the Golden Horn. Here are headquarters of the Far Eastern Steamship Company, the Far Eastern Fisheries Trust, and the Pacific Fleet. Every second resident of Vladivostok is involved in ocean-related work.

Vladivostok is a major center for scientific research in the Soviet Far East. The Far East Science Center of the USSR Academy of Sciences was established here in 1970. Several of the center's twenty-one institutes are based here. Nine institutions of higher education, including the Far Eastern University, are also located here. The Oriental Faculty of the university has a tradition of Asian studies dating back to the Oriental Institute, founded in 1899 to train students in Asian languages, history and culture.

There are three theatrical companies, four museums, some forty
cultural clubs, and about three hundred public lending libraries in
the city. Ample opportunities for sports exist, among the favorites
being swimming, sailing, tennis, skiing, and ice-skating. During the
"velvet season," the period from late August until October when
Vladivostok is blessed by warm, dry, sunny days, thousands of tourists from near and far flock to its sandy beaches.

## Khabarovsk (pop. 568,000)

Located near the juncture of the Amur and Ussuri rivers, Khabarovsk is the administrative center of the Khabarovsk Territory.
Machine building and metalworking stand out among the city's
industrial enterprises. Locally manufactured diesels are used nationally and are exported throughout the world.

Khabarovsk has twenty-four scientific research institutes and
eleven institutions of higher learning which train some forty thousand students. The city also has thirty-three technical and vocational
schools.

Cultural life in the city revolves around three drama theaters, a
philharmonic and a symphony orchestra, a well-known dance ensemble, and many cultural clubs and societies. Among the city's
notable museums are the Local History Museum, the Far Eastern
Art Museum, and the Alexander Fadeev Museum of Far Eastern
Literature. The internationally renowned Local History Museum is
associated with the life and work of the distinguished explorer, naturalist, and ethnographer, Vladimir Arseniev (1872–1930).

Sports facilities include ten stadiums, 130 sports clubs, and several public swimming pools. The Lenin Stadium is the site of major
all-Union and international competitions, notably in ice hockey.

Khabarovsk is the Far East's principal air transportation center.
The city has air service to Japan and North Korea. Some twenty
thousand foreign tourists visit the city annually.

## Nakhodka (pop. 172,300)

Stretching for thirty-five miles along well-sheltered Bolshaia Bay
(formerly Amerika Bay), Nakhodka is located fifty-five miles south-

east of Vladivostok, a distance that is covered in less than three hours by hydrofoils. The city's name derives from the "find" *(nakhodka)* made by officers and crew on the Russian schooner *Amerika* while surveying the Maritime Territory coastline in 1859.

In the late 1930s, Nakhodka became an important port when some shipping operations were transferred from Vladivostok. Expansion of the port resumed after World War II. In 1950, Nakhodka was given municipal status. Today it is the USSR's main commercial port on the Pacific, and ships from forty countries with thirty thousand crewmembers call there annually. Nakhodka is in fact a complex of specialized ports (fish, fuel, general trade, containers). Nearby Port Vrangel handles coal and wood chips, mostly for shipment to Japan. Also nearby is Vostochnyi Port, a trans-shipment point for containers sent to and from Japan, Hong Kong, the Philippines, and Western Europe across Siberia.

Nakhodka is the headquarters for Dalintorg, the all-Union commercial organization handling coast trade between the Soviet Far East and Japan, North Korea, Australia, and the People's Republic of China. Several Japanese and one American firm have regional representation in the city.

By A.D. 2000 Nakhodka's population is expected to reach three hundred thousand.

## Birobidzhan (pop. 76,800)

Birobidzhan, which takes its name from the rivers Bira and Bidzhan, is the administrative, economic, and cultural center of the Jewish Autonomous District. Formed in 1931 on the site of the village of Tikhonkaia, it was designated a city in 1937. Birobidzhan is located on the Trans-Siberian Railroad just over a hundred miles west of Khabarovsk.

Birobidzhan's main industries include railway construction and repair shops, power generators, textiles, shoes, clothing, woodworking, food processing, and construction materials.

Cultural life there is enriched by the Sholem Aleichem Library with its fine collection of works in Hebrew and Russian, as well as the Russian and Jewish national theaters, a philharmonic orchestra, chamber music ensemble, a Jewish music theater, and newspapers in Russian and Yiddish.

## Blagoveshchensk (pop. 195,200)

Administrative center of the Amur region, Blagoveshchensk lies at the junction of the Amur and Zeya rivers. Established in 1858, it lies directly across the Amur River from the Chinese town of Aigun (Aihun). The city's industrial enterprises (metals, ship construction, electronics, textiles) have found international as well as national markets.

Blagoveshchensk has a drama theater, a puppet theater, a philharmonic, music conservatory, the Amur Folk Choir, and a nationally popular Far Eastern Children's Ensemble.

The city's people tend to be young. Every fifth adult is a full or part-time student. There are pedagogical, medical, agricultural, and polytechnic institutes, two military academies, and fourteen secondary specialized schools. One of the latter, the Blagoveshchensk River Navigation School, is the oldest institution of its kind in the Far East.

Blagoveshchensk is connected to the Trans-Siberian Railroad by a seventy-mile branch line. The city is linked by air service to central regions of the country.

## Komsomolsk-na-Amure (pop. 291,400)

In the 1930s the Soviet government decided to build a new industrial and cultural center in the Far East. It chose as the site of this center the village of Permskoye, located deep in the taiga on the banks of the lower Amur. The first Komsomol (Young Communist League) construction units arrived on 10 May 1932. On 10 December, Permskoye was officially renamed Komsomolsk. Today the "city of youth," as Komsomolsk is popularly called, is a major metallurgical center. The eastern terminus of the Baikal-Amur Railroad, the city also has rail connections with Vanino and Sovetskaia Gavan, ports on the Sea of Japan.

The city's natural setting on the majestic Amur embankment is enhanced by tree-lined boulevards, parks, and squares. The House of Youth was opened in 1967 by cosmonaut Yuri A. Gagarin. Educational institutions include a pedagogical and polytechnic institute, five vocational schools, forty-five middle schools, and scores of lending libraries and cultural clubs.

## Magadan (pop. 150,800)

Magadan is the administrative seat of Magadan District and a center for processing nonferrous metals, furs, marine products, and meat (largely from reindeer). The city is linked to the resource-rich interior—the Kolyma Basin—by an all-weather highway. Local architecture is designed to create a normal living and working environment in a region where winter lasts ten months and the thermometer plunges to minus sixty degrees Fahrenheit.

Magadan's most notable industry is the manufacturing of mining equipment. The city is also the location of the Northeast Complex* Scientific Research Institute, the All-Union Scientific Research Institute for Gold and Rare Metals, the Institute of Biological Problems of the North, and the Agricultural Institute. There are also a pedagogical institute, a polytechnical institute, and several vocational schools. Local writers and poets publish a literary journal, *Na Dal'nem Severe* (In the Far North).

Separated by over six thousand miles from European Russia, Magadan has direct air service to Moscow, the Caucasus, and the Crimea.

## Petropavlovsk-Kamchatskii (pop. 252,400)

Petropavlovsk is nestled in Avacha Bay on Kamchatka's western coast. It is one of the oldest settlements in the Far East, established in 1740 during Vitus Bering's Second Kamchatka Expedition. Petropavlovsk is the only major city in the Soviet Far East to face directly on the Pacific Ocean. The city is surrounded by volcanoes, some of them active.

As Kamchatka is the center of the Far Eastern fisheries industry, Petropavlovsk serves as a base for trawlers and factory ships that operate in all the world's oceans.

At the Institute of Vulcanology, scholars investigate the earth's interior and look for practical applications of geothermal energy. Geothermally heated greenhouses provide city residents with year-round fresh vegetables. Several branches of the Far Eastern Science

---

*"Complex" when applied to scientific institutes indicates that the institute in question conducts research in a number of different scientific disciplines.

Center are found in Petropavlovsk, notably the Institute of Ocean-ography and Institute of Physical Geography. There are also peda-gogical, fishery, navigation, medical, and musical institutions of higher education.

A popular hot springs sanatorium, Paratunka, is located a few miles outside of the city.

## Yakutsk (pop. 203,000)

Yakutsk is the administrative, economic, cultural, and scientific cen-ter of the Yakut Autonomous Soviet Socialist Republic. Founded as a fort by Cossacks in 1632, Yakutsk served during the seventeenth and much of the eighteenth centuries as a base for the exploration of the Okhotsk seaboard and North Pacific. Thanks to its location on the Lena River, Yakutsk has for three centuries been an important supply center for Northeastern Siberia.

Yakutsk has a continental climate. The mercury has been known to plunge below minus seventy degrees Fahrenheit. Summers are short but warm and dry. Yakutsk falls within the permafrost region, and frozen soil around the city reaches depths of over two hundred meters. Construction problems associated with permafrost have given rise to considerable research and architectural innovation. Buildings rest on pilings so as to cope with the melting and refreez-ing of the ground.

In the city are found the Yakutsk Branch of the USSR Academy of Sciences, Yakutsk State University, and institutes studying perma-frost, atmospherics, and northern zone agriculture. Yakutsk has a drama theater, a musical theater, and a Russian drama theater. The A. S. Pushkin Library contains nearly two million volumes.

## Yuzhno-Sakhalinsk (pop. 163,700)

Yuzhno-Sakhalinsk is the administrative center of the USSR's only island district. The town has a complex history. It started as a settle-ment named Vladimirovka in 1881. In 1905, Vladimirovka was occupied by Japanese forces. During southern Sakhalin's period of Japanese rule (1905–1945), Vladimirovka was renamed Toyohara and grew to be a city of 38,606 by 1940.

Today Yuzhno-Sakhalinsk is a modern city. It serves as regional center for the construction materials, machinery, and food products industries. The secretariat for the Soviet-Japanese Committee on Offshore Energy Resources and the Sakhalin Complex Research Institute are located there.

The Chekhov Theater is the city's pride, as are the Palace of Sports and Pedagogical Institute. For relaxation local residents stroll in the Yuri Gagarin Park of Culture, enjoying its artificial lakes, fountains, and wildlife. The Local History Museum (formerly Kara-futo Museum) with its traditional Japanese architecture is another local landmark. On the outskirts of town is Gornyi Vozdukh (literally "mountain air"), a tourist base and mecca for winter sports enthusiasts. National ski-jumping championships are held there, attracting the country's finest skiers and thousands of sports fans.

Yuzhno-Sakhalinsk has regular air service to Khabarovsk and to settlements in the Kurile Islands.

# Contributors

JOHN E. BARDACH is a research associate at the Resource Systems Institute, East-West Center, Honolulu, Hawaii, and an adjunct professor at the University of Hawaii. Formerly director of the Hawaii Institute of Marine Biology, Dr. Bardach has since 1971 been a member of the Council and Executive Committee of the Pacific Science Association as representative of the U.S. National Academy of Sciences. His publications include *Aquaculture* (1972) and *Harvest of the Sea* (1968).

WILLIAM B. BEYERS is professor of geography at the University of Washington. He conducts research on economic geography and regional development with a primary interest in interregional structure and structural change. His works include contributions in *Economic Geography* and *International Regional Science Review*.

KATHLEEN BRADEN is assistant professor of geography at Seattle Pacific University, Seattle, Washington. Dr. Braden received a B.A. in Russian from Boston University and an M.A. and Ph.D. in geography at the University of Washington. A regular visitor to the USSR, she has contributed a chapter to Robert Jensen's *Soviet Natural Resources in the World Economy* (1983).

VALERII PETROVICH CHICHKANOV is the director of the Institute of Economic Research, Far East Science Center, USSR Academy of Sciences, in Khabarovsk. A Doctor of Economic Sciences and corresponding member of the USSR Academy of Sciences, he is the author of *Main Directions for Long-term Development of Productive Forces in the Far East* (1980),* *Labor Efficiency Among Managers* (1982), and *Social-Economic Problems of Raising the Efficiency of Social Work* (1983).

EVGENII BORISOVICH KOVRIGIN is head of the Section on Economic Problems of Pacific Basin Countries, Institute of Economic Research, Kha-

---

*Unless otherwise indicated, all publications of Soviet contributors listed here are in Russian.

barovsk. A Candidate of Economic Sciences, Dr. Kovrigin's publications include *Japanese Capital Exports* (1977), *Japan's Economic Expansion* (1980), and *The Pacific Community: Contradictions and Prospects* (1985).

Elisa B. Miller is a doctoral candidate and lecturer at the School of International Relations, University of Washington. A specialist in Soviet-East Asian economic relations, Ms. Miller has published articles in *Asian Survey* and *Soviet Geography.*

Pavel Aleksandrovich Minakir is deputy director, Institute of Economic Research, Khabarovsk. A Doctor of Economic Sciences, he is the author of *Economic Development: A Programmatic Approach* (1983) and *Analyzing and Projecting Regional Economic Development* (1984).

Franklin C. L. Ng is professor of anthropology at California State University, Fresno, California. Trained in history and East Asian studies at Johns Hopkins University, Harvard, and the University of Chicago, Dr. Ng is a contributor to *American Diplomatic and Public Papers, the United States and China* (1974–).

Aleksandr Borisovich Parkanskii is a senior research associate at the Institute of the USA and Canada, USSR Academy of Sciences, Moscow. A Candidate of Economic Sciences, Dr. Parkanskii's publications include *Economic Interests of the USA in Asia and the Pacific* (1983) and *USA-China: Economic and Scientific Aspects of Washington's China Policy* (1982).

Robert H. Randolph is assistant director of the National Council for Soviet and East European Research, Washington, D.C. Dr. Randolph was trained in history at Yale and Stanford universities and was formerly a research associate at the Resource Systems Institute, East-West Center. In 1978–1979 he was a member of a joint U.S.-Soviet research team at the International Institute for Applied Systems Analysis in Laxenburg, Austria. His publications include *Scientific and Technological Forecasting in the USSR* (1980).

John B. Richards completed his B.A. and M.A. degrees at the University of Washington, where he is currently a Ph.D. candidate in the Department of Geography.

Nadezhda Leont'evna Shlyk is head of the Section on External Economic Ties of the [Soviet] Far East, Institute of Economic Research, Khabarovsk. A Candidate of Economic Sciences, Dr. Shlyk has published articles on international economic relations of the Soviet Far East.

Boris Nikolaevich Slavinskii is the editor of *Social Sciences,* an English-language journal published in Moscow. Formerly chief deputy to the Academic Secretary of the Far East Science Center in Vladivostok, Dr. Slavinskii is a Candidate of Technical Sciences and a contributor to *Interna-*

*tional Relations in the Far East, 1945–1977* (1978), edited by S. L. Tikhvinskii; and *USA and Problems of the Pacific* (1979), edited by V. P. Lukin.

Viktor Grigor'evich Smoliak is head of the Section on Socio-Economic Problems of Pacific Basin Countries, Institute of Economic Research, Khabarovsk. A Candidate of Historical Sciences, Dr. Smoliak has published articles on the modern history of the Soviet Far East.

John J. Stephan is professor of history at the University of Hawaii. Trained in Russian and East Asian history at Harvard, the University of Hawaii, and the University of London, Dr. Stephan has been a regular visitor to the USSR for many years, lecturing at the Institute of Oriental Studies and the Institute of the Far East, USSR Academy of Sciences, Moscow, and at the Institute of Economic Research, Khabarovsk. His publications include *Sakhalin: A History* (1971) and *The Kuril Islands: Russo-Japanese Frontier in the Pacific* (1974).

# Index

**Production Notes**

This book was designed by Roger Eggers. Composition and paging were done on the Quadex Composing System and typesetting on the Compugraphic 8400 by the design and production staff of University of Hawaii Press.

The text typeface is Baskerville and the display typeface is Compugraphic Palatino.

Offset presswork and binding were done by Vail-Ballou Press, Inc. Text paper is Writers R Offset, basis 50.